Making Our High Schools Better

ALSO BY ANNE WESCOTT DODD

A Parent's Guide to Innovative Education (One of 10 Best Books for Parents, *Child Magazine,* 1992)

Footprints and Shadows (A children's picture book illustrated by Henri Sorenson; ABA Pick of the Lists [Fall 1992]; Junior Library Guild selection; Outstanding Trade Book, National Science Teachers Association, 1992)

Beachcombing and Beachcrafting

A Handbook for Substitute Teachers

Practical Strategies for Taming the Paper and People Problems in Teaching

From Images to Words: A Visual Approach to Writing

Write Now: Insights into Creative Writing

Making Our High Schools Better

How Parents and Teachers Can Work Together

Anne Wescott Dodd
Jean L. Konzal

St. Martin's Press
New York

MAKING OUR HIGH SCHOOLS BETTER

ISBN 0-312-21335-2

Library of Congress Cataloging-in-Publication Data

Dodd, Anne W.
Making our high schools better: how parents and teachers can work
    together / Anne Wescott Dodd and Jean L. Konzal.
        p. cm.
    Includes bibliographical references and index.
    ISBN 0-312-21335-2
1. Home and school--United States. 2. Parent-teacher
relationships--United States. 3. Community and school--United
States. I. Konzal, Jean L., 1944- . II. Title.
LC225.3.D63 1999
373.119'2--dc21   98-46121
                                                             CIP

First edition: May, 1999
10 9 8 7 6 5 4 3 2

To
Anna Marotta, Anne's godmother, a teacher of children,
and a PTA member for fifty-plus years
and
In memory of
Paula and Alex Stein, Jean's parents and first teachers

Contents

PART I:
UNDERSTANDING THE OFTEN PROBLEMATIC
RELATIONSHIPS BETWEEN PARENTS AND SCHOOLS

PART II:
UNDERSTANDING TENSIONS CREATED BY
DIFFERENT OPINIONS ABOUT TEACHING AND TESTING

PART III:
BUILDING BRIDGES TO PARENTS AND THE COMMUNITY

Acknowledgments

This book never could have been written without the help of many people. First and foremost, of course, we thank the parents, teachers, and administrators in Eastland and Grover's Corners for taking time from their busy lives to share their knowledge and experiences with us. We are forever indebted to Eileen Landay, a mutual friend who realized that both our studies involved parents of high school students and put us in touch with each other in the first place.

We also thank other researchers and colleagues who helped in various ways: Pam Shufro (whose study in a suburban high school led to some of the same conclusions as ours); Lois N. André Bechely (who used readers' theater scripts from Jean's study to find that diverse urban parents shared concerns like those of parents in Eastland and Grover's Corners); and Pam Kay and other members of the American Educational Research Association School, Family, and Community Partnership Special Interest Group.

Members of our doctoral committees deserve our heartfelt thanks for their support and direction. Assisting Anne Dodd were Gordon Donaldson, Dick Barnes, Lynne Miller, David Silvernail, and Fran Wills; and helping Jean Konzal were William E. Bickel, Noreen Garman, Bruce Anthony-Jones, Leslie Cox-Salmon, and Carol Wishcamper. Jean also wishes to thank Robert Donmoyer and June Yennie-Donmoyer for their help and encouragement in the creation of the readers' theater scripts that were central to the success of her dissertation.

Thanks to those who contributed their skills and expertise in the production phase: copyeditor Debra Manette, Marilia Oliver, indexer Lisa Rivero, Susan Martin, Susan Bean, Lucrecia Gilman, Sarah Potter, and others who contributed to the book at various stages. Of course, we are indebted to those at St. Martin's Press who made this book possible, especially our editor, Michael Flamini, who encouraged us to submit a proposal and then remained enthusiastic and supportive when we felt like giving up; Mara Nelson; Jennifer Simington; and Alan Bradshaw.

Finally, we thank our families for their love and unwavering faith in our work: James Dodd, Vickie Dodd Gehm, and Suzan Dodd de los Heros; William Konzal, Gregory and Angela Konzal, and Philip and Cathy Stein.

Preface

In order for readers to make more informed judgments about the information and ideas we present, we would like to tell you a little about ourselves and the studies we independently conducted on which this book is based.

About the Authors

Anne Wescott Dodd

I sometimes tell my student teachers that I am a dinosaur because I have been involved in education since I graduated from college with a B.A. in History and Government more than three decades ago. After teaching high school English in Maine for one year, I went to Southern California. There I spent six years teaching English, social studies, and conversational French in two junior high schools—both of which included students from very diverse backgrounds—and earned an M.A. in English. Upon returning to Maine in the late 1960s, I worked as an elementary supervisor and English teacher in a small rural school district and then moved to the more prosperous and populated southern part of the state. I continued to teach English in two high schools and served as acting principal/assistant principal at a high school and principal of a middle school. Since 1984 I have taught education courses and worked with student teachers at Bates College, a liberal arts college in Lewiston, Maine. I am also on call as a consultant any time one of my two daughters has a question or problem about educating their six children in schools in Florida and Massachusetts.

Throughout the years I have been actively involved in several state and national professional organizations, conducted workshops for teachers in many school districts, and presented my work at state and national conferences. My publications include seven books (five of them in the field of education) and more than a hundred articles on educational topics in a variety of general interest publications, such as *The Christian Science Monitor*, *The Maine Sunday Telegram*, and *The Baltimore Evening Sun*, and in many professional journals, such as *Phi Delta Kappan*, *Educational Leadership*, and *Education Week*. My book *A Parent's Guide to Innovative Education* (Noble Press, 1992) was named one of the "Ten Best Books for Parents" by *Child Magazine* in 1992.

When I began work on my doctorate at the University of Maine in 1990, I already knew I wanted to focus my research on parents. I had seen from my own experience how important parents were to the success and smooth operation of schools, but I also wondered why the educational pendulum kept swinging—from progressive practices to "back-to-basics" approaches. As a middle school principal, for example, I encountered parents who refused to let their children participate in a five-day outdoor education program at a nearby camp. Instead, each year a few children were forced to sit in a self-contained study hall for a week while all of the other sixth graders were learning about nature firsthand, developing group skills, and building bonds with each other as they camped out and cooked their own food. These parents told me they didn't want their children to "have a vacation on school time." Yet other parents thought this week was the best part of the sixth-grade curriculum. Why did parents think so differently about what counted as "good" educational practices?

When I began looking for answers in the research, I was surprised to find that, although there were many studies on parents of young children, very few had been conducted with parents of secondary students. My dissertation, *Parents as Partners in Learning: Their Beliefs about Effective Practices for Teaching and Learning High School English*, an attempt to address this gap in the research, was named the 1996 Outstanding Dissertation by the Families as Educators Special Interest Group of the American Education Research Association.

A mutual friend put me in touch with Jean, who was also involved in learning more about parents' perspectives on secondary schools.

Jean L. Konzal

Although I am only in my second year as assistant professor of elementary and early childhood education at The College of New Jersey, I too have worked in education for many years. After graduating from Queens College's urban teacher preparation program in 1964, I taught in East Harlem in New York City for five years. Following that I gave birth to my son, and, after almost two years at home, I moved with my husband and son to New England because we wanted to experience more of the world than just New York. Since then our travels have taken us to New Hampshire, Arizona, Vermont, back to New Hampshire, to Maine and, most recently, to Pennsylvania and New Jersey.

As a result of this journey, I have the advantage of multiple perspectives of the American educational landscape. I have taught poor inner-city children in New York and in Tucson. I have taught poor rural children in New Hampshire. I have been a classroom teacher, a reading specialist, an educational consultant on a multidisciplinary team working with children with special needs, a consultant to teachers about mainstreaming, a staff development specialist for a school-university partnership, a state-level school reform consultant, and an evaluator of urban school restructuring efforts.

Parallel to and intertwined with my role as an educator has been my role as a parent. As a mother, I have struggled to find schools that are congruent with my beliefs about what should go on in "good" schools or to influence the schools that my son attended—and it hasn't been easy. I tried a variety of approaches: one-on-one conversations with my son's teachers and principals, participation on task forces, and volunteering in school. In retrospect, the only way that I actually was able to achieve my goals was to carefully investigate a number of schools and then to move to the community where the school most closely matched my ideas of a "good" school. It was this strategy that led us to move to Westminster West, Vermont. My son spent his second and third grades in a one-room country school in a town populated not only by longtime Vermonters, but also by a growing number of "flatlanders"—people like me from more urban areas who fled to rural Vermont in search of the good life. This school became my model for a "good" elementary school; the teacher there, Claire Oglesby, my model for a master teacher. My attempts to influence the public schools my son attended after this school, so they looked more like Claire's school, were not as successful. I found it was not easy for a parent—even one like me with many years as an educator—to influence school teaching and learning practices.

After working for seven years with Maine's Department of Education, I returned to school and in 1995 I earned a doctorate in Policy, Planning, and Evaluation from the University of Pittsburgh. At the time I decided to return to school, I had been working with teachers and principals of high schools in Maine who, in their attempts to change their teaching and learning practices, had run into countless problems. I wanted to gain a deeper understanding of these concerns. As I began reading about previous attempts to change schools, I became aware of a relatively unexamined issue, one that resonated with my own experiences as a parent—the role parents play in school change—and decided to examine this issue more fully. In writing my dissertation, *Our Changing Town, Our Changing School: Is Common Ground Possible?* I chose to break with tradition and present my findings in the form of two readers' theater scripts.[1] These scripts, designed to be used to open discussion about educational issues in any community, make my research accessible not only to scholars but also to practitioners, policymakers, and parents. My dissertation was awarded the 1997 Outstanding Dissertation Award by both the Families as Educators Special Interest Group and the Division D/Qualitative Research Special Interest Group of the American Education Research Association.

About the Studies

Both of our studies are qualitative case studies informed by our concerns for social justice. They were conducted in two small-town New England high schools, both of which had made changes in their teaching and learning practices. These studies, however, reflect but a moment in time at both schools. Since their completion, other changes—both in teaching practices and in ways of involving parents—have been introduced. While the results of our studies, like those of other qualitative studies, cannot be generalized to other schools and communities, the questions raised are questions that all schools should consider. (Appendix B provides further information about how we conducted our studies.)

Even though our studies used different methods and were based on different assumptions, we came to similar conclusions. We share our work to help readers understand why it is so important to make room for parent voices in the dialogue about school reform. As in the case of any disempowered group, parent voices have been marginalized in this discussion.

We describe the responses of our participants in depth in order to capture and better understand the complexities of their ideas—complexities that could not be uncovered with anonymous survey data—and to learn from them.

Because these communities are small and relatively homogeneous in terms of ethnicity (European American), religion (primarily Christian), and language (English in almost all cases), some might question whether the views of our participants represent those of others in larger, more diverse schools elsewhere. Interestingly, when Jean's two readers' theater scripts were presented to more diverse groups, both parents and educators said that the concerns mentioned in the scripts sounded very familiar to them. In any event, whether the issues raised by the parents we spoke with are the issues of importance in other places or not, we believe that readers will see that they probably do not know enough about the views of parents in their own communities. In fact, the areas of misunderstanding and lack of knowledge we discovered may be even greater and more problematic elsewhere.

About Our Purpose

This book is for parents, educators, and community members who are committed to school improvement. Differences in the ways people think about education in general and high schools in particular too often create conflict about school change. Instead of working together to improve schools for students, people join one side or the other in a war of words. No group—neither parents nor teachers—speaks with one voice. Yet we discovered that what appears to be lack of agreement may be the result of a lack of information or a misunderstanding. Thus we hope that by presenting in some depth the differing perspectives in two communities, readers will gain a better understanding of different ways of thinking in their own communities and begin to consider positive ways of resolving conflict. Students everywhere need and deserve better schools, not endless debate and dissension.

Most books written exclusively for parents seem to be "how-to" books with lots of advice about what parents should do in different situations—usually in relation to helping their own children succeed. These books typically do not discuss or provide a rationale for dealing with larger educational questions that every community must address. On the other hand, books written for educators tend to present a great deal of theory, but they offer little in the way of concrete suggestions for applying these theories in real schools. In this book we attempt to do both, but we should warn readers that we devote many more pages to parents than to teachers. We let parents speak throughout this book because their voices have not been heard. Teachers are also parents, and, even with professional knowledge, some will see their views expressed in the words of the parents we quote.

We begin by introducing Eastland and Grover's Corners (pseudonyms), the two communities in which the studies were conducted, and the parents from those communities whom we interviewed.

Introduction

About the Communities

In order to encourage open and honest conversations, we promised all those we interviewed anonymity. Therefore, all names of places and people have been changed. In some cases we have also changed other characteristics that might make either people or places identifiable.

We chose "Eastland" to signify a general geographic location within Maine. We borrowed "Grover's Corners" from Thornton Wilder's play *Our Town*, the story of a New England town at the turn of the century, in order to remind readers that today's town is rooted in memories of life in small-town New England. The Grover's Corners of *Our Town* casts a nostalgic shadow of life "as it was" on the Grover's Corners of today and influences how longtime residents respond to changes in the schools.

One group of parents interviewed for our studies lived in the New England town of Eastland; the other in the town of Grover's Corners. As a result of grants from the state and other sources, high schools in both communities had begun to make significant changes. The following descriptions of these communities and participants provide a context for understanding parents' views, which will appear throughout the book.

Eastland

I am bitter because when he was in middle school, the teachers told me it was the best class to come along in seventeen years. . . . Now so many of his friends have left to go to private school that he begs, "Dad, I really would like to leave."

—*Parent of a High School Student*

[When it was a factory town, other schools] made fun of the kids who lived in this town, especially when they came to play basketball in the "carpet barn" [a hangar-type gym building with a carpeted floor].

—High School Teacher

When I took drafting . . . you did everything by hand. You don't do that nowadays. You plug all your information into a computer. . . . The old way is gone. I'm not really very keen on it because you have a computer doing the work and you get very lazy.

—Parent of a High School Student

Nothing in school worked for me. That's why I dropped out in ninth grade.

—Parent of a High School Student

Eastland, a small coastal town in southern Maine, has a population of just under 7,000. At one time many of its citizens worked in factories, but the character of the town has changed in recent years as most of these factories have closed. Once a "mill town" and still home to some people who could be classified as working class, Eastland also serves as a bedroom community for many professionals who work in a nearby city. A coastal residential area in town is almost entirely upper-middle-class professional families, who for many years were able to choose a small (100 students) progressive elementary school in the neighborhood for their children. Although this school has since closed, the new elementary school building now houses three separate programs from which parents can choose: ungraded, multigraded, or classroom-based ("traditional"). Each program has its own wing and teaching principal. After the children graduate from Eastland Middle School, however, some of these professional parents send them to private schools rather than to Eastland High.

Eastland, perhaps best known today for its proliferation of retail shops, is a popular destination for many tourists. Downtown traffic is so heavy during the summer months that local residents often find it difficult to take care of routine business. The renovated school building that houses the town manager and other town officials is situated right in the center of the shopping district. (At the time of the study the office of the superintendent of schools was also located there; it has since moved about a block off the main street.) Few local residents shop in these designer stores, but some adults and teens depend on them for employment.

According to the 1990 U.S. Census data, which classifies Eastland as "rural" rather than "urban," the population was 99.1 percent white; other groups, represented in very small numbers, included Hispanic, black, American Indian, and Asian or Pacific Islander. Although most residents (63 percent of the population five years and older) were born in Maine, there was a small number (2.8 percent) of foreign-born residents. Eastland was better off economically than the state as a whole: Its median family income ($37,150) was almost $10,000 above that for the state, and only 2.5 percent of the families lived below the poverty line as compared with 8 percent for the state. Of the people twenty-five years and older, 14.5 percent reported not having graduated from high school, 85.5 percent were high school graduates, and 32.2 percent had graduated from college.

The Parents and Their Children. Educational background is the best way to show the range of parents interviewed, because among these parents there was sometimes little or no connection between their occupations and educational backgrounds. For example, one college graduate worked as a cabinet-maker; another repaired appliances for a major department store. Of the parents who participated in the study, a slightly lower number have college degrees (20 percent) than the U.S. Census lists for Eastland (32.3 percent) because, as noted above, by grade 11 some professionals had chosen to send their children to private schools and hence were not included.

Of the twenty-five parents interviewed, one was a grade school dropout, and two had dropped out of high school, while two others had later earned a high-school equivalency diploma (G.E.D.). Six parents were high school graduates, nine had some college or vocational/business school experience, and four were college graduates.

Finally, one parent, a former school administrator, held two advanced degrees.

The children of the parents interviewed represented an even number of males and females, but only nine of the participating parents were male. It was very difficult to find men to interview, in part because of the large number of single-parent families headed by women. Several married women explained that their husbands could not be interviewed because they worked out of town. One man agreed to an interview but was not home at the scheduled time for it. His wife did not give any explanation for his absence, but, when asked if she would be willing to talk, she said, "I'm here, ain't I?"

Most of the parents (64 percent) were Maine natives although only some of them had attended Eastland High. Twenty-eight percent were from out of state, and three parents originally came from outside the United States: one from Canada and two, surprisingly because they did not seem to know each other, from the same European country.

According to their parents, 37.5 percent of the children enrolled in grade 11 were "excellent" students while the others were described as "good" (29.1 percent), "fair" (16.6 percent), and "poor" or "very poor" (16.6 percent). Four children were enrolled in special education classes. Parents indicated that about half of the children planned to attend college after graduation while a third intended to go right into the workforce. Others were undecided about future plans.

All except two of the interviews were conducted in parents' homes, and the directions they gave for navigating Eastland's back roads were interesting and revealing. One man said to look for a "human-sized man with a rifle," a wooden cutout with the family name painted on it, in his front yard. Another said he lived in "the first trailer on the right with a green addition . . . a lot of Maine cars around there and a goat on the front lawn." Another parent lived in a beautiful old house that had been in her husband's family for years. The old part of the house reflected the way people lived in days gone by, but the interview took place in a skylighted family room–kitchen addition, a wonderful example of the best in contemporary design.

The District and the School. Unlike many other communities, for many years Eastland schools had actively involved parents. Thus there were a number of ways parents might learn about innovative practices. For over twenty years the district had offered parents the option of enrolling children in the very progressive ungraded elementary school mentioned earlier—and parent involvement there was so extraordinary that some called the school a "private public school." Seven of the children of parents interviewed had attended this ungraded school; while some praised the education their children received there, others were critical. One parent transferred her children from this school to a parochial school for "more structure and discipline."

All district schools for some time had had parent advisory committees, which often functioned most effectively in winning community support for proposed school budgets. Parent representatives were included on search committees when new administrators were hired. High school parents received copies of *News from Eastland High School*, a well-designed newsletter, which included articles about school activities and programs. Parent-teacher conferences, especially at report-card time in the fall, were encouraged. So, even though Eastland High had not involved parents directly in its restructuring effort, many had some information or background for understanding some of the changes that had been made there.

Some changes had been initiated by a former principal and were continued (and expanded) by the next principal. Other changes, as in Grover's Corner, began with the teachers. The American Studies course, for example, had been created by the teachers—one English and one history—who taught it. Although the entire high school faculty had participated in workshops and retreats on topics related to school reform and restructuring, parents had not been involved in these.

Grover's Corners

> I've been here thirty some odd years. I graduated from Grover's Corners High School, went a year to a business college, because my dad made me—I hated it. Now I work in the local market. I'm raising

my two kids on my own and it's not easy. They're both in high school and need a lot of things. You know, my dad gave me a piece of land, but I can't afford to keep it. I'm a third generation and they [those people from away] would just as soon turn around and say to me or my dad, who has major farmland, "Hey, if you can't cut it, then move the hell out." Well, if it wasn't for the people like us who had the land, where would they have gotten their land to build on and then they turn around and tell us to move? No way. They bring these yuppie couples in, add more kids to the school system, our taxes go up more, and it's just a vicious cycle.

—Parent of High School Student

My parents started out in Massachusetts and moved up here. I was born here. But there was just never any doubt that you would do the best you could do, be involved and expose yourself to different things. I would consider us being old Grover's Corners people. We're old Grover's Corners for sure, but we're not afraid to change. We're just forward-thinking people.

—Parent of High School Student

I have lived in five countries but find Grover's Corners a very comfortable place to live. It is very reminiscent of where I grew up. I was born in a working-class section where I went to school and eventually I went to one of the best universities in the country. I was in business for thirty-two years and have come here with my family to indulge my hobby of boat building.

—Parent of High School Student

Grover's Corners is a town in transition—a New England town of 11,856 residents trying to hold on to the strengths of its past as it moves into the future. It is home to one of the campuses of the state university, originally a two-year normal school for training teachers. Grover's Corners is a town much like any other small New England town—Main Street boasts a pizza restaurant, a sub shop, a convenience store, and a flea market at one end of town and a supermarket, a drugstore, and a five-and-dime at the other end. Scattered along the street are some hairdressers, insurance companies, banks, and the post office. Nothing on the street would tell a passerby that there was a university campus in town.

Driving through, one is struck by the ambivalence with which the town struggles today. New restaurants with a decidedly "yuppie" flavor have opened, as have a whole-foods market and a bookstore. These businesses are run by and cater to the "people from away"—a New Englandism for people not born in the state—whose numbers have increased during the past fifteen years. Living in new developments carved out of the rich farmland with magnificent vistas of rolling hillsides, these new people have brought new values and demands to the town. On the other hand, the old houses that line the main streets, the farm stands, the greenhouses, the sawmills, the gravel pits, and the farms reflect the great agricultural past. Grover's Corners was the last town in Newland County to hold on to its agricultural base. Late into the 1980s, more operating farms were located in Grover's Corners than in any other town. Disquieting images of this transition are impressed on the mind's eye: the lines of beautiful old homes distorted by modern awnings displaying the name of a Chinese take-out restaurant or a Subway chain, a weathered old farmer slowly driving his tractor down Main Street during the nightly rush hour followed by a stream of disgruntled drivers in a hurry to get home.

Negotiating the marriage between the "old" and the "new" in Grover's Corners has not been easy. Debates rage about how to maintain the small-town flavor of the village as commuters from outlying communities travel through the town's major crossroad to get to the nearby metropolitan center. Shrinking state revenues and increased taxes due to property reevaluation put citizens in a quandary. They need more economic development, but they don't want the development to spoil their small-town environment. New housing developments have brought in more young families who want more and more services, but they also want to preserve the bucolic quality of life that drew them to Grover's Corners in the first place. The school population is growing, requiring more staff, but the taxes raised by the new homes don't cover the costs of the increased services. The townspeople voted to recall the budget twice during the early 1990s because they thought the town council was not prudent enough and demanded more budget cuts. Longtime landholders in town, feeling the pressure of higher taxes, were forced to sell off acreage to developers. One farmer said, "These newcomers move into town for seven years, raise our taxes, and then move on. And we're stuck with the higher taxes." Some say that the dynamic tension has been healthy and has forced the town to respect the old while trying to accommodate the new. Others are not so sure it has been a positive experience.

The Parents and Their Children. Grover's Corners is a town in transition; some residents were born and raised in the town; others were born and raised elsewhere. Attempts were made to interview a cross-section of parents of high school seniors. Parents of seniors were selected because these students had experienced fully the new math and social studies curricula changes. Parents interviewed represented all socio-economic levels, as well as those from town and "from away."

Thirty-eight parents (twenty-eight women and nine men), including eight couples, two single mothers, and one grandmother were interviewed. Even though they look relatively homogeneous in terms of ethnicity (100 percent European American), when examined more closely they are a diverse group. One way they differed is in where they were raised: Ten, or 26 percent, were raised in Grover's Corners; thirteen, or 34 percent, were raised in other towns in the state; three or 8 percent, were born in the state but spent many years away; and twelve, or 32 percent, were raised out of state, including two who were born and raised in European countries. These differences influenced the diversity of experiences they had as children in school and their mental models of "good" schools.

The parents also differed in their occupations: seven (18 percent) were educators; five (13 percent) were in professions other than education; four (11 percent) were independent business consultants; four (11 percent) were small business owners; five (13 percent) were skilled tradespeople; five (13 percent) were entry-level white-collar workers; two (5 percent) were unskilled workers; one (3 percent) was a farmer; and five (13 percent) were homemakers or volunteers. Their different occupations and education influenced their aspirations for their children and the "cultural capital" they brought to their interactions with the schools. The parents also differed, although to a lesser degree, in terms of their children's academic success. Of the fifty-three children represented by the thirty-eight parents, the majority (thirty) were viewed as "good" students—their parents were satisfied with their academic progress. In addition, parents identified ten of the children as outstanding or gifted students, ten as children with learning problems, and three as "average" students who were not motivated. While children were identified as "outstanding" and as "good" by parents from all geographic origins (in town and from away), all but two of those children identified by their parents either as having learning problems or as being average but unmotivated came from families rooted in Grover's Corners or its surrounding towns.

The District and the School. Since 1983 the district has had two superintendents recognized for their skilled leadership of the change efforts. As one teacher said, "Grover's Corners has been blessed to have a couple of superintendents who not only stay on top of [the changes] and are articulate and are in favor of [them] . . . they [also] try to educate [the public] about what's going on and I think that's very important as well."

From 1983 through 1990 the district was led by a female superintendent who believed that raising the voice of teachers was important and who encouraged teachers to reflect on their teaching and take risks to make changes to increase students' learning. The superintendent who followed her continued and expanded on her emphasis on teacher leadership and began to bring together the disparate teacher-initiated change efforts into a more systemic district-wide effort. In reflecting on the change efforts the second superintendent said:

> [I]t was teacher voice, it was respect of teachers, it was a sense that
> teachers can make decisions, they can be trusted to make decisions.
> . . . I heard that over and over again. It wasn't hard to synthesize that.
> That was a key cornerstone of what [she] had brought to this
> organization. She'd never say this, but those were radical ideas in

1983 when supply closets were locked up. You were not allowed to go into supply closets unless you asked the principal to go in and get some construction paper. Think about it for a minute. . . . We've built upon that, both because we believe in it, but [also] because of the need for capacity. In order to change, in order to have capacity and adjust and improve and to grow as an organization and as individuals, we've taken teacher voice and teacher decision making [and moved] towards teacher leadership. [We've] really stretched that work in a number of directions that I'm very proud of.

In 1992 the district was chosen to be a pilot site for one of the New American Schools Development Corporation (NASDC) design teams—the National Restructuring Project (NRP).[1] While districtwide strategic planning had been initiated in 1990 with the arrival of the new superintendent, the project galvanized the district's efforts to develop a systemwide plan to create a results-oriented educational program for all students. Not all teachers viewed project participation as an opportunity. As one teacher said, "Imagine this, the first day the NRP staff arrived in a squad of Volvos with out-of-state license plates. They don't live here, what in the world do they know about us?"

Others, however, did see it as an opportunity to bring together all of what they had been working for individually and in small groups for the last ten years. Teachers took active roles in the project as a result of the superintendent's commitment to developing teacher leadership. Site developers were chosen; design teams were formed; school planning and management teams consisting of teachers, parents, administrators, and students were formed at each school; teachers, parents, and students attended summer institutes, conferences, and meetings at the other pilot sites. A very busy and exhausting three years ensued.

About the Book

Like people everywhere, parents in Eastland and Grover's Corners want good schools and good teachers for their children. Many recognize that schools must change to prepare students for living and working in a rapidly changing society, but the parents aren't always pleased about specific changes educators introduce in these high schools. Such disagreements, of course, can and do create conflict, but, as readers will see in the chapters that follow, other factors also complicate the relationships between parents and high school educators. Even the reasons parents disapprove of specific practices are more complex than one might guess.

Part I provides a context for understanding the problem: why improving relationships between parents and educators matters (Chapter 1), how what has happened in the past explains the situation today (Chapter 2), how teachers as professionals and parents as active participants in the life of a school have competing and contradictory roles that complicate their relationships (Chapter 3), and what influences parents to have different opinions about high schools (Chapter 4).

Part II focuses on understanding the tensions created because people have different ideas about teaching and testing. Chapter 5 presents profiles of four Eastland parents to show the range of opinions about teaching and learning—from the most traditional to the most progressive views. It is easy to see why educators face a difficult challenge in finding common ground when people think so differently. Chapter 6 looks more closely at different perspectives on what and how students should learn in three specific subjects: English, social studies, and mathematics. By presenting different opinions on how student learning should be assessed, Chapter 7 helps explain why there is so much debate about establishing standards for learning and high-stakes testing to measure student achievement.

Part III moves from research and theory to concrete suggestions that may help educators and others build bridges from schools to parents and the community. To show that high schools can involve parents in meaningful ways, Chapter 8 describes what four very different programs have actually done to bring people together. In Chapter 9 readers will find snapshots (short versions of programs and practices across the country) and other suggestions for inviting parents and community members to work with educators. In the last chapter, "A Call To Action," we explain what we think are principles to guide the difficult but very important process of going beyond simply "involving" parents to building democratic communities. Ideally all stakeholders will participate in the process of creating a caring and democratic high school in which *all* children learn. We invite readers to share their knowledge of communities and high schools where similar efforts are underway by writing to us at our respective institutions (Bates College, Lewiston, ME 04240 or The College of New Jersey, Ewing, NJ 08628) or by e-mail (adodd@bates.edu or konzal@tcnj.edu).

We hope that, when readers think about the issues we raise and the suggestions we offer, they will commit themselves to inviting parents and others into conversations about schools in their own cities and towns. Although making decisions about schools in the United States is a local function, improving the quality of schools and the education of children should be a goal all Americans share.

PART ONE

Understanding the
Often Problematic Relationships
between Parents and Schools

Why Focus on Improving Relationships between Parents and Educators?

An ideal relationship between parents and teachers has to be based on some mutual respect, mutual trust—that we understand their point of view, they understand ours. Not that being skeptical is bad, but there's got to be that underlying trust that we're trying to do the best job we can do. It's when it appears that trust isn't there, from either side, or that we're not listening to them or we're not listening to their interests, that we have gotten into trouble with each other.

—*High School Teacher*

Parental involvement, defining it. That is tough. Does [a parent] get to go in there and be the veto power?

—*High School Teacher*

Every parent wants to know that their kid is getting a good education, but it is hard to get involved at the high school level.

—*Parent of a High School Student*

I'm thrilled to be doing this interview. It's about time someone asked parents what they think.

—*Parent of a High School Student*

Despite the fact that many teachers believe a lack of support from parents makes teaching more difficult than it used to be, all parents want their children to be successful in school. And contrary to the opinions of many parents, teachers are just as interested as parents are in assuring that every child succeeds.

Parents and educators have good reason to join together in a common cause because both desire good schools where all students can learn, where what is good for "my" child is what is good for all children. For a variety of reasons, however, relationships between educators and parents of high school students are often nonexistent, prickly, or problematic.

Conflicts Threaten the Public Schools

Because parents and educators have not had closer relationships with each other, no one should be surprised that any attempt to change schools may generate bitter conflict. You may recall a headline in your local paper that echoes the concerns reflected in one of these: "California Parents Target Math Frameworks," "Harbor Creek Parents Knock School Board's Move towards Block Scheduling," or "Requiem for a Reform: Shifting Winds Uproot a Colorado District's Plans."

The debate over setting higher standards for all students provides a good illustration of the types of conflicts brewing in many communities. While most would agree with the idea of setting higher standards for students and realize that such standards will require significant change in schools, parents and educators may not agree on what this change would mean. For many parents, "higher standards" means more discipline in schools and an increased focus on learning the "basics." On the other hand, many educators interpret the phrase to mean encouraging students to become self-directed learners and developing higher-order thinking skills. These conflicting ideas can be like simmering coals, ready to flare up at any time.

On a national level, many people worry that, if education does not improve, the United States will lose its edge in the global economic competition. Thus there seems to be widespread support for higher standards and more tests—especially tests showing the performance of

U.S. students in relation to those in other countries. But as soon as Michigan instituted a test based on newly adopted higher standards, some parents opposed their children's participation in the testing, believing that it would harm rather than help them.[1] The rule of thumb seems to be "Institute a change, and someone complains."

A few years ago educators in Littleton High School in Littleton, Colorado, embarked on an ambitious plan to revise their curriculum, to raise standards, and to require students to meet rigorous new graduation requirements. Teachers and administrators received accolades from other educators, both locally and nationally. The district was considered a bellwether—leading the way toward a new mode of teaching and assessing learning at the high school level. There was one problem, however. When parents learned about the high-stakes nature of the innovations—that some students wouldn't graduate on time as a result of not meeting the new requirements—they rebelled against the changes. All of the hard work of the teachers and administrators accomplished nothing. The school board rescinded the new practices, forced the superintendent to resign, and pushed schools to return to more traditional practices. While some say the schools didn't do a good job of informing the public, school board member Karen Kaplan said the district did reach out: "[S]ometimes you forget . . . that the stakeholders change. . . . The major issue underneath all this stuff, is that there are major philosophical differences in the community, and we don't know how to address them and talk about them with each other."[2]

These differences among people's perspectives also show up in other places. Besides the frequent attacks on the public schools by Rush Limbaugh and others, a number of recently published books, such as *The Schools We Need and Why We Don't Have Them* by E. D. Hirsch, a proponent of cultural literacy, and policy scholar Dana Mack's *The Assault on Parenthood: How Our Culture Undermines the Family,* argue that schools should go back to the "good old days." Mack, for example, criticizes nearly every aspect of the current school improvement effort—from setting standards to cooperative learning—because she believes these changes serve the needs of the workplace, not those of children and their parents. Her main point is that institutions cannot raise children as well as families can. Parents, not professionals, know what is best for their children, and, Mack argues, we need policy changes to support parents' interests.[3]

Many of the parents we interviewed share some of Mack's concerns. They say that the schools don't want to hear their point of view because it isn't "politically correct." When they feel their views are discounted, they don't see the value of getting involved in school activities—even the ones specifically designed for them. "What's the use?" they ask. "They won't listen to us." Then, when parents don't participate, teachers and administrators say "See? We invited them to come and nobody came. Parents are not interested in being involved."

In addition to attacks in the media and the lack of participation in school-sponsored parent involvement activities, there are other indications of a lack of support for public schools. More parents are choosing to home school their children—in 1997 for the first time ever a home-schooled student won the National Spelling Bee. More people are speaking up for school choice in the form of charter schools and vouchers, which might give parents the option of sending their children to private (perhaps even including parochial) schools at public expense.

If teachers and administrators continue to attempt to make changes in the teaching and learning practices in schools without the understanding and support of parents and the public, they face the potential of seeing their work come to naught, as did Littleton High School educators. And if parents continue to choose not to be involved except to protest a change, they give up their opportunity to influence what goes on in schools. Or perhaps even worse, as educator Philip Schlechty suggests in *Inventing Better Schools: An Action Plan for Educational Reform*: "[I]f schools are not changed in dramatic ways very soon, the public schools will not be a vital part of America's system of education in the twenty-first century."[4] How important are the public schools?

The Survival of Democracy
Requires Finding Common Ground

Democracy rests on the quality of the local schools. Providing an effective and accessible system of public education is the only way to guarantee that all children, regardless of family background or income level, will have equal opportunities to become the best citizens and parents they can be. Although charter schools and voucher plans undoubtedly would help some children, they may hurt the children of parents who lack the practical knowledge and know-how to take advantage of these options. Many scholars worry that the creation of educational alternatives will draw so many students and resources away from existing schools that the neediest children will be the only ones left to learn in even more intellectually and financially impoverished environments.

Clearly, the variety of opinions about the purpose and design of public schools suggests that public education may need to be reinvented; the preservation of the nation's democratic way of life requires that citizens try. This challenge is not just for educators. Everyone must get involved, for the quality of every American's life will depend on the quality of education offered to all.

Democratic Society, Democratic Schools

A democratic society requires actively engaged citizens—citizens who accept responsibility to care for those who live in their communities, their state, and their nation as well as those in their own families. In a strong democracy there will always be a tension between the rights of the individual and the rights of the community; between honoring and celebrating differences while seeking common threads that bind people together. Schools, as public institutions, are places where these tensions have been played out and where together Americans have struggled to find resolution for them in daily life.

Americans have not always succeeded in dealing with these tensions in honorable ways—but people have continued to try. However, if more and more of our children are educated in schools that separate them by religion, by race or ethnicity, by values, by class—as will many of the new alternatives to public schools—citizens will lose the opportunity to struggle with these tensions, to learn to live with differences, and to assume civic responsibility for each other. And everyone will pay for these losses. As families and schools have failed, there have been increases in crime, substance abuse, and domestic violence—and, as some have said, it costs the same amount to imprison a person for a year as it would to send him or her to Harvard University. Schools cannot solve these complex problems alone, but improving schools is certainly a way to take the first step.

While we support the right for all parents to choose the schools they believe are best for their children, we also believe that perhaps there is a way to entice more parents to choose the public schools—to re-create the public school as the new common school, serving the interests of all the children in the community. We propose that public high schools become a model of democracy—a place that carefully nurtures a culture where all voices are heard and respected, where civic engagement is the norm, and where people struggle together to resolve the tensions between the good of the individual and the good of the community.

In the ideal democratic school, the voices of teachers, administrators, parents, and students would be sought out, listened to, and respected; there would be an ongoing effort to seek agreement about the school's purpose, practices, and outcomes; and differences of opinion would be respected when agreement couldn't be reached. A democratic school community would be one in which all members feel welcome, know each other, care for each other, and trust and respect each other.

Common Values, Beliefs, and Ideals—Or Not

Researchers and theorists—and common sense—tell us that, when parents, educators, and students share values, beliefs, and ideals about schooling, there is a better chance of creating schools everyone will support.[5] Perhaps even more important, other studies have shown that students are more likely to be successful when parents and educators agree on what a school should be. Sociologists James S. Coleman and Thomas Hoffer, for instance, found that "Catholic high schools do a better job of educating students and have lower dropout rates than public schools." They speculate that the difference lies in "the strongly supportive community built up between parents and teachers . . . based on a shared set of beliefs and values. Such cohesive communities of adults are almost totally absent from most public schools."[6]

History, however, reveals that both locally and nationally, Americans have found it difficult to form and sustain such a shared vision of schooling. The history of American education in this century can be viewed as the story of competing visions for schools.[7] At any given point one vision is more dominant, but, as time passes and circumstances change, power shifts to a competing vision. Consider how, in the last few decades, for example, policymakers, legislators, school boards, and others have made decisions that reflect particular visions of education. For a variety of reasons, once highly-touted reforms disappear. Some readers will recall these attempts at school change.

- The effects of *Sputnik* on schools in the late 1950s and early 1960s led to concerns about making the curriculum more rigorous with particular emphasis on science and "new math."
- In the late 1960s and early 1970s, a reaction to this focus on "academics" resulted in a push for open classrooms, more electives, and the adoption of more humanistic teaching practices, such as values clarification and small-group projects.
- These changes caused people to worry about the erosion of standards, so in the late 1970s and early 1980s, it was "back to the basics" again.
- Reform efforts in the early 1980s—standardized tests, more requirements—gave way to the current push for "restructuring," a very loose umbrella under which can be found everything from innovative teaching practices and school choice to strategies that redistribute power and responsibility in the classroom, school, and larger community.
- "Restructuring" has continued in the 1990s with a particular focus on setting standards and developing more authentic assessment for student learning.

As the current reform movement leads to the adoption of many nontraditional practices, the potential for community conflicts about schools, reminiscent of earlier efforts to introduce more student-centered practices, is likely to increase.

The views of the parents with whom we talked are, no doubt, shared by many other parents across the country. When teachers focus on teaching students how to solve problems, parents fear their children will not learn "the basics." When teachers teach writing as a process, they ignore errors on first drafts, causing parents to worry their children will never learn to spell correctly. Even though parents may agree with the idea of computer literacy, many fear that children who become too dependent on technology will not be able to cope when the power goes off. When schools eliminate tracked classes, parents of honor students fear their children will be held back, while others are concerned that children who may have learning problems will be pushed ahead too fast.

Of course, parents do not all speak with one voice, but many parents think that these and other changes are being introduced into schools for no good reason, as these comments from parents we interviewed suggest:

> Our kids just seemed to be getting "guinea pigged" all the way along into these new concepts.

> I say, "Let's not fix it if it's not broken."

> I know that's really an old-fashioned way of saying things but that has worked for years and years.

> I go along with the old school. That's the way I did it. Why change it?

When parents don't understand or accept the value of the changes introduced into schools, they are likely to object, as some parents in Eastland did when their children were forced to study English and history together in a required American Studies course. These parents demanded that the school board get rid of the course and go back to teaching the subjects as two separate courses.

History is likely to repeat itself: When educators rush to change their practices without involving parents in the process, opposition may cause innovations to pass from schools. Americans' failure to agree on a common vision about the purpose of education and what constitutes a "good" school for students may prove to be the Achilles' heel of school improvement efforts. It also may undermine the very foundation of our democracy. If people believe that public schools are important enough to preserve, then parents and educators must work together to find some common ground. Both groups have much to contribute: Parents have personal knowledge of their children and their communities that educators lack, and educators have professional knowledge about teaching and learning that most parents do not have.

A Process for Beginning

A journey of a thousand miles begins with a single step.
—Chinese proverb

Because parents and educators must work together to create schools where all children can learn, in this book we will share what we have learned from studying their differing perspectives on schools, teaching, learning, and curriculum and classroom practices.

We recognize that schools are complex institutions and that there is no shortage of serious and thorny issues. For example, some suburban schools offer students clean, well-lighted buildings with computers and sometimes even swimming pools; well-educated teachers; and opportunities for students with special interests and talents, such as Advanced Placement courses and extensive art and music programs. On the other hand, as author and reform advocate Jonathan Kozal shows in *Savage Inequalities,* inner-city students get the short end of the stick: grim school buildings in need of repair, classes in lunchrooms and bathrooms, and teachers, who, even when they are well prepared and dedicated, struggle to teach larger classes with fewer resources.[8]

These inequities in school funding and resource distribution must be addressed, but doing so will take a multifaceted and aggressive response at both the national and state levels. However, even without a solution to these difficult educational problems, we believe that, at the local level, parents and educators can begin to make schools better by joining together in a concerted effort to build school communities where all voices are heard. We have chosen to focus on this challenge: the need to rethink the roles and relationships of parents and educators in high schools.

Why high schools? Although much has been written about the importance of involving parents in elementary school communities, and in many areas this has begun, very little has been written about high schools, and even less has been done. Some people take the position that once children reach high school age, they object to having their parents involved. Others accept as a *fait accompli* the commonly held belief that parents are less likely to become involved in high schools and so it is not worth the effort to try to get them involved. While both points may be partly true, it is also true that parents are particularly concerned about what goes on in high schools, for, as their children get closer to graduation, parents focus more and more on how well the school is preparing their children for life after high school, whether it be for the workplace or further education. Because the stakes are higher, parents are less tolerant of educators' experiments with their children, experiments that may prevent them from later getting good jobs or being admitted to good colleges.

We believe that if educators, parents, and policymakers have a better understanding of the complex crosscurrents—differing images of schools; differing ideas about the roles of parents and educators; differing beliefs about the nature of the teaching and learning process; differing opinions about what students should learn, how they should be taught, and how achievement should be measured—that underlie the tensions, they may be able to avoid full-scale conflicts about schools. Educators can help move their communities from dissension about education to dialogue about teaching, learning, and classroom practice. Through this process we hope everyone also can learn positive and productive ways of interacting that may lead to resolving other important educational and community issues beyond the walls of individual schools.

Because educators must work *with* parents to make these needed changes, we would like them to think in a new way about building trust and common ground with parents. We hope they will see the need to engage parents and other community members in ongoing conversations about teaching and learning practices. And we hope that parents—or others who care about good schools—will see why they must get involved. It isn't enough for them to sit back and say nothing until the school does something that seems wrong for their children. Both parents and educators have much to learn from and with each other.

Readers should not expect to find a solution in this book because there are many "solutions"—what is best in any community must be decided by the people in that community. Even when the issue is similar, the resolution may be different. Instead, we present the perspectives of some educators and parents to increase readers' understandings and suggest some ideas that may help them find ways to collaborate in making decisions to improve their schools. Because parents' voices often have not been heard except when educators are distracted by the immediate need to appease critics of a particular practice, we have given a great deal of space to parents' and educators' comments and concerns. We hope that readers will take the time to reflect on those perspectives and, in the process, see new ways that parents and educators might collaborate in making decisions to improve their own schools.

The process best begins with conversation. Conversation is the first step to building a common vision and finding ways that everyone—people from differing socioeconomic, cultural, racial, and ethnic groups and with differing political interests and ideas about schools—can participate in a democratic process to work together toward the important goal about which there is no disagreement: providing the very best education possible for America's children.

What Can Be Learned from Looking at the Past?

We had great success, up until twenty-five years ago, using this method of teaching. . . . Who put it into kids' minds that they shouldn't like it? In the 1960s, every tradition was out the window, everything. . . . We don't pay attention to anything that ever happened past yesterday.

—Parent and Community Activist

When I came up here and saw what they had here and heard people say "What was good enough for us back then is good enough for our kids now," I thought, "Well, gee, it wasn't like that for me!" And so I like seeing them become more progressive. I feel like we're becoming part of the world rather than this little closed community."

—Parent of a High School Student

My kids respect teachers. If my kid ever said anything [disrespectful] to a teacher, I'd want to know about it. And I guarantee it's going to get taken care of. But there's too many people who are not doing that. It's a very serious problem today.

—Parent of a High School Student

I remember being afraid of my teachers. They were so stern and military looking. . . .They were a lot stricter back then. Teachers are a lot different today. I think it's easier for kids nowadays than when I went to school.

—Parent of a High School Student

Many people believe that public schools are not as good as they once were. They remember—or maybe just wish for—the "good old days" when teachers were in charge, students behaved, and the focus was on making sure that all students learned the "three Rs." Some would say the "good old days" never really existed—everything is more complex and problematic than it first appears. It is true that at one time communities, schools, and families were more closely connected than is the case today. When schools were smaller than most are now, they could, of course, more easily adapt to community norms. We tend not to remember that the current system of public schools people take for granted was not always in place and that conflict about schooling— not just about teaching methods and curriculum but even about the existence and design of public education—is nothing new.

Although this country was established to reflect a democratic ideal, Americans have not always agreed on what *democracy* means in practice. Nowhere can this be seen more clearly than in the changing ideas about public education. Reformers today argue that not only should equal access to a free and appropriate education be provided for all children, but also ways must be found to ensure that they all will learn—regardless of ability, learning style, or ethnic or racial background. This is a worthy and ambitious goal, given the diversity and complexity of schools and society. Setting this as a national goal seems a logical approach to mobilize widespread support for it, but public education always has been the province of state and local agencies, not the federal government. And while some states, such as California and Texas, have exerted a large degree of control over their schools, others, like New Hampshire and Maine, lean much more toward local control.

Thus, in diverse ways, depending on who they are and where they live, people continue to struggle with the same difficult questions that challenged Americans in the past: How do we educate for a democracy? Who gets educated? For what purpose? And who decides?

As readers look back to see how public education developed into what could be described as a universal, bureaucratic system offering something for everyone, it may help to remember that there is a difference between *schooling* and *education.* Children are learning all the time from many sources—family, peers, the media, to name just a few. *Education,* then, occurs outside of schools as well as in them. When people talk about public education, they are discussing only one aspect of education, *schooling,* and that was not always as important for children of the past as it is for today's children.

One reason why answering questions about public education seems so difficult is that, over the years, people have come to expect public schools to educate more children, for more time, and for more purposes. Author and scholar Kieran Egan believes that some of the nation's problems stem from the fact that schools have been expected to serve three distinctive but incompatible purposes: "to serve as a significant agency in socializing the young," "to teach particular forms of knowledge that will bring about a realistic and rational view of the world," and "to help realize the unique potential of each child."[1] For example, if educators decided to focus on the socializing function, providing students with knowledge and skills needed for life, and changed the curriculum in order to do that well, they might not at the same time be able to prepare students with the forms of abstract knowledge and thought also considered important. Or, put another way, if the main goal were to foster the personal and intellectual potential of each individual child, schools would look very different. By trying to serve all of these purposes simultaneously, schools do none of them well. Furthermore, people with differing ideas about which purpose is more important will disagree when others with a different purpose in mind push for change in schools.

Regardless of how the problem is framed, it is clear that designing a system of public education for everyone presents a greater challenge than it did when schooling was thought to be necessary for only a privileged few. And if more people are invited to participate in making decisions about schools, the additional challenge arises of figuring out how individuals with varying—and perhaps even contradictory ideas—can work together to create schools that can accommodate multiple perspectives and multiple purposes. Given these complexities, it's no surprise that people might wish things were as simple as they were in the past. But was there ever such a time?

Education in Colonial America

When the country was first settled, all children were "educated," but very few were "schooled." In addition to learning, primarily from family members, the skills they needed for daily life—everything from growing crops to cooking food and making clothing—children were educated in moral virtue. As historian Lawrence Cremin puts it: "At the outset, preaching and catechizing were the forms of education most widely practiced" in the colonies.[2] Since many of the colonies were established for religious reasons, education differed depending on the particular religion in each colony. Schooling came later when the communities were more stable, but, as Cremin points out, it was not long in coming because "it was viewed by the colonists as the most important bulwark after religion in their incessant struggle against the satanic barbarism of the wilderness."[3]

For a long time the family and the church remained as the most important educational institutions because schools, when they were established, were not available to everyone. The first schools, which usually copied the models colonists knew in European schools, were diverse as were the teachers who taught in them, "ranging from the literate but relatively untutored housewives who maintained 'dame schools' in their kitchens to the cultured university graduates who presided over the better grammar schools."[4] Intellectual qualifications were perhaps less important for teachers than piety and good character.

However, except for the students who were preparing for the university, children attended school for only a few years. School was in session intermittently—when there were no other more pressing demands, such as crops to be harvested. Nonetheless, these schools did enable students to become literate and opened the doors "to new ideas, new occupations, and new lifestyles" beyond those of a particular family or neighborhood. At the same time, however, as Cremin suggests, wherever schools were established, they were viewed as a way of "promoting uniformity."[5] This purpose was more easily achieved in the relatively homogeneous communities of Colonial America than it would be today.

Nowhere was this more true than in New England, where the town was "essentially a body of householders organized for political, social, and religious purposes—an association useful for communal defense, desirable for local government, and utterly indispensable for the creation of an exemplary Christian society." Within such a society, Cremin points out, family, church, and school could be mutually reinforcing because "responsibilities moved easily from one institution to another."[6]

New England took the lead in promoting schooling. In 1642 Massachusetts became the first colony to require that all students be taught to read; in 1647 it was the first to require that every town of over fifty families establish an elementary school and that those of one hundred families have a Latin grammar school. Massachusetts could also boast of having the oldest secondary school—Boston Latin, established in 1635—and the oldest college—Harvard, chartered in 1639.

In general, however, opportunities for formal schooling in Colonial America were limited. Even where there were schools, African Americans and Native Americans usually were not included. An exception was Pennsylvania, a Quaker colony, where some schools were open to all children. Most Americans today would call Colonial attitudes about educating females sexist. Since girls would be wives and mothers, most people did not think much formal education was necessary—or even desirable—for females. They were taught to read and write to fulfill religious and family duties, but they were not allowed to attend the grammar schools or colleges whose curricula were designed to prepare males to be ministers and lawyers, professions not open to females.[7]

The Common School: Basic Education for Everyone

In the first part of the nineteenth century, most people still viewed education as a "luxury."[8] Thus, as Cremin points out, schooling varied greatly due to variations in instruction and the difficulty of deciding what could be called a "school." He notes, though, that "there were individual teachers of reading, writing, ciphering, grammar, book-keeping, surveying, navigation, fencing, dancing, music, modern languages, embroidery, and every conceivable combination of these and other subjects; that these teachers taught part time and full time . . . in their homes, in other people's homes, in rented rooms, in churches . . . , in abandoned buildings, and in buildings erected especially for their use. . . ."[9] Some children also learned through apprenticeships; often children as young as seven years of age were sent to live with a master from whom they learned a trade.[10]

The elementary or district school provided basic literacy, but it did not offer children any opportunity to improve their social status. With very few exceptions, only males from upper-class families attended the Latin grammar schools in preparation to enter college. Yet throughout the nineteenth century, "forces of frontier egalitarianism, political democratization, and economic change" eroded the two-track system, which had been copied from the European model of education.[11]

After the Revolutionary War, many Americans began to realize that a patchwork system of public, private, and religious schools would not foster the unity necessary for the newly created democracy. The movement to establish common schools was the basis of the contemporary American belief in the power of a free universal education to improve both the individual and the society. The common school was established to provide the "basic tools of literacy that could be used in everyday life and for ongoing practical education." It was "common" in that it was "open to all children of all social and economic classes."[12] However, privileged students (read: white males), who needed a classical ("college prep") curriculum because they were being groomed for positions of leadership, attended academies or Latin grammar schools.

But it took a long time to establish a system of free public education. The movement, intended to develop "a unifying bond of culture" was energetically led with a missionary zeal by noted educator Horace Mann. The effort to establish these free (paid for through taxes) common schools, however, was often hindered by bitter political struggles.[13] "[F]or twenty-five years the outcome [whether or not to establish public schools] was uncertain. Local elections were won and lost on the school issue. The tide of educational reform flowed in one state, only to ebb in another. . . . State laws requiring public schools were ignored by the local communities that were supposed to build them."[14]

Where there was consensus about creating public education in the nineteenth century, historians David Tyack and Elisabeth Hansot report that it stemmed mainly from a belief system described as "a Protestant-republican ideology, a source of unity in a highly decentralized nation."[15] The contemporary concern about separating church and state was not an issue. Strong ties between education and religion served as a base for the first public schools. Children learned moral character from stories in *McGuffey's Readers*, and, even today, some older Americans can probably still recall reciting Bible verses as part of the opening activities in school when they were young. It was perhaps this appeal to people's moral sensibilities and their desire to instill Christian virtues that eventually led people to be convinced that creating a system of public schools was the right thing to do. The consensus in favor of public education was greatly influenced by the compelling rhetoric of speakers like Horace Mann, whose speeches can be described as "secular sermons."[16]

Yet there were people for whom the reformers did not speak. Since these reformers were typically "British-American in origin, Protestant in religion, and entrepreneurial in economic outlook, they wore blinders of their class, religion, and ethnic background. They were intolerant of the Roman Catholic Church and so alienated Catholics that they hastened the growth of a separate parochial-school system. . . . Of course, many leaders assumed their own values were the only moral ones."[17] While all groups shared the idea that children should be educated formally and moral training was important, they disagreed about the actual content and approaches for education. Then, as now, there were questions about whose values, whose views, would prevail, and, as Tyack and Hansot describe the debates, there is yet another indication that the past was not so much different from the present day: "In reading the debates over such issues one is struck by how much both sides talked past one another, perhaps because the values they expressed were so deeply embedded in their own cultures that they believed them to be the only ones reasonable people could hold."[18]

By 1860, though, a majority of states had established public school systems, and free elementary education was widely available. A few communities also provided secondary education by then. The small-town common school, usually with one room, not only served as a place to educate young people, it also became a center of community life. Historian David Tyack describes a number of ways the one-room school met the community's needs: "[M]inisters met their flocks, politicians caucused with the faithful, families gathered for Christmas parties and hoedowns, the Grange held its baked-bean suppers, Lyceum lecturers spoke, . . . and neighbors gathered to hear spelling bees and declamations."[19]

In the small rural community everyone knew everyone else. Teachers, even if they came "from away," were part of the community; they often boarded with local families. As one researcher notes in his book about small-town rural schools and communities, "schools d[id] more than educate children; they also maintain[ed] communities."[20] Because most rural people encountered it daily, "the common school both reflected and shaped a sense of community."[21]

Yet such close relationships were not always positive. If the families got along, community life could be fairly harmonious. On the other hand, if there were feuds or animosity, the school could be caught in the middle of warring factions. Sometimes community arguments were about the schools themselves. For example, the location of a new school was a common reason for disagreement. Tyack writes about the night a group of Iowa farmers actually moved a schoolhouse to their preferred location, a mile away from its original site. And in a small Oregon town, three feuding groups each tried to maintain its own separate school. Despite these problems, the rural school usually served to build rather than diminish the sense of the community in small towns.[22]

The smaller any community was, the greater the opportunity for citizens to have a say in who the new teacher would be or how schools should be run. Even if parents didn't actively participate in making the decisions about school, they knew what was going on. They could trust educators to provide the kind of education they believed their children needed because most teachers lived in the community. Teachers were neighbors who knew and respected the community's values, customs, and beliefs. Relationships and personalities were more important than formal status. The people believed the school was "theirs to control (whatever the state regulations might say) and not the property of the professional educator."[23] Then, as now, however, well-liked teachers without any positional power could exert considerable influence through their own personal power.

Ultimately, though, the teacher served at the pleasure of the local board, and there could be conflicts. Tyack provides some interesting examples to illustrate:

> [An] Oregon teacher followed the state course of study which required her to have the children write their script from the bottom of the page up "in order to see the copy at the top of the page." An irate committeeman warned her that "if you don't have the kids write from the top down, I'll have you fired." He won. But when other trustees objected to building two privies—one for boys and one for girls, as the state law said—the same teacher convinced them to comply by showing it would cost only twenty dollars for the two privies together.[24]

Small rural schools may have had benefits that the larger consolidated schools, which came later, couldn't offer, but all was not idyllic. Teachers in these schools were not well educated nor were the schools well financed. Historian Herbert Kliebard writes: "At the heart of America's educational system in the nineteenth century was the teacher. It was the teacher, ill-trained, harassed and underpaid, often immature, who was expected to embody the standard virtues and community values and, at the same time, mete out stern discipline to the unruly and the dullwitted."[25]

Another historian, Lawrence Cremin, is also critical of rural schools of the 1890s:

> Everywhere the mundane problems . . . had become overwhelming. Rural schools . . . had been allowed to fall into disrepair and disrepute. Cut off from the pedagogical mainstream and frequently beset by problems of rural decline, they remained ungraded and poorly taught. Recitations averaged ten minutes per subject per class, and untrained teachers continued to concentrate on "the same old drill in the same old readers."[26]

Urban schools of that time weren't any better. Buildings were "badly lighted, poorly heated, frequently unsanitary, and bursting at the seams [with] young immigrants." Superintendents wished they could reduce class size to "sixty [students] per teacher."[27] It might be thought that these schools would not be the model a community would want to copy, but, in fact, a scaled-down version of the more bureaucratic urban school eventually became the norm everywhere in this country except in the smallest, most geographically isolated communities.

The High School:
Expanding the Idea of Basic Education

Public schooling during most of the nineteenth century could best be described as rural, unbureaucratic, and "dependent on hundreds of thousands of lay promoters and school trustees."[28] The schools were small, often containing only one room, and their major purpose was to provide basic literacy and skills for living. Only a few students attended grammar schools or academies (which today are called "prep schools") as preparation for higher education and professions.

In some areas students were able to extend their education beyond this basic level, but only a small number of public high schools existed until the second half of the nineteenth century. Gradually, however, the high school began to replace the academy, providing educational opportunities for more students, despite the resistance of taxpayers who did not want to pay for it. After a series of court rulings in the 1870s ensured that public funds could be used to pay for high schools, the movement to create them spread more rapidly. By 1890 more than 200,000 students were enrolled in the nation's 2,526 public high schools; fewer than 95,000 students were enrolled in the 1,600 private secondary schools and academies.[29]

Because the high school at the beginning of the twentieth century began to serve as a response to the particular educational needs of American society, it was different from European secondary schools, which separated students according to their future plans.[30] American high schools served students who planned to go on to college and those who would enter the workforce by differentiating the curriculum (college prep, vocational, etc.) in one school rather than by establishing separate schools.

Because urban schools had to serve so many more students than those in small towns and villages, educators looked for new ways to organize them. And because of the great influx of poor immigrants to the cities, the schools took on a new purpose: to socialize students into the American culture. This meant not only teaching them English but also teaching them what today would be called white middle-class values.

Coping with students from other countries was a great challenge for urban educators. In 1908 investigators for the U.S. Senate Immigration Commission, who counted the ethnic origins of students in thirty-seven cities, found more than sixty nationalities, and fifty-eight percent of all students had fathers who had been born abroad. Particularly hard hit was New York, a major port of entry. Historian David Tyack writes that "from 1899-1914 there was a 60 percent increase in school enrollment. . . . [C]hildren were denied admission to school for lack of space, and . . . [some] attended school only part-time. Inside the classrooms it was not uncommon to find sixty to eighty students. Educators joked that teachers should have prior experience in a sardine factory before being hired to work in the New York schools."[31]

To make educating so many students more efficient, schools separated students by age into grades. Teachers, like their counterparts in other urban agencies and institutions, began to specialize, teaching only one grade or one subject. And in response to social problems, such as boys leaving school too early and hanging out on the streets, schools attempted to defeminize education by creating vocational programs for boys (and, to be fair, home economics courses for girls). As the number of options grew, students were scheduled into different types of classes, usually based on their future plans—work or college. Later, when standardized tests were introduced, students could be placed in classes based on ability or special needs.

Schools in small towns resisted many of these changes for a long time, but early in the twentieth century educational reformers took advantage of a newly adopted belief in scientific management as a more efficient and effective way to run businesses and solve social problems. To make schools more efficient and less costly, they began to persuade rural communities to join together to establish consolidated schools—schools that served more than one town. Politicians, who worried about the increasing costs of providing new programs, could see an economic advantage in having larger schools. Others were convinced to support the change when they were told that their children were not getting the opportunities available to students in the larger urban schools, which could offer so many more options.

Change, however, did not come quickly. Many people wanted to hold onto the local school because the small-town grade or high school served as a community center. Even today the local high school remains an important focus for community life in rural small towns. For example, the basketball team of a high school (enrollment about 130 students) in one small Maine coastal district has long been an important unifying force for the whole community. Nearly everyone in town regularly attends the games and, when the team makes the state tournament, a large caravan of cars heads to the city auditorium almost a hundred miles away. Because the school brings everyone together, people are not easily persuaded to give up control or community. While efforts to consolidate schools continued for decades, by the 1950s most American schools were consolidated.

The movement to consolidate schools was a paradox, according to one Oregon educator in 1926. "[American education] asks for education for all, yet urges that control be placed in a bureaucracy, as if educated citizens can't be trusted to control their own schools." On closer examination, historian David Tyack goes on to say, "the rural-school reform becomes not so much a paradox as a transfer of power from layman to professionals." Even though people in rural communities were dissatisfied with their buildings in need of repair and a curriculum in need of revision, they did not want to give up control of their schools. Thus they resisted consolidation and standardization, and political battles were waged. In the twentieth century consolidation of rural schools became a "major source of controversy."[32]

Schools, however, eventually had to change because American life after the Civil War had changed. As a result of industrialization, villages grew larger—some became crowded urban areas—and cities attracted people from the farms and immigrants from Europe, many of whom got factory jobs. And city life was different from life in small towns. Increasingly, society became more complex and fragmented. People began to turn to specialists or impersonal agencies for things neighbors and family members once did for each other. Because work was no longer centered in the home or even close by, transportation and communication systems were needed. And then there was a need for services: police and fire protection, water supply and sewage systems, public health agencies. Gradually the modern bureaucracy was born, despite serious group conflict and ambiguity of political authority.[33] Of course, these great societal changes also affected the schools. Educators early in the century commonly believed that "[t]he problem of the city is the problem of a revolution—a revolution brought about by an industrial evolution with an immigrant invasion."[34] In creating a school to serve the needs of students in urban areas, educators designed a model for schools that eventually was adopted everywhere in the United States. Thus the comprehensive high school with a multiplicity of programs to serve a variety of purposes became the American norm.

The Comprehensive High School Today

Other political and social forces impacted the American high school in the twentieth century; their effect has been to make education more accessible and appropriate for more students. Desegregation of schools, which began with the U.S. Supreme Court decision in 1954 on *Brown v. Board of Education of Topeka* and the Civil Rights movement that followed, led to immediate changes in school demographics and to later changes in curricula and programs. The 1975 federal law (PL 94-142) mandating that all children receive an appropriate education in the least restrictive environment meant that children with all kinds of needs—ranging from hearing and vision impairments or severe physical handicaps to all manner of learning differences or disabilities—had to be accommodated in some way. Schools now have a large number of special programs and a well-entrenched system of policies, procedures, and specialists to provide them. Finally, the women's movement led to other changes, such as those mandated by Title IX legislation requiring that females be given more opportunities, as well as an increasing sensitivity on the part of educators to curriculum and practices that do not seem to serve girls as well as they should.

What this means is that high schools, in cities as well as small rural districts, have become much more complex. Because of the proliferation of special education and other programs to serve students with various needs and desires, today's high schools have been compared to factories or "shopping malls."[35] Such schools can offer something to every student—although this arrangement creates both winners and losers in the educational marketplace because only some students from middle- and upper-class homes get to shop in quality stores, that is, get to take the best classes. Quality is lower for students in the low-track classes. When the organization is so complex and the programs so numerous, the school can no longer maintain close connections with parents and the community.

With the arrival of the comprehensive high school came other changes in education with which people still struggle today. The larger the school, the more difficult it becomes for parents to know their children's teachers and the curriculum. Many parents may be recent immigrants who do not speak English. High school teachers, assigned to teach several large classes, no longer know students and their families as teachers in the small ungraded schools did. While schools offer students more opportunities, they have grown more distant from the community.

Schools and Community

Public schools have evolved from institutions that educated most children for basic literacy and only a selected few to go on to higher education, into school systems that attempt to educate all students for many purposes. Some would argue that this dramatic change in the size and scope of public education is more democratic. While enabling more students to have access to education certainly is more democratic, at the same time fewer schools today may actually be democratic. When schools become larger and layered with programs, the intimate connections between the school and community members are lost. Parents are less likely to participate in the daily life of the school and increasingly are forced to accept decisions made by professional educators, legislators, and policymakers. In this way democratic participation has been lessened rather than enhanced, and the connection between the school and the community almost erased in many places.

Many American educators, such as the philosopher John Dewey, viewed American society in the first decades of the twentieth century as "a community of neighborhoods in which a social consensus arose that united and integrated American life, institutions, and values."[36] The many social and technological changes that transformed small-town rural America into the urban, industrial, fast-paced technological world of today have improved the quality of life in a material sense. On the other hand, these changes have not been good in other ways. People no longer know their neighbors as they once did. Changes in the workplace and families moving from one place to another have lessened the sense of community.[37]

Worse, few parents of high school students know their children's teachers, and, high school teachers have a difficult time even getting to know their students. Most high schools today could not be called "community schools" in any sense of the word. In the many large and bureaucratically structured high schools, students—especially those from less privileged families—become anonymous names on rosters, numbers to schedule. Educators tend to keep parents—many of whom are poor, do not speak English well, and lack the knowledge necessary to negotiate better educational opportunities for their children—at or outside the schoolhouse doors.

Some critics argue that schools also create rituals, such as the annual open house and parent conferences controlled by teachers, to keep parents at a distance. Certainly many parents, some of whom had unpleasant experiences when they were in school, do not feel comfortable there. Too often principals and teachers contact parents only when there is a problem with students, or they schedule informational meetings at which they announce a change in program or practice they have already made without any input from parents or community members. Given these barriers—which are all too common in high schools across the country—how can "community" be re-created or rediscovered?

The Challenge:
Creating More Effective School-Community Connections

In order to create a community, people must talk to each other. John Dewey argues that forming a community requires communication. For him, communication is "the process of sharing experience till it becomes a common possession."[38] Communication is identical with social life, and from it people can learn. Through their conversations, parents and educators actually could teach each other, but the comprehensive high schools make such interaction difficult, if not impossible. Without better communication people are unlikely to develop the common understandings needed to improve schools and strengthen communities.

Unfortunately, communities also are not what they used to be. In the small town or urban neighborhood of yesteryear everyone knew everyone else. Communities had norms of behavior and values that everyone shared and enforced with all the young people of the community.

As time passed and people moved more frequently for jobs, community and family relationships began to splinter. It may be that people can't make the same kind of commitment to any community if they know they won't be there very long, but researchers also argue that adults now give less and less time to community concerns.[39] The symbiotic relationship between schools and communities that researcher Alan Peshkin once described no longer exists.[40] When schools were the center of community activity, a strong fabric of familiarity was woven between and among parents, students, teachers, and administrators. People who remember how it used to be tell children, "If I misbehaved down the street, my neighbor would straighten me out and tell my mother" or "If I misbehaved in school, it was quite likely that my mom would find out about it that afternoon when she met my teacher in the local grocery store." Children today will not have memories like these because the social fabric has been weakened; the strength of both communities and schools, dissipated.

While community offers benefits, it should not be romanticized as an ideal, because community also has its dark side. Communities are wonderful places for those who belong, but they can be very lonely, even hostile, places for those who do not. American history is replete with examples of school communities that provided a nurturing environment for some but excluded others, of school communities comfortable with those who were the same but fearful of anyone who was different. At different times and in different places those who were viewed as different—because of race, ethnic group, religion, gender, disability, sexual orientation, or social class—have been, and often continue to be, excluded from community and school life.

What makes the idea of *community* so problematic today is that there are many communities; "excluded" can mean not being part of the group that controls the schools, read: "white middle-class." Nearly everyone belongs to some community, but the shared sense of community people once had when the school and community were almost synonymous seems no longer to exist. Researchers Carol Merz and Gail Furman believe that "[t]he education world seems generally unaware that its responses to the loss of community have been to create more specialized and complex systems."[41] Bureaucracies, though, cannot replace the earlier social groupings that usually were based on kinship, place, or ethnicity. Citing another source, Merz and Furman remind us that many high school teachers "encounter more students in one day than the number of people who lived in a whole tribal village."[42] The large comprehensive high school is too impersonal to give people the same sense of belonging they can get from social groupings.

The prevailing view of society may provide another barrier to community. When immigrants flooded the schools at the beginning of the twentieth century, America was viewed as a melting pot. Parents wanted their children to learn English, to adopt new ways of being and behaving.

> To deal with the task of educating thousands of immigrant and rural children who had little in common, urban schools were set up as efficient organizations to socialize children to be good, productive American citizens. As in the village school, there was a widespread

assumption about the role and values of the school. While many of the values were not shared by families at home, there was little question about the melting-pot philosophy. . . . [I]n many ways these schools were established to create a culture that was distinctly different from the culture of the home.[43]

But today the United States seems to be seen as a salad bowl in which various groups will mix but retain their individual characteristics. In fact, during the last few decades there has been a proliferation of social groups that have publicly tried to maintain their own identities. Americans are divided, for example, by socioeconomic class; ethnic and racial background, including differences in language and custom; gender and sexual orientation; and religious and political views. Because each group wants to preserve its identity and promote its values, there are enormous pressures on schools to adapt programs and curricula in different, often contradictory, ways. Since one school cannot at the same time serve so many masters well, increasingly there are calls for vouchers and charter schools, and the number of home-schooling parents grows.

How can the desire of so many people to maintain their own "private" communities—the social, political, or religious groups with which they choose to identify—be reconciled with the need to create a "public" community—some sense of shared values that a school can represent? The writer Robert Bellah speaks of "real communities" as "communities of memory."[44] As people tell stories of a community, they identify with them and feel they belong. Yet because of people's geographic mobility today, these communities are not real: according to Bellah, "the longing for the idealized small town is really a longing for meaning and coherence."[45]

The bureaucratic organization and specialized programs of the typical comprehensive high school fail in several ways. First, the ties between the school and the local community are often weak—in part because there is not one local community but many. Some parents do not feel welcome in schools, and others—religious conservatives, for example—may feel their values are not represented or respected. Second, relationships within schools themselves tend to be impersonal and fragmented. High school teachers, isolated in separate classrooms all day, have little time to interact with colleagues and many deal with over one hundred students each day, making it difficult to get to know them—much less their parents—well. Moreover, both the organizational structure and building design keep teachers in one discipline from talking to those in any other. Add to the mix the facts that the United States is a geographically mobile society, that Americans highly value individualism and free choice, and that there has been a growing lack of trust in democratic ideals and public institutions. This seems to be an impossible situation. Yet finding some way to redefine community to suit the realities of contemporary society is essential. Because the public school is intended to serve the needs of everyone in the community(ies), it is the best—perhaps the only logical—place to begin.

The public school itself may be working at cross purposes. Merz and Furman describe the paradox of the school's need to be both more organized and more personal: "[t]hese characteristics have certain polar pulls such that as we increase one characteristic, we may be decreasing the other. As we try to bring more organization to a school, we are probably causing it to become less intimate, and, as we increase proximity and intimacy, we reduce the uniformity and efficiency of our organization."[46] This paradox begins to show the difficulty of the challenge to re-create community, but there are other issues to resolve as well.

Today people are part of many communities simultaneously. Americans often live and work in diverse and fragmented groups. People don't stay in one place so schools must accommodate mobility. Some reforms have addressed only "a few aspects of community without acknowledging that community must compete with other connections in people's lives or the deeper issues that divide us."[47] If schools, for example, try to create a "professional community" of teachers, they exclude parents and other stakeholders who should also be involved. And people do not agree on the responsibilities schools should take on. When a school offers student health centers that provide condoms to teens, for example, or after-school care, some will say these are not appropriate roles for public schools. So what should a "school community" be? How can people decide? Can people ever agree?

Perhaps the answer lies in learning to live with paradox and ambiguity. Merz and Furman argue that, because people live in a multiplicity of settings, from neighborhoods, to nations, to the world as a whole, they must learn to live with ambiguity and divided affiliations. Thus, they suggest this mission for schools:

- to teach students to live satisfying lives as participants in groups at various levels;
- to learn to live and work in groups in which differences are accepted and respected;
- to learn to form groups that provide satisfaction, identity, and security without destroying choices and opportunities for others.[48]

If this can be the mission with regard to students, what role can the wider community play in making it a reality?

The challenge is to find a way to reconceptualize the school as a community where differences are valued rather than feared and in which everyone is invited and encouraged to participate. This is a difficult challenge—one with many obstacles to overcome—obstacles that may affect people's values or aspects of their lives they are not willing to change.[49] However, it is a challenge worth the struggle.

If communities where children see their parents and neighbors involved in the concerns of the school can be created, both the community and the school can be strengthened. In the words of John Dewey, the school itself can be "a miniature community" in which children practice democratic living.[50] When students learn to work with each other in schools that also extend learning into the larger community, the school becomes a microcosm where children practice the behaviors they need as citizens. If students also see their parents, teachers, and others model democratic engagement, they will understand what is required of them as future citizens in a democracy and how their active participation in community life can improve the quality of life for everyone. And perhaps adults also should consider including students' voices in community conversations about schools. Not only do students bring knowledge of schools that adults do not have, they also have the strongest motivation for improving them: Their education today will shape their lives tomorrow.

At the same time the country has moved away from small community schools to larger and more bureaucratic institutions, the history of school/parent relationships over the past century has been one of growing imbalance. Americans' love affair with science and efficiency has led educators to create an environment that privileges expert knowledge over public participation. Educators who believe they are the experts on teaching and learning are less likely to care what parents and other community members think. So, instead of inviting people to join them in two-way conversations about schools, they set up meetings where they tell parents and the public what they have already decided to do. When educators-as-experts keep parents at the margins, the only way left for them to participate is to oppose the decisions they've had no part in making. Because this tension is important, it will be explored in detail in the next chapter.

So citizens face a Catch-22 situation. On one hand, educators complain that people don't care about schools, but they act in ways that keep people away. On the other hand, parents and the public feel that since educators don't really care what they think, why should they bother to get involved?

The lack of public engagement in civic life has seriously impacted all of the nation's institutions—including schools. It is time to reexamine the role of the professional in democratic institutions and look for ways to find a balance between expert knowledge and public engagement. Some argue that, in order to find this balance in schools, educators, parents, and other stakeholders must engage in serious discussion built on a foundation of mutual trust and respect.[51] Perhaps people should begin, as philosopher Kenneth Strike suggests, by changing the question from "Who is in charge?" to "What kinds of communities do we want our schools to be?"[52]

This question is as important as the others that must be discussed: How can schools educate for a democracy? Who gets educated? For what purpose? Who decides? There is no way to go back to a less complex time—nor, if people believe in democracy, should they want to. Americans shouldn't lose sight of the fact that over the years, schools have become more democratic by expanding educational opportunities for more students. Can this positive aspect of schools be retained as citizens decide what vision to have for schools in the future? Can

Americans find a way to create a twenty-first century version of the common school—one that reclaims the closeness of past communities while exchanging the exclusion that went along with some of them for a school community that welcomes everyone's participation?

Some Milestones
in the History of American Education

1635	Boston Latin Grammar School established.
1639	Harvard College chartered.
1642	Massachusetts requires that children be taught to read.
1647	Massachusetts requires towns of over fifty families to establish elementary schools and those of one hundred families to have a Latin grammar school.
1821	First public high school opens in Boston.
1872	Michigan court decides that taxes can be levied to support high schools.
1892	National Education Association Committee of Ten recommends a four-year high school with a traditional curriculum for all students and the "Carnegie Unit" as a way to assign credit.
1896	*Plessy v. Ferguson:* U.S. Supreme Court supports racially separate but equal schools.
1909	First junior high school established in Berkeley, California.
1918	Commission on the Reorganization of Secondary Education report, *Cardinal Principles of Secondary Education,* leads to the view of the high school as both an academic institution and an agency for social development.
1954	*Brown v. Board of Education of Topeka:* U.S. Supreme Court outlaws racially segregated schools.
1958	As a result of *Sputnik,* launched by the Soviet Union, the National Defense Education Act provides funds

	for improving science, math, and foreign language programs in schools.
1964	Job Corps and Head Start begin.
1972	Title IX prohibits sex discrimination in schools.
1975	Public Law 99-142 passed by Congress requires education for all handicapped children in the least restrictive environment.
1979	Cabinet-level Department of Education established.
1983	The report of a blue-ribbon commission, *A Nation at Risk,* cites the mediocrity of public schools and calls for higher standards for students and teachers and other educational reforms.
1989	Goals 2000: National Governors' Association and President George Bush agree to work to establish national goals for education.
1996	President Bill Clinton calls education a national priority and pushes for the establishment of voluntary national educational standards.

THREE

How Do Competing Roles Complicate Relationships?

> "Teachers know Everything! Since you are a teacher, you know Everything!" "No," I say [to my five-year-old niece], "teachers know Some Things. Nobody knows Everything."
>
> —*Judy Logan, Author and Middle School Teacher*
> in Teaching Stories

> I share the opinion that parents should trust educators to make the right decisions because they are the professionals.
>
> —*High School Teacher*

> The older you get, the more you realize they [teachers] don't know everything. Just because teachers have a degree and an education doesn't mean they are the experts.
>
> —*Parent of a High School Student*

Once upon a time teachers were teachers and parents were parents— or so it seemed. Teachers taught children to read, write, add and subtract, and parents taught their children practical life skills and their family's beliefs and values. Roles were clearly defined and compatible. However, as society has become more complex, families have become more diverse, and schools have taken on more and more of the roles once left to families. The roles and responsibilities of teachers and parents have become less clearly defined. In fact, teachers and parents now share many of each other's roles. Who is responsible for what is no longer as certain as it once seemed.

At the same time that roles have blurred, everyday life has become more complicated and the problems people face, less easily solved. Many people—business leaders, parents, politicians, teachers, and college professors—wonder whether schools are up to the challenge of educating an increasingly diverse population for the twenty-first century. Many conclude that American schools need to change. This call for reform has taken two competing and sometimes conflicting paths: teacher professionalism and active parent participation. Both paths—and their implications for the roles of parents and teachers—have further blurred the line between the responsibilities of home and school and added new complications to the relationships of parents and teachers.

Teacher-as-professional implies teachers boldly taking a more active role as decision makers in their schools and classrooms. Rather than doing what the experts tell them to do, they are encouraged to use their own judgment about teaching and learning practices. They are urged continuously to seek better ways to meet the needs of all of the children they teach by meeting and learning with their colleagues about best teaching practices; by testing out new educational theories against what they do in their classrooms; by developing a repertoire of more effective teaching strategies based on theory, research, and reflection on their own teaching. In other words, this path to reform leads teachers toward the goal of becoming the experts on teaching and learning.

On the other hand, *parent-as-active-participant* implies that parents also have something of value to add to the conversation about good teaching and learning practices for their children. Rather than just taking the word of the "experts," parents are encouraged to become advocates not only for their own children but for *all* children in schools. They are urged to participate in deciding what will be done in schools and classrooms by serving on decision-making councils, by becoming informed consumers, and by learning about new teaching practices along with teachers. They are encouraged to contribute their knowledge about their children and the community to the mix of information used to make decisions about what is taught and how it is taught in local schools. In other words, this path to reform leads parents toward the goal of gaining an equal voice with teachers in deciding what goes on in schools and classrooms.

It is easy to see how these two paths to reform can, if not carefully managed, create conflict between teachers and parents. Just as teachers are finally gaining a voice in what goes on in their classrooms, parents are demanding an equal voice. Who knows best? Teachers? Parents? Does it have to be either teachers or parents? How did this dilemma arise in the first place? In this chapter we look at the changing roles played by teachers and parents in the education and schooling of youth and the implications of these changes for home-school relationships.

Changing Roles of Teachers

Until the recent interest in reforming schools, most teachers had not taken an active role in deciding what should be taught and how it should be taught. Instead, university researchers developed new programs, textbook companies created "teacher-proof" guides, and administrators determined what and how teachers should teach. Teachers were supposed to do what these "experts" told them to do. Of course, behind the closed doors of the classrooms teachers did what they wanted to do, but this was a clandestine operation not to be talked about with others. The notion of teaching as a profession—one in which teachers base classroom decisions on a growing knowledge base of teaching and learning theory, participate in ongoing discussions with their colleagues about what they do and why, and engage in action research to better understand how children learn—is relatively new. What has kept teachers in this subservient role? Some say that the increasing bureaucratization of schools and the feminization of teaching over the past century have been the major culprits.

Early in the twentieth century the influence of a network of powerful men—referred to by historians David Tyack and Elisabeth Hansot as "the educational trust"—set the stage for schools as we know them today.[1] These men—university presidents and professors, school superintendents and policy analysts and researchers in foundations—enamored with the notion of the scientific management of schools, believed that schools could be made more efficient by the standardization of practices. Frederich W. Taylor's scientific management techniques, which revolutionized factories by introducing assembly-line manufacturing and scientific efficiency practices, intrigued these men. Following Taylor, they created bureaucracies to manage and regulate what went on in schools and classrooms. For example, students were grouped by age and grade, and, once standardized testing was introduced, they were also grouped by ability. Unfortunately (from the perspective of these experts), children don't act like widgets: They have the uncanny and charming ability to act in unique and idiosyncratic ways. Even though uniform practices don't work with all children, this didn't stop the educational "experts" from trying.

Along with the bureaucratization of schools in the early twentieth century came the feminization of teaching. The number of women who entered teaching increased as did restrictive regulations that governed their lives. For instance, well into the twentieth century certain districts would fire a teacher once she married. This system reflected the role of women in the larger society: They were expected to do the bidding of men. Thus they had to resort to covert resistance. In schools, when teachers (mostly women) were observed by administrators (mostly men), they put on their "company's coming" behavior and taught according to the dictates of the "experts." Sadly, this need to retreat behind closed doors prevented teachers from learning with and from each other and perpetuated the illusion of a school with standardized practices. To this day, passive resistance continues to sabotage innovations introduced in highly bureaucratized school systems.

The legacy of the attempt to apply scientific-management principles to schools can be seen today. Teaching is conceived as intellectual factory work where teachers are told what to do, expected to apply standardized routines in their classrooms, and are monitored to make sure they do as they are instructed. Breaking this pattern and asking teachers to take a more active role in their classrooms—to assess the unique learning styles of each of their students and to base their decisions on their personal knowledge of theory and on their own experiences—requires both a different conception of teaching and a different school structure. The challenge is complicated. It requires teachers to rethink their roles, administrators to rethink their leadership styles, and teacher educators to rethink their programs.

As a result of the most recent school reform movement, which traces its beginnings to the publication of the provocative 1983 report *A Nation at Risk*, some teachers, administrators, and teacher educators are attempting to meet this challenge.[2] Many teachers across the United States are being encouraged to take a major role in decisions about what they do in their classrooms. Metaphors such as "teacher-as-decision-maker," "teacher-as-reflective-practitioner," "teacher-as-researcher" all recast teaching as a profession in which teachers actively construct knowledge about teaching and learning rather than receive knowledge generated by others.[3] And teachers in many schools are taking these calls for change seriously. Many are joining study groups, working with their colleagues to develop new teaching strategies, speaking at professional conferences, and publishing articles in educational journals. In short, they are becoming the experts about teaching and learning. In both of the schools we studied in Eastland and Grover's Corners, the curriculum reforms were the result of teacher initiatives—designed and implemented by teachers, not solely by administrators or outside experts.

Are Teachers Professionals?

Central to a conversation about teacher-as-professional are these questions: Is teaching a profession? Are teachers professionals? What exactly does it mean to be a professional? The dictionary defines a profession as "a vocation regarding knowledge of some department of learning or science."[4] It implies specialized knowledge not held by the general public. Linda Darling-Hammond, a leading proponent for the professionalization of teaching, extends the definition: In addition to specialized knowledge, a profession "incorporates . . . self-regulation, special attention to the unique need of clients, autonomous performance, and responsibility for client welfare."[5] Using this definition, Darling-Hammond and her colleague A. Lin Goodwin conclude that teaching is not yet a full-fledged profession because, while teaching has moved forward on some of these dimensions, teaching has not yet fully realized all of them.[6] For example, even though states have increased requirements for teachers, in times of teacher shortages they continue to provisionally certify teachers who do not meet these standards. Despite the fact that professional teachers need to have autonomy in their classrooms to make informed decisions about teaching and learning, many times they work in highly bureaucratized schools in which they are told what and how to teach. And while one mark of a profession is defining the standards for those who enter it, teachers do not have this responsibility. Decisions about standards for licensing teachers still remain the province of legislatures, state boards of education, state departments of education, and central offices.[7]

Darling-Hammond and Goodwin suggest that teaching can be conceptualized in ways other than as a profession: teaching-as-labor (where one does what one is told to do); teaching-as-a-craft (where one is specially skilled at implementing proven methods); and teaching-as-an-art (where one is especially sensitive to intuitive knowledge about teaching). However, they do not question the idea that teaching could and should strive to be a profession in which teachers diagnose the needs of clients (students) and develop strategies (curriculum and practice) to meet them, as other professionals typically do.[8]

Others do not share this view. Most teachers applaud the move to a more professional stance because for so long teaching has not been taken seriously, but others, such as university professor Kenneth Strike, argue that teaching is not really a profession.[9] Teaching, they argue, does not have a clearly defined knowledge base, as does medicine and law, nor a universally agreed-upon technology. For instance, there are many conflicting theories about how children learn and what constitutes best teaching practices. An example of this can be seen in the ongoing debate between "phonics" and "whole language" advocates: How can children best learn to read? Each camp views learning differently and cites research supporting its claim to the superior approach. Doctors, on the other hand, do not debate the best way to set a broken arm. Therefore, the argument goes, if teaching is not a profession with a commonly held knowledge base, then teachers should not claim privilege in decisions about what should be taught and how.

Even some people who accept the premise that teaching is a profession raise questions about the role of teachers precisely for that reason. Educators argue that as a profession, teaching shares some of the same problems other professions are coping with in the latter part of the twentieth century. For instance, scholar and author Seymour Sarason describes how professionals try to maintain boundaries between themselves and their clients: "However a 'professional' is defined, that person's training makes clear that there are boundaries of responsibility into which 'outsiders' should not be permitted to intrude. Those boundaries are intended to define and protect the power, authority, and decision making derived from formal training and experience."[10]

Today professionals of all kinds—doctors, lawyers, ministers, government officials, and educators—are struggling to maintain these boundaries in the face of a populace less inclined to accept the notion that the "experts" know best. Individuals are becoming more knowledgeable and proactive about their own needs.

Whether people agree that teaching is—or should be—a profession, teachers, for the most part, have embraced the idea, and this change has implications for how they interact with parents and the roles they want parents to play.

Teacher-as-Professional: Implications for Teacher/Parent Roles

Teacher professionalism casts parents in two roles: client and customer. As clients, parents are expected to accept the word of the expert, the teacher. The teacher knows what's best for the student and the parent. However, casting parents as clients is problematic for a number of reasons.

First, it implies that the teacher has access to a well-defined knowledge base necessary for making educational decisions. And, as was mentioned earlier, while the knowledge base is growing, many believe that it is not clear cut and that it continues to evolve.[11] In order to make use of this evolving knowledge base, teachers need to be in an environment that encourages and supports continued learning. However, most teachers are still not working in such environments. Many school districts commit a very small percentage of their budget to professional development for teachers—certainly much less than most corporations allocate—and these funds are often the first to be cut when budgets are tight. Because the legacy of the teacher-as-intellectual-factory-worker model still is so common in many schools, there is a very uneven distribution of research-based knowledge about teaching and learning. Some schools are breaking down the barriers presented by an overly bureaucratized school system, but others are still mired in a system that prevents teachers from developing the knowledge they need to make more informed professional judgments in their classrooms.

Another problem with the parent-as-client model is that it suggests that parents don't have anything to contribute to the conversation about good teaching and learning practices. Just as the medical profession is under attack for failing to include patients in a partnership to decide on the best course of treatment for an illness, the educational profession is under attack for not including parents in the dialogue about what's best for their children. For just as patients know their bodies well, parents know their children well. It seems only logical that for the best plans to be made, both parental and professional expertise should be considered.[12] The teacher-as-professional role, by casting parents as clients, runs the risk of falling into the same trap that doctors and lawyers have fallen into—a trap that leads to perpetuating an unequal relationship between themselves and their clients. As Kenneth Strike says: "To be a client is to be someone who is consulted and considered in decision making and who may have some rights to informed consent, but it is also to be someone who is not a full participant in decision making. Thus, the relationship is conceptualized as one of unequal status and power."[13]

There are also problems with conceptualizing the second role, parents as customers. The parent-as-customer model derives from a business metaphor: Schools are businesses, and marketing educational programs is a high priority. In this scenario, schools have something to sell to parents. Schools create programs based on professional knowledge and marketing plans to sell these to parents. Educators can find out what parents want by using focus groups—another successful business strategy—to glean information to help them develop effective plans to sell their products. Schools operating from this perspective tend to view parent/school relationships from a public relations perspective. As public policy researcher Robert Crowson notes: "To some educators, the terms *community relations* and *public relations* are synonymous. The effective communication of school goals, activities, and achievements to a (hopefully) receptive public would be the simple definition of community relations, from a decidedly public relations (PR) perspective."[14]

In an earlier study of the Grover's Corners School District, administrators seemed to think of parents as their customers. While they talked about using multiple approaches to educating parents about the changes in classroom practices, they described the goal of the interactions as "selling" parents on the value of these new practices rather than working with them to build common understandings of "good" classroom practices.[15]

Cast in either role, client or customer, parents are expected to view the educator as the expert. They may be consulted about changes, but the consultation usually comes after the fact, giving parents a chance to comment only on an already decided-upon practice. As educators become more immersed in their professional organizations and seek to maintain a professional status by casting parents either as customers or clients, boundaries between parents and educators will become even more marked, and the gap between their ideas of what constitutes "good" teaching and learning practices will grow.

The Growing Gap between Teachers' and Parents' Understandings

Teachers who have responded to reformers' calls to become more professional in their role as teacher probably have become more involved in local, state, and national associations. And as they have worked in these ways, they and their colleagues have developed new ideas and a new language about schooling that many parents don't understand. Teachers' views about what goes on in "good" classrooms may now be quite different from those of most parents.

The Public Agenda Foundation, an organization founded by pollster Daniel Yankelovich and former Secretary of State Cyrus Vance to help citizens understand policy issues and to help policymakers understand what citizens think, recently published three reports, all of which demonstrate that the gap between parent and professional views about education is indeed wide and growing.[16]

In the surveys of parents, teachers, and other community members conducted for these studies, differences between teachers and parents are clearly visible. Many of the differences are related to the newly introduced innovations in schools, such as the early use of calculators, teaching writing in a way that focuses first on getting down main ideas and then on the mechanics of spelling and proper usage, and grouping students with others of different abilities. For instance, while many educators today advocate the early use of calculators, most parents surveyed believed children should first learn how to do arithmetic without calculators: In a 1993 study, for example, 82 percent of math educators favored the early use of calculators; only 12 percent shared the public's doubt about their value.[17] This finding may have been a forewarning—one not heeded by many educators—of things to come. By the end of 1997 a major backlash had developed against the new math curriculum innovations in California, long the leader in educational change in this country. The innovations were abolished, and the math curriculum reverted to the drill and skill many adults remember from their own schooling; the early use of calculators was outlawed.

Similarly, there has been a backlash against new approaches to teaching reading and writing. Forewarnings about differences in the public's ideas about the teaching of reading and writing also went unheeded. Researchers Jean Johnson and John Immerwahr noted that parent beliefs about how children should learn to read and to write—by learning phonics, spelling, punctuation and grammar rules—differed markedly from those of educators. Educators didn't pay attention, and again California acted. Again the public prevailed: The teaching of phonics was mandated.

Parents and educators also disagree about how best to group children for learning. Many parents, especially those who have children who excel in school, favor homogeneous grouping—grouping of children with similar abilities.[18] It makes more sense to them. While California has not yet mandated homogeneous grouping, can that be far behind? Will the state act again? Our interviews revealed that parents (and educators) do not speak with one voice on these matters. For instance, Eastland parents were not opposed to heterogeneous grouping as long as the needs of individual children were met in the mixed-ability classes. Although opinions of parents and teachers vary on each of these issues, it is fair to say that in California, more educators favored innovative practices than did parents. And the public's view—at least the one that got the attention of the California legislature—was decidedly against these practices.

Where did this gap come from? What contributed to it? One response is that as teachers develop more expertise about teaching and learning from their professional associations, their understandings diverge further and further from those of parents and others not involved in such professional networks. And as teachers become more and more involved in these networks and convinced that they possess professional knowledge that others don't, they are less willing to increase parental participation in school decision making and to listen to parents' concerns. They ask, "Why should parents be involved when they know so little about teaching? We are the professionals. We have the expertise about teaching and learning." Or, as one teacher put it: "It would be fairly rare, in modern medicine, for doctors to bring their patients together and ask them which kind of technique or medicines would best help the healing process. . . . Why is education different?"

Is education different? Many teachers argue that it is not. Based on their newly emerging acceptance of themselves as professionals and on their experiences with parents, teachers are struggling to understand and to define parent involvement within this context.

Teacher's Ambivalence about Parent Involvement

Parental involvement, defining it. That is tough. Does somebody get to go in there and be the veto power? What happens when they are opposed? Do they just stop everything or is their role to present their concerns?

—*High School Teacher*

I don't give a tinker's damn what parents think! That's the problem with asking parents for their input. They think that we will use it all—when they're just thinking about what's good for their kid. We have to think about what's good for all kids.

—*High School Teacher*

For the most part, the educators with whom we spoke are ambivalent about the roles they think parents should play. On one hand, they listen to the current call for more parent participation in schools and agree that parents should be more actively involved. On the other hand, they seem sure that parents should play a supporting rather than a starring role in schools, leaving teachers to decide the best ways to teach. "Trust our professional judgment!" they say. "Talk with your children, visit the school, visit our classrooms. Make sure children do their homework, and support our decisions." These are the jobs educators wish parents would take more seriously. In addition, there is a growing belief among teachers that many problems are the result of parents' abdicating their responsibilities. They say, "If only parents would do their jobs at home, we would be able to do our jobs in school."

Educators, especially those who are parents themselves, do understand the need for parents to advocate for their children by making sure they get the courses they need or a favored teacher. They may encourage parents in this regard. But when it comes to influencing what gets taught or how it gets taught, educators resist because they believe that parents should trust their professional judgment. Influenced by a view of themselves as professionals, teachers try to maintain a boundary, keeping parents outside the arena in which issues of teaching and learning are decided.

In addition to their ambivalence about parents playing a role in decision making, Grover's Corners educators also expressed distrust of some parents. They recounted stories that echo the reasons why scholar Ellen Lagemann reminds people not to romanticize parental involvement in education: Not all parents can be counted on to be caring, interested, committed, and reasonable.[19] The experiences of these educators with a *few* parents led them to want to keep *all* parents at arm's length. In these instances, educators saw parents acting as the child's accomplice, protector, and even victim.

Educators recalled parents who would lie for their children or who would fight against a school policy intended to protect the child. One principal remembered a parent who disagreed with the school about an attendance policy saying, "I'll lie for my child because I disagree with this." Sometimes the lies can be humorous, as was the case when a parent sent this note asking the high school assistant principal to excuse her *son's* absence on the unsanctioned "senior skip day": "Please excuse Johnny's absence yesterday. He had an appointment with his gynecologist."

Other educators told stories of parents calling them to ask them to tell their children that they can't do something because they—the parents—are afraid to confront their own children. One teacher said: "A lot of parents have a hard time saying 'No' to their kids. I had a parent last year who called me and said 'I want you to take my kid out of sports because she's not doing well in her classes.' And I said, 'Well, she's eligible. . . . Why don't you tell your kid? You have more authority to pull your kid off. I don't have the authority to just pull the kid off the team.' For some parents it's hard to draw the line. They want the school to do it."

According to many of Grover's Corners teachers, parents should work in support of the school's goals and programs as a client or as a customer, but they should not participate in making decisions. Because many educators have had past experiences with parents they saw as less than reasonable and now believe more in their own professional expertise, they resist the idea of more parental input.

Starting with the Vietnam War and increasingly so during the past twenty years, the general public has grown more suspicious of experts. As American society grows more and more complex, science fails to solve some very difficult societal problems—the HIV epidemic, drug and alcohol addiction, hunger, ethnic genocide, and persistent gaps between the academic achievement of different ethnic groups in our country. As citizens struggle with these problems and try to make sense of how and if to make use of new scientific technologies, they realize that professional technical knowledge alone probably will never be enough.

The emergence of professional teachers has influenced opinions on the roles parents should play in the education of high school students. The issues are complex and multilayered. Teachers have embraced the idea of professionalism at a time when our society has begun to question the power of professionals and families and family relationships are changing in dramatic ways. Taken together, these conditions lead to teachers feeling a great deal of ambiguity about the role parents should play. The next section examines this same dilemma through the eyes of parents.

The Call for More Active Parent Participation

Just as the recent educational reform movement has led to the call for a more professional teaching corps, the reform movement has embraced the belief that improved schools require more active parent participation. Parents are now being asked to share in school decision making—including a say about what should be taught in schools and how. The changing society, the growing distrust of professional knowledge, the increased perception of failing schools, and the growing concerns about who knows what is best for children have led to a renewed call for parent activism in schools at the same time teachers demand that their voices be heard. These conflicting calls for reform will lead to an impasse at best or, at worst, to full-scale conflict between teachers and parents about whose voices should count most.

Just as teachers were silenced during much of the twentieth century, so, too, were parents. Changes in the political landscape and in schools led to the distancing of parents from school decisions and the blurring of responsibilities of home and school. How did the United States change from schools that distanced parents to those that called for parents to be more active?

Two shifts in the early part of this century led to the distancing of parents from schools: One was in the school governance; the other, in the curriculum. Just when professionals—first administrators and university professors and then later teachers—gained a voice in the debate about what should go on in classrooms and in schools, parents in both urban and rural areas were losing theirs. In the cities, political progressives—as the leaders in the movement for scientific efficiency were known—were frustrated by the overtly corrupt behavior of the local school boards that dotted the city. They petitioned for a new, more efficient system, one that would be controlled by one school board rather than many. This model was quickly adopted throughout the country. Soon the many school boards, comprised of local common people—laborers, small businessmen—were consolidated into one centralized board comprised of the city's elite, leaders of business and industry.

As mentioned earlier, in rural areas the move to consolidate school districts took control farther and farther away from local residents—farmers and workers—and put it into the hands of the town's elite—doctors and lawyers—because many believed these people had the necessary skills to manage the business of a large district efficiently. With each consolidation, parents lost power to influence decisions.

In addition to the changes in the governance of schools, other changes affected home and school. Prior to the 1900s, secondary schools strictly taught academic subjects primarily to students who were planning to go on to college; parents taught values and practical life skills. Older children often left school before high school to go to work. At the turn of the century, not long after the first major restructuring of the high school curriculum occurred, schools took over some of the responsibilities formerly left to parents—but not all at once.

Because a lack of consistency among high schools' curricula made college admissions decisions very difficult, Charles Eliot, president of Harvard University, chaired a group of prestigious university presidents who came together in 1892 to deliberate the negative effects of the lack of a coherent, rigorous, and universal high school curriculum. Faced with entering students from all over the country who attended high schools with significantly different curriculum and course requirements, these presidents wanted to define a required curriculum and level of rigor that would be the standard for all high schools. This "Committee of Ten" defined a course of study for high schools that all students, whether they planned to attend college or not, would take. It consisted of the disciplines as we know them today: English literature, history, science, math, and foreign languages. The committee also suggested the now-infamous Carnegie unit, which granted credit based on the number of hours a student sat through class.[20]

Today school reformers criticize this "seat time" because credit earned depends primarily on the amount of time students sit in a class but does not take into account what or if they actually learn. Critics argue that Carnegie units contribute to a decline in student achievement.

The Committee of Ten's decisions have influenced the high school curriculum for the past century. Although every school did not change its curriculum immediately to meet the new standards set forth by this committee, its recommendations eventually became the standard by which schools across the country were measured. The curriculum defined by the Committee of Ten endures as the core curriculum in most high schools today.

Perhaps the idea of a standard academic curriculum made sense at the turn of the century when those who attended high school came from similar backgrounds and had similar goals, but things rapidly changed in the early 1900s. The country and the schools were flooded with immigrants from eastern and southern Europe seeking a better life for themselves and their children. Mainstream Americans, fearful of the new immigrants, their different languages and ways of living, saw the schools as a way of "Americanizing" (read: "civilizing") the new arrivals. Thus schools were assigned new purposes. Schools became places where children were prepared for family and community life and for work, and as such they now had to add more practical courses to the academic ones in the high school curriculum.

In 1918 the National Education Association convened another influential committee to evaluate the high school. Unlike the Committee of Ten, this one included representatives of the new professionals—high school principals and education professors as well as the United States Commissioner of Education. The group created the Cardinal Principles of Secondary Education, a new vision for schools that marked the beginning of the expansion of the school's purpose beyond the development of the intellect into what had previously been the domain of the family and the church. Now the schools were concerned with the development of the total person, including health, ethical character, family life, citizenship, and vocation.[21] This shift reflected the prevailing bias that the new Americans with their foreign ways couldn't be trusted to shape their own children's lives. The schools had to step in to socialize the student to American values.

Immigrant parents also bought into this idea because they believed that education was essential for making the American dream come true for their children.

This radical switch of curricula emphasis grew out of the growing belief that schools should provide different programs for the new and diverse populations they were serving—especially the children of the new immigrants. Those students who weren't going on to college were offered a decidedly different curricula—one that emphasized practical over academic knowledge. The high school began to differentiate programs for students. Rather than changing the core college-bound curriculum, however, it merely added new programs to meet the needs of different populations. As educator Ernest Boyer puts it, high schools have added programs like "barnacles on a ship."[22] When college-bound students were offered courses to prepare them for family and civic life, they took them as electives, as add-ons because the core curriculum did not change. Students who were not going to go on to college were offered a watered-down version of the core curriculum and took other courses to prepare them for work (vocational training) and family (home economics, health).

New Roles for Parents

Over the course of the twentieth century, these changes have led to a diminishing role for parents. Not only do experts decide what should be taught, but schools have taken over more of the roles once considered to be the family's domain. Parents were co-opted into believing that others did, indeed, know what was best for their children.

In the 1960s, however, some people began to think the experts did not always know best, and research pointed to the importance of parent involvement in their children's education. When schools— especially those in the inner cities—began to decay, parents, less inclined to accept the experts' decisions, began to demand a greater voice in the schooling of their children. When school reformers talk about parents as active participants, they cast parents in two roles: parent-as-customer and parent-as-political-actor.

Thinking of parents as customers can be threatening to educators, for now many parents are not merely customers to be pleased but savvy consumers who have the power to *choose* schools for their children. With the publication of policy analysts John Chubb and Terry Moe's controversial book, *Politics, Markets and America's Schools*, and their call for replacing school boards with a market economy came a new panacea for school reformers: school choice.[23] The argument is that if parents are given the power of the marketplace, good schools will bloom; bad schools will wither on the vine.

Politicians jumped on ideas of choice, such as vouchers, charter schools, and privatization (hiring private businesses to run public schools or school programs). These alternatives to the public high school found legitimacy on the legislative agendas of many states. Conservatives especially find the idea of school choice attractive. State voucher plans vary. Some allow parents to send their children to public schools other than those in their school district; state money follows the child to the new district. Others allow parents to choose private nonsectarian schools; the school is paid a flat rate (i.e., $1,000) from the state, and the parent has to pay the rest of the tuition. In 1995 Ohio and Wisconsin passed legislation issuing vouchers to parents who can spend them in any private school setting they choose, including religiously affiliated schools.[24] Cleveland and Milwaukee have initiated voucher programs of this type—despite arguments that such programs are unconstitutional because they violate the separation of church and state. Even though some courts have recently ruled in support of vouchers for religious schools, this issue will likely be before the courts for many years.

Charter schools, which are publicly funded, may be started by groups of educators (including private educational companies) and/or parents. The initiating group develops a plan for a school and applies either to the local school district or directly to the state for a charter. Regulations vary, depending on the state. Once chartered, however, these schools are usually freed from the authority of the local governing body. A school's board of trustees is held accountable to the local district or the state for achieving desired outcomes. Twenty-nine states and the District of Columbia had charter school laws on their books as of September 1997.[25] Although parents choose to send their children to charter schools, in some places entering a lottery may be required because of limited space. The charter school movement has spawned all kinds of schools that represent the full range of educational philosophies.

If parents are customers who have the power to shop for the school that best meets their children's needs, schools have to produce what parents want or they will not survive. This argument is seductive to a parent like co-author Jean Konzal, who shopped for schools for her son even before charter schools existed. It is also attractive to parents of children who are locked into schools that are dismally failing students, such as many inner-city schools. And, indeed, it is the coalition of some strange bedfellows—conservative rural politicians and inner-city African American politicians, who both put vouchers and school choice proposals on legislative agendas.[26]

The parent-as-customer role, however, has its downsides. Critics argue that some parents lack the ability to choose appropriate schools for their children. Being a sophisticated consumer is not easy in a commercial environment where slick marketing pitches prevail. Researcher Annette Lareau notes that some parents—primarily those from the middle-class—understand and have contacts within the social and political systems and know how to access them for their children. This "cultural capital" necessary to make informed choices about the best school for a particular child may not be available to all parents.[27] On the other hand, others counter that, with the right support services, parents can and will make appropriate choices. For example, District 4 in New York City, one of the first districts to offer parents choice among the public schools there, devotes considerable resources to making sure that all parents are informed about the available choices and provides information so they can make suitable choices for their children. Or perhaps, some say, it doesn't matter what reasons parents have for choosing a school for their children: Just by the act of making the choice, parents are more likely to be satisfied with the school and to support it, and the children are more likely to be successful.

A second concern about choice programs is related more to the needs of society than to the needs of individual children. This argument suggests that the goals of society are not necessarily protected by schools of choice. Its proponents believe that democratically controlled schools (with elected representative school boards) assure that societal needs and values are considered. Schooling serves society by preparing children to be participating members in it. Citizenship in a multicultural society requires the ability to interact with those who differ, but choice plans potentially segregate children and their parents into small communities where differences are minimized. Segregation by class and race may be exacerbated rather than ameliorated. That is why scholar Kenneth Strike, in his argument for charter schools, calls for the continuation of school boards, albeit in a redefined role. He believes the voice of the larger society must be included in the conversation and decision making about schooling.[28]

The parent-as-active participant model also casts parents into the role of political actor. Support for this role is based on the premise that a democratic society requires that parents have a say in what goes on in their children's schools. Researchers Seymour Sarason and Michelle Fine both argue that until the issue of political power is addressed in schools, fundamental school reform will not be possible. However, after agreeing on this point, they quickly part company. Fine argues that parents cannot have power unless they hold the majority vote on a legislative school council.[29] However, Sarason seeks to build a community—not a legislative body—where all members have power.[30] Sarason concludes that the only feasible way to deal with these issues of power is to eliminate school boards and to replace them with decision-making processes that include parents and other involved community members. He argues from what he calls the "political principle"—that all those who are affected by a decision must have a voice in it—and therefore, parents must have a voice in decisions affecting the education of their children. But he does not suggest a legislative body where vested interests are pitted against each other; rather he says that decision-making bodies should be places where "participants [are] there to learn, to help others learn." He adds: "I do not have *an* answer to the question of how the decision making should be organized, who should have what role about what kinds of education decision. If I do not have an answer, I do have a starting point: a confronting and discussion of the predictable problems that can or will arise *in any group*, the members of which vary in terms of status, power, professionalism, and acquaintance with each other."[31]

On the other hand, Fine takes a different tack and uses researcher Nancy Fraser's examination of those who are excluded from the public sphere in a democracy as the foundation for her belief that parent voices have systematically been excluded from the public discussion on schooling. Fine argues that "[t]he presumption of equality between parents and schools, and the refusal to address power struggles, has systematically undermined real educational transformation, and has set up parents as well as educators involved with reform."[32] She suggests that the "asymmetry" of power relations between parents and teachers must be repaired and that the only way to do that is to do what Chicago has done: give parents a majority voice on school councils that make decisions about what goes on in schools. Chicago has, since the early 1990s, experimented with the most radical of governance reforms. The parents there have a majority voice on councils with the power to hire and fire principals. While the results— in terms of student achievement—are mixed, some schools have made significant improvements.

It will be interesting to watch the progress of charter schools, vouchers, and schools in which councils are dominated by parents. Will they lead to better student outcomes? Will they grow and thrive? Or, as some argue, will they sap the public school system of resources? Will they lead to the further disintegration of schools along ethnic and class lines? Will students fare better academically? Will parents feel better satisfied with the education their children are getting? Will public schools improve as a result of the competition? Some say that the public school system as we know it will disappear. Will it? While awaiting the results, many parents in more traditionally governed public schools continue to play the roles they have always played, and, in some cases, they will likely attempt to make their voices heard in new ways. How do parents view their roles in these schools and what barriers must they overcome to take on new and different roles?

Parent-as-Active-Participant: Implications for Teacher/Parent Roles

Parents who have heeded the call by school reformers to become more involved and have begun to take an active role in school decision making—participating on task forces or on parent councils—may be convinced that they have a great deal to offer schools. They may say, "We parents know our children better than teachers do. We know what they need. Because decisions about teaching and learning affect our children, we should be involved." They may be angry with teachers who don't seem to welcome their involvement.

And parents who have ideas about what goes on in "good" schools based on their own experiences in school and on what they think is best for their children, may find the new language used to talk about schools difficult to understand. What do teachers mean when they talk about "authentic assessment," "rubrics," or "literacy" and "numeracy"? One parent interviewed characterized this educational jargon as nothing more than "power words," language used to distance or exclude parents, keeping teachers in control of what goes on in schools.

Above all else, parents want to be sure that their children's high school education will prepare them for the future. When we asked parents to talk about what roles they want to play in their children's high school education, they most often mentioned being in a position to monitor their children's program and to advocate for their needs. At the high school level, the role takes on an added importance because no parent wants their children shortchanged when it comes to meeting future demands of college and/or the workplace.

Parents Involved as Advocates/Monitors

I was on the school committee so I've taken a broader approach. . . . I think it's an evolving thing. I think it's hard to make effective change if one gets just everybody's singular opinion. I think people are mostly concerned about their own child[ren], their own sel[ves], their own family. It's pretty hard to have a philosophy or a program that satisfies all.

—*Parent of High School Student and School Board Member*

The parent quoted here is an exception, perhaps because school board members have to think of the needs of all children while most parents think only about their own children. Parents and educators always will bring different perspectives and priorities to any discussion: Teachers think in terms of the universal ("all children") while parents have particular concerns about individual children ("my child"). Parents, of course, have always been advocates for their children. Even when they seem to be acting on behalf of all children in the school—for instance, by volunteering in classrooms—many say that their primary reason for being there is to monitor what the school is doing on behalf of their child. Both parents and teachers with whom we spoke agreed that advocacy was an important role for parents. Yet only a few suggested that parents need to think about all of the children in the community as well as their own children. For example, Eastland parents said that, even if they knew that heterogeneous grouping might be best for children generally, they would be in favor of it only if it met the needs of their children. This hesitancy to think more globally may be a difficult barrier to overcome. However, if the roles played by parents in schools are to be redefined, perhaps the role of advocate will have to be changed as well: from advocacy for "my child" to advocacy for "my child and all children."

What barriers prevent parents from more fully participating in their children's schools once they reach high school? What barriers prevent parents from broadening their perspective beyond what's good for their children to what's good for all children? In the next section we suggest some of these barriers using a model developed by Joyce Epstein, a noted scholar in the field of parent involvement, as a framework with responses of Grover's Corners and Eastland parents to illustrate the problems.

Barriers to Parent Participation in High Schools

To examine the many different roles parents can play in schools, Joyce Epstein identified six types: parenting (providing a supportive parent/child relationship that provides for the nourishing and nurturing of their children), communicating (maintaining open communication with teachers), volunteering (actively working in the classroom), learning at home (providing learning experiences in support of the school program at home), decision making (participating in school governance), and collaborating with community (participating in activities that bring the school and the community together).[33]

While Grover's Corners parents and educators agreed on many of these roles, they disagreed about parent involvement in school decision making. Educators were more likely to question whether parents should be involved in decisions about teaching and learning, but parents usually thought they should be involved in these decisions. Some parents, however, did say that the teachers, as the experts, should make the decisions.

Grover's Corners parents described how they fulfill many of the roles defined by Epstein at home and in school. They spoke mostly about being either an advocate for their own children or a monitor of their children's programs, but they also expressed their frustrations about constantly struggling against a school whose doors seemed to be closed to them.

The first role Epstein cited, that of nurturing parent, is important because it takes up a great deal of a parent's time. Whether a single parent, a grandmother raising her grandson, or a married couple—all parents spoke of how hard they worked to maintain the family unit and to provide for their children. They told of caring for elderly parents, of working two jobs, of struggling to make ends meet, to feed their families—time-consuming tasks that left little time for active participation in schools. Their first priority was maintaining their households, feeding and caring for their immediate and extended families. Schooling, while important, was not the center of their very busy lives. They were also concerned with their children's activities outside of school, their family obligations, church responsibilities, and jobs.

The second role Epstein discussed, maintaining open communication with the school, is difficult at the high school level since teachers and parents barely know each other. Because many high school teachers deal with over one hundred students, because most high schools limit parent participation to ritual events, such as open houses and teacher-controlled conferences, and because older students may discourage their parents from appearing at school, parents and educators have few opportunities for informal get-to-know-you conversations. Even teachers with children of their own usually leave their "parent hats" at the school house door. Thus both groups tend to fear and/or misunderstand the intentions of the other.

Many parents talked about their struggles to maintain open communication with the schools and were frustrated by what they perceived as one-sided communication. Some mentioned their delight—and surprise because it was so unusual—when they received postcards from teachers (a new initiative by the Grover's Corners principal) praising their children for something they had done. They also spoke with enthusiasm about the parent conferences that were scheduled during the fall that the interviews took place—the first parent/teacher conferences held in the high school! They welcomed these exceptions to their past experiences.

Parents, however, complained about the difficulty of communicating with guidance counselors and teachers. Eastland parents echoed these concerns. One Eastland parent had never had any contact at all with her son's high school teachers, and the principal called only when her son was in trouble. Yet she felt comfortable enough with her daughter's middle school teachers to visit when classes were in session. But almost all Grover's Corners parents told of their perseverance in terms of advocating for their child's needs—not being shy about speaking even to the superintendent of schools if necessary.

No matter how consumed they were with other matters, all parents—whether professionals or those barely eking out a living as laborers—recalled instances when they had approached the school to advocate for their children's needs. Contrary to some notions that poor parents are less able to approach schools or less concerned that their children do well in school, these parents seemed able, willing, and committed. There were differences, however. Middle-class parents with more of the cultural capital previously described chose different issues to advocate for and usually were more successful in their approach. For instance, one parent who grew up "on the other side of the tracks" in town was concerned that her son was being unfairly disciplined by the assistant principal. She related: "She had me in tears and stuff. Everything I said, she made it look like it was mine or [my son's] fault, . . . she must think I'm an imbecile or stupid, I was . . . I was crying!"

Compare her words to those of a professional, whose focus was on getting the best teacher for her son: "Our son wanted a certain teacher.

His whole schedule had to be rearranged because of that and that's something [advocate for his needs] that [I] would do. I would encourage him to do [that]. I said, 'If you're in trouble, I will be in.' And a kid whose parent won't do that sometimes gets the worst teachers and probably won't have as good an experience because of that."

Both parents advocated for their children, but the parent who was a professional exhibited a sense of efficacy. She believed that she would get what she wanted for her child, and she knew how to approach the school in order to do so. The other parent was not confident in her approach to the school, and her experience probably increased her doubts about ever being successful. Through these two examples, the invisible advantages available to different members of the community are clearly apparent.

Fewer parents talked about the third Epstein role, volunteering. Those who did, however, spoke of volunteering in the high school not out of altruistic motives but rather as a way to a better chance to influence what happened for their own children. As mentioned earlier, volunteering was also another means to monitor the school's performance in relation to their own child. It is commonly accepted that students don't want their parents involved in their schooling once they hit high school. In fact, many parents and teachers with whom we spoke agreed with this idea. However, a few parents were actively involved in the high school with their children's support. They felt that other children would not resist participation of their parents if more moms and dads followed suite. If involvement were a common practice, no child would be singled out as the only student whose parent took an active role in the school.

Educators routinely express support for the fourth Epstein role, that of providing learning experiences at home to support the school's program, and parents also saw this role as important. One mother, for example, tutored her daughter, who had learning disabilities, at home each day in order to help her keep up with her lessons. Others talked about providing learning experiences at home, but not necessarily in support of the school's program. For instance, one mother—against the advice of her daughter's teacher—made sure that her children studied Greek language and culture after school one day each week so that they would retain their culture and language.

The fifth role suggested by Epstein, that of encouraging parents to be involved in school decision-making bodies, seems to be the most problematic. A few parents told of participating on task forces and on advisory boards, while others talked about trying to participate but being discouraged by what they perceived to be a lack of sincerity among the teachers and administrators. Most who participated reported a less-than-positive experience. They talked about being "tokens"—the only parent in a sea of educators; they spoke about being "listened to" but not heard, of being presented with already decided-upon outcomes and of the difficulty of understanding the jargon used by educators.

On the other hand, some parents said they were too busy with other commitments to take an active role in school decision making. While they may not necessarily trust educators to do what they think is best, a lack of time, not a lack of interest, prevents their greater involvement. One parent said: "If they were to come to me and ask me my opinion, as you did, I would be very willing to do that. I would be very willing to give it. But because of time constraints and my activities surrounding my son outside of school, I'm not sure how much more I could do."

And, finally, although some parents want a greater role in school debates about teaching and learning practices, our studies revealed that many parents do not. Some parents accept the idea that teachers are the experts and should make the decisions.

Lack of time also affects the way many view the final role in Epstein's model, parent involvement in community-based activities to bring schools and communities together. Some parents were very involved in community activities—some to the degree that they felt they didn't have enough time to be more actively involved in the schools. However, few of these activities seemed to be devised to bring the school and the community together.

The views of Eastland parents in some ways mirror those of Grover's Corners parents. All of the Eastland parents who were interviewed had responded to requests for information from the high school or helped children with homework on occasion, and some had contact directly with teachers, such as attending a conference at school. Many attended school events, such as athletic competitions, and a few had served as volunteers. Only one had ever served on an advisory committee. One Eastland mother talked about the difficulty of communicating with teachers, noting that talking to teachers "was impossible." She had talked only with the principal, and that was because her son was in trouble. She asked to be notified if her son was failing, but, even though he did fail a course required for graduation (the controversial American Studies class), she never heard from anyone before she got her son's report card! Needless to say, she was not happy with the school-home relationship.

So while many parents were trying to be involved in a variety of ways, they felt they were in an uphill struggle—attempting to make connections with an un-enthusiastic partner. When parents find communicating with schools about their own children's needs so difficult, they certainly will not be willing to take on the added responsibility of advocating for the needs of all the community's children. Their children, of course, will always come first.

The Challenge

I think teachers are basically frightened to contact parents because I think it holds them accountable. Also . . . we hear stories about certain parents at times, and it puts us on the defensive. It's tough to deal with. . . . I also think parents are frightened to come in to talk to teachers.

—*High School Teacher*

It is often suspected that, for some reason, teachers have ulterior motives for wanting to make changes. The public has a hard time believing that we are looking out for the best interests of their children.

—*High School Teacher*

This chapter has traced the evolution of the roles played by parents and teachers in high schools during the past century. Over the course of this century parents have been distanced from schools due to changes in governance and in curriculum. Teachers, on the other hand, after many years of being locked out of decision making about teaching and learning practices, now have begun to raise their voices and to be heard. Will teachers be willing to share their newly found influence in matters educational with parents? For over the past fifteen years, parents have asked more and more to be included in the conversation about schools.

Some researchers argue that parent voices will not be heard until issues of mutual trust and respect are sorted out.[34] The educators we spoke with talked a great deal about the lack of trust that permeated relationships between parents and teachers. They believed parents didn't trust them, and they admitted that they didn't trust some parents. Parents, too, spoke of their lack of trust of teachers and administrators. Both groups felt that they weren't respected by the other. This lack of mutual trust and respect undermines any real efforts at building bridges between parents and educators. Unless this issue is addressed, all other efforts will be to no avail.

One theme running through the interviews in Grover's Corners was a general sense of suspicion: Are teachers acting in the best interests of my son/daughter? Why don't parents trust that teachers will act in the best interests of the children we teach? This suspicion clearly limited the ability of parents and teachers to work together for both individuals and for all children.

Changing views about roles and relationships will require that people commit themselves to the complex and time-consuming process of getting to know each other better, of building trust, and of examining and sharing their own beliefs about the proper roles for each group and about the best ways to teach and learn. We believe that it is time for educators to take heed of what researchers such as Robert L. Crowson and Mary Henry have suggested: They need to rethink their role as professionals and to find ways to involve parents in discussions about teaching and learning.[35]

One important role, implied but not specifically mentioned by Epstein, that needs more attention is that of parent-as-learner. In the new concept of teacher-as-professional, one of the main attributes of professional educators is that they are continuously learning— continuously seeking new and better ways of teaching. We suggest that parents also should be viewed as continuous learners. Perhaps the dilemma of teacher-as-professional v. parent-as-active-participant could be resolved if both groups learned side by side; if together they discovered more about children, about child development, and about approaches that will help children learn.

The challenge, then, is how to build a school climate where parents and educators trust and respect each other so that parents are able to move from advocacy strictly on behalf of their own children to advocacy for all children in the school community; where teacher professionalism is defined as learning with and from parents; and where parents are included in the school's learning community. Not only do we believe it can be done, we argue that it *must* be done if high schools are to improve.

What Influences Parents' Opinions about High School?

A good teacher will bring Shakespeare . . . up to date. And there's [other] things to be learned—even social things. Kids should read technical books too: how to build a house. . . . If it was up to me personally, I would have one week every semester for each class in vocational school. They gotta survive. They're not all going to have the money to pay their own plumber.

—*Parent of a High School Student*

I'm very pro-business. What I'd like to see them do . . . is take groups of kids and put them together and study, do everything as a group. . . . When you get out into business, that's the way the world works.

—*Parent of a High School Student*

I think students need to know how to think critically, to read and analyze good literature—not those "young adult" novels—no matter what they plan to do after high school.

—*High School Teacher*

I think you need to teach kids about life. You give kids a checkbook and they don't know what to do with it. Living—everyday experiences. They don't have the common sense about basic everyday things like doing laundry and cooking meals.

—*Parent of a High School Student*

All they're learning is push this button . . . rather than learning the principle. I have nothing against typewriters, but as far as using a computer to figure out your problems for you, I mean if all of a sudden the computer blew up, they [students] should know how to do it themselves.

—Parent of a High School Student

What is the primary purpose of education and the goal of the high school? Should schools focus mostly on preparing students for college or the workplace? Or is helping them develop skills and habits of mind to survive in an unknown future more important? Or can they do both?

People—both parents and educators—have different opinions about the purposes of education. Neither parents nor teachers speak with one voice. Many parents (and teachers) believe that the major purpose of high school is to prepare children for the future by offering them basic subject matter and college prep and vocational courses. On the other hand, some teachers (and parents) do not agree with this exclusive focus. They wish that people would see the importance of learning for learning's sake and be concerned with the intangibles, such as the development of problem-solving skills, the ability to work independently on self-chosen projects, and a greater understanding and appreciation of cultural differences.

Even though they do not always agree on what high school is for or how it should be, the parents we interviewed want their children to be successful in school and to gain knowledge and skills that will prepare them for the future. When they talked about education, they usually were thinking about the needs and experiences of their own children, and, of course, children have different future plans: Some wish to go on to college while others plan to enter the workforce right after graduation.

To further explain why there is conflict about a variety of educational matters, this chapter explores the basis for the different opinions people have about high schools and the criteria parents use to evaluate curriculum and practice.

People's opinions, of course, are shaped not only by their personal histories but also by the communities in which they live. Yet despite vast differences between life in these New England towns and in other towns and cities across the United States, the comments and concerns of many parents in Eastland and Grover's Corners are similar to the perspectives of a much larger and more diverse group of parents in studies conducted by Public Agenda, an organization whose researchers focus on public policy issues.

According to the Public Agenda report, Americans across the country, regardless of geographic or demographic characteristics, believe that safety, order, and the basics should be the top priorities in public schools. Although study participants said they were satisfied with their local schools, many were less satisfied when they were asked to compare today's schools to those they attended. In fact, 60 percent complain about a lack of attention to the basics. Focus groups suggest that the public definition of what is basic is "rather straight-forward—basics are the ability to read and write and spell the English language and do basic arithmetic."[1]

As the following chapters show, the parents with whom we talked echoed these findings. Moreover, their views about how and what students should learn are remarkably similar to another finding from a Public Agenda study with regard to teaching innovations: "Ideas such as using calculators to teach math, teaching composition without teaching spelling, and grouping students with different skills together in one class don't make intuitive sense to most Americans. And they seem to have another strike against them: most Americans don't seem to think they are working very well."[2] While our studies confirmed the Public Agenda's findings that many parents believe this way, we also found that there were parents who didn't. What influenced how parents thought about these changes?

A major reason many Americans have concerns about the wisdom of school and classroom change can be traced to the fact that people have different mental images of school which they unconsciously use to evaluate what they see and hear about schools today.

The Importance of
Mental Models in Shaping Opinions

[In my school] we were always in rows. . . . The rows would be fine as long as you feel comfortable and don't always feel watched. I had to be quiet. Made me uptight.

—*Parent Born and Educated in Europe*

My family has farmed land in Grover's Corner for many generations. Grover's Corners High School was a lot more relaxed when I was there in the early 1970s.

—*Parent of a High School Student*

I think kids need to have a teacher at the head of the class . . . so they are less likely to get off the subject. Maybe it has to do with how I was brought up. . . . Eastland High then was a "freedom school" where kids could do whatever they want and didn't have to do homework if they didn't want to.

—*Parent of a High School Student*

I teach in a nearby town. My high school experience was unbelievable. I went to this very, very progressive high school—probably more modern than Grover's Corners is at this point. It was known as the Country Club. It had just a fabulous music program and an art program. I had extra time in my day added to the beginning and to the end so I could fit in extra courses. But for the kids who weren't interested in school they could get out at one and go to work.

—*Parent of a High School Student*

I had a good high school experience. It was a very traditional school. I remember three-quarters of my teachers were very good and one-quarter were terrible. There was one teacher there who was very progressive. She taught a class called Projects. It was an independent study. We could study anything we wanted to. We were under the gun, so we read, read, read, and made a presentation, a good presentation.

—*Parent of a High School Student*

Mine was a traditional high school twenty-five years ago. Teaching was traditional. You were in the classroom, you'd get a lesson, you'd do your homework, and then "See you tomorrow."

—*Parent of a High School Student*

I come from a French background. My mother could barely speak English, and my father still speaks broken English. . . . I go to public schools and I don't speak any English. I flunk the first grade so they put me in with nuns that spoke French and I didn't learn English. . . . so I think vocabulary is important. . . . You don't want to go through life talking like me all the time.

—*Parent of a High School Student*

Parents' own school experiences are a major influence on their beliefs about how school should be for their children, and these experiences varied.

Parents who differ, as these parents did, in terms of their experiences with schools, develop different "mental models" about what goes on in good high school classrooms. They then evaluate school programs and practices through the lenses of these "mental models," which may differ considerably based on past experiences.[3]

Another way of thinking about mental models is that they create internal images—what people see in their mind's eye when they think about what should go on in "good" high school classrooms when they hear a word or think about an idea. For example, what do people picture when they hear the word classroom? When college students were asked this question, most pictured a room with desks in rows and a teacher standing at the front. Readers with a similar mental image of a classroom, like some of the parents we interviewed, may have difficulty understanding how a couch in a classroom might facilitate learning.

People develop differing mental models from different experiences, influenced by where they grew up and went to school, the success they had (or didn't have) in school, their parents' past experiences with schools, and experiences with their own children's schooling. Aspirations for children also contribute to these unarticulated internal images. Because these mental models are unconscious, and thus unexamined, people make assumptions based on them but don't think about the basis for them. They don't talk to others about mental models—even though these lead them to different understandings of school.

These many different images of "good" high schools and class-rooms contribute to the difficulty parents and educators have in communicating with each other. In one parent's mind the English teacher is going over a grammar exercise to help students understand the mistakes they made on their essays. Another pictures students acting out scenes from *Romeo and Juliet*. And yet another imagines the students and the teacher engaged in an emotional discussion about Toni Morrison's *Song of Solomon*.

Mental models also can lead to using different words to express similar ideas; for example, as we mentioned earlier, parents talk about "reading," "writing," and "arithmetic" while teachers talk about "literacy" and "numeracy." Or the same words may be used to talk about different ideas. For example, both parents and teachers agree that "higher standards" are important. But while parents may mean correct spelling and usage, teachers might mean that students can write a logically constructed argument for or against a position. For some people history is facts, that's the way it was, and that's the way it still is. When teachers, believing that students should understand past events from different perspec-tives, teach American history from the points of view of African Americans or Native Americans, these parents complain that teachers are distorting the truth as they know it.

An illuminating example of how words have different meanings to different people emerged during interviews with the parents of Grover's Corners High School. The discussion had turned to the topic of multigraded classrooms, and three of the parents had attended one-room schoolhouses when they were children. Eric Roskowski liked the idea of multigraded classrooms, while Phil Whitney and Martha Shaw didn't. Why? Further questioning revealed that their views were based on their own personal experiences.

For Mr. Roskowski the one-room schoolhouse was a wonderful experience:

Well, I think one of the finest things about the one-room school-house was the fact that the older kids helped the younger kids and there was a togetherness . . . which is not a school competitiveness but there is a togetherness, and they're all one big family. So the older kids help the younger kids and I think that children learn to read a lot faster in that kind of concept, because then you have kids that know the words teaching the younger kids the words and teaching them how to sound out the sounds. In a one-room schoolhouse, the teacher couldn't teach everything. The teacher had maybe fifteen minutes for each class . . . and [to] teach everybody something relevant was a real art. And those kind of teachers were real teachers and . . . would make the best master teachers today if they were still around; there are not too many of them around. But teaching, I think it's wonderful. I fairly enjoyed school when I was teaching somebody else how to do something, 'cause I knew, because it helped me learn too. So nothing stopped me from learning. Nothing would stop a person who wants to inquire, learn, to continue learning in that kind of environment.

For the other parents, however, the one-room school was a terrible experience. Mr. Whitney explained:

But down in the lower grades, and again I'm conservative, but I really don't like the idea of combining one, two, and three. . . . Maybe that's because, you know, I was in a one-room schoolhouse. That shows how old I am. But I was in the one-room schoolhouse . . . until third grade. And I can remember back being a third grader, well [my teacher] says I have to do this for an hour. While I'm doing this she's dealing with a first grader or second grader or other kids. I just have a hard time comprehending that as an advantage to have two or three different grades at one time. Basically the teacher would give an assignment to the third grade and the second grade and work with the first grade. There was a designated time, you know, like this half hour was for them, this half hour, she might combine the math to all three grades. But what good would it do to have a third grader learning how to add one plus one? The third grader was trying to multiply nine times eighteen, something like that. That's where I just feel, if a child is in the third grade—not all third graders are the same, so how can you have seven third graders that vary in ability and then have seven second graders who vary in ability and then have seven first graders? I mean, you've got twenty-one kids. You could have ten different levels of learning amongst those twenty-one kids, and I think if you have fifteen or eighteen third graders whatever the class sizes, you're only going to have two or three levels of learning, you're not going to have more than that. And for the teachers, it's got to be very difficult.

Mrs. Shaw shared Mr. Whitney's negative take on the one-room school:

If anyone had come to me and said, "I want to put your third grader or your second grader into a multiage situation," there is no way I would have ever gone for it. I would have thought, "Oh, he'll get lost, they won't tend to him. How can they possibly tend to him?" I wouldn't have done it. I wouldn't have done it with my oldest kid who read when he was three. And see, I went to one [one-room schoolhouse] where the eighth-grade kid who couldn't read had to sit next to me in the first grade. And I knew even then that that was horrible for him. I did, I sensed that even then. And when that teacher died, a couple years ago, I was home. I wouldn't go to the funeral. My friend that lived next door to me called me and said, "Let's go," and I said, "No, I'm not going." And I wouldn't, I just wouldn't. And I know that [the teacher] didn't know any better than to do what she did. I know it was how she was trained [but] I don't have good feelings about that whole experience.

These parents had different mental models of multiage classrooms because their different experiences with one-room schools created very different internal images about the concept of educating children of different ages together. Without some discussion, however, the differences would not be apparent. Even when everyone uses the same word, people may be assigning very different meanings to it. Thus, to understand parents' opinions about school and classroom practices, it is important to recognize that individuals have different mental models about what should go on in "good" high school classrooms and they unconsciously evaluate the new programs based on these images.

Differing Mental Models Explored: How Parents Evaluate Curriculum and Teaching Methods

Parents do not always agree on what students should be taught, but all parents would like their children to be successful in school and to gain knowledge and skills that will prepare them for the future. When Eastland parents talked about education, they were usually thinking about the needs and experiences of their own children, and, of course, children have different future plans: some wish to go on to college while others plan to enter the workplace right after graduation. So, do all students need the same education? No, said most of the parents in Eastland.

Like the parents in Grover's Corners, when Eastland parents explained their views on what should be taught and how, they talked about themselves, about students, and about school as preparation for life. Although some spoke favorably about a practice they had experienced, most parents had been exposed to a very limited number of different teaching methods in their traditional classrooms. For example, what one parent said about those he believed should be used in the ideal English class was probably true in varying degrees for most parents: "A lot of these ideas I'm talking about now are coming from my own experience—things I would like to have done, some things I did [but] I've done just a few."

Parents also drew on the experiences of their own children and what parents believed students needed to survive and succeed in school and in the real world. These perspectives were shaped by their positions and background. For example, Randall Cromwell, an educator with two advanced degrees, was the only parent interviewed who mentioned research studies as the basis for some of his views. He advocated a greater emphasis on oral communication because he had looked at studies of "success models" that showed "correlations between what they found in school and successful people. . . . CEO's . . . don't write or read, but they're scanning volumes of stuff and they have to communicate verbally." Other parents looked to their reality rather than research; for instance, "The kid who is going to work in a gas station doesn't need algebra, chemistry, or Shakespeare!"

Regardless of whether these parents talked about themselves, students in general, or the very specific needs of their own children, they thought students should have curriculum and teaching methods that would (1) capture their interest or engage them, (2) address their needs and personal characteristics, (3) have real-world relevance, and, in only a very few cases, (4) preserve a tradition.

Student Engagement

What would interest or engage students? Parents thought that discussion was a good way for students to develop an understanding of a book they had read, but they did not agree on the form that discussion should take. Some parents said students would be more likely to participate in the discussion if they were in small groups. Fourth-grade dropout Robert Foster explained why he would have been more likely to participate in a small group, something he had not done when he was in school: "If there had been only three or four of us, I probably would have had to do it. You know here [in the whole class] I could get away with more because . . . she [the teacher] was paying attention to the other kids and I never raised my hand or anything."

Others said whole-class discussions would be better because students in small groups would not stay on task—although most also said it would be all right to use small groups occasionally to provide a change in routine. Judy Johnson said the small group without the teacher there "would not be as productive [as whole-class discussion]. I think it gives too much to be able to wander off the track . . . end up talking about different things. [The teacher] kind of keeps their train of thought going." Or, as Ralph Jones said, students discuss: "What did you do last night? Are you going to the dance?"

Students' Characteristics

One reason that parents favored different practices seemed to stem from their views of students. Those parents who believed students were intrinsically motivated (and didn't need the promise of rewards or the threat of consequences) thought they could be trusted to work with their peers and would benefit from doing so. On the other hand, some parents, believing that students were extrinsically motivated, preferred a whole-class discussion because the teacher would have more control and be there to keep students on task. Even those parents who preferred small-group discussions explained the teacher's role in ways that showed they thought different levels of teacher control were necessary. Some said the teacher should carefully monitor the small groups to keep students focused and on task; others thought the teacher only had to stop by once in a while, as Alex Lamonte explained, so "she could assess where they are" and "drop a couple of things to get them off on a completely different tack."

Similarly, parents had different opinions about the amount of choice students should have with regard to books they read. Those who favored giving students the least choice often explained that, left on their own, students would choose easy, short books. As Mary Andrews put it, "Give a kid a choice between a book that's got fifty pages and *War and Peace*, they're going to choose the one with fifty pages." Some suggested that the teacher could force students to make good choices by providing a list of books from which to make their selections. Others said simply that students should be given few opportunities to choose.

Where do parents get their theories of motivation? Most seemed to be derived mainly from their own experiences with children. Some parents, though, talked about children generally while others talked about the characteristics of particular groups or individual students. Ralph Jones, for example, discussed the students generally: "[O]utside classrooms are too loosely structured. . . . there are too many outside distractions. . . . there has to be some sort of control, [not] just turning the kids loose."

Other parents said small groups meeting outdoors would work well for the "A students," but those with lower grades might fool around too much. A few parents talked in terms of specific children being motivated differently. Pat Wilson noted that a small-group discussion might not work well for her daughter Martha, who was failing nearly everything, "unless she had incredibly strong-minded students . . . who would keep her focused," but "that works for Tanya [another daughter] because she's a very motivated student." Unlike other parents who said the teacher needed to keep students focused, Pat Wilson seemed to think that Martha's peers could handle that responsibility. Some students would be intrinsically motivated to stay on task, but others would need someone else (the teacher or other students) putting pressure on them to do that.

Parents also discussed other student characteristics that teachers should take into account. They mentioned, for example, levels of ability, talents, interests, and learning styles, often noting that these factors were related to motivation. For instance, they felt students would be more interested in learning when the curriculum and methods suited their personalities or learning styles.

Once again, though, parents had different opinions about how these characteristics could be addressed, as in the case of whole-class or small-group discussions. Nora Kendall favored small groups: "I think they'd open up more. . . . They'd be more comfortable. . . ." A few parents who described small groups as problematic, believed that some students would sit back and let one or two students with a stronger work ethic do everything. Mary Andrews, who had been very upset about her daughter's recent experience in a small group, said: "Those [small groups] I have a problem with . . . because it seems as though one person does all the work and the other three people just don't do anything. And they [meaning her daughter] get a poor grade because it's supposed to be a group effort."

The comments of some parents showed that they were making distinctions among types of students rather than thinking of "students" as a universal category. Parents' comments about evaluating students' understanding of a book provide another example of this point. Because some students would test well and others would not, some parents said that students should be allowed to demonstrate what they had learned with something other than a test. Karen Shelley, for instance, said that teachers "could tell by class participation and the way they talk" whether students understood what they read. She did not favor tests "[b]ecause some kids freeze. And there's one answer." Students might view a book differently from the teacher and be marked wrong on a test.

A few parents talked specifically about the unique characteristics of particular students. For instance, Pat Wilson, after explaining that her daughter Martha learned best with right-brain techniques, said that all the students' work should not be written "because you can artistically and physically demonstrate your knowledge." Laura Hunnewell pointed out that while having a choice of writing topics is fine for her son David, her daughter "thinks differently" and "might be confused" because she "needs to have the teacher tell her what to do."

Real-World Relevance

What curriculum and methods are relevant to the "real world"? Parents said students were likely to learn best when they could connect what they were learning with their own lives or when it would improve their chances for success in school or survival in the real world. Some curriculum should be included or a particular method used because it would help students do well in other subjects, prepare them for college or jobs, or generally help them get along well in everyday life. Lucille Farnum, for example, said students should learn how to balance a checkbook and do laundry. On the other hand, Randall Cromwell, who talked about the real world in terms of chief executive officers, advocated that schools place greater emphasis on oral communication.

Parents' views about the value of grammar provide another good example. Most parents believed that grammar study will help students express themselves correctly and more effectively in speaking and writing—although what parents called *grammar,* English teachers would probably refer to as *usage.* Many cited examples from the real world to support their positions. For instance, if students did not use correct grammar in letters, applications, and résumés, they would not be hired or get into college. Ralph Jones favored giving students many grammar exercises because "the more you do, the more proficient you eventually become." He talked about a letter a college student had written to his company with "things like *ain't,* double negatives, and [incorrect] spelling. . . . What sixth grader wrote this? . . . I don't want this person working for me."

Parents did not agree, however, on the best way that students could develop these skills. Only four parents believed that diagramming sentences and labeling parts of speech would help; most thought students did not need formal grammar study. Randall Cromwell commented: "We had to take the sentences apart. I think our kids can use the rules. They have a far better understanding of what's appropriate than I did." Some parents thought, as Ralph Jones did, that students should practice applying rules by doing exercises, while others thought students could learn the rules simply by correcting the errors in their own writing.

As before, differences among parents were apparent in the degree to which they talked about practices for students universally or for particular groups or individual students. Because some parents did not think the classics were relevant today, they thought they should be taught only to college-bound students; or, as Lucille Farnum put it, the student who was going to work in a gas station did not need algebra, chemistry, or Shakespeare.

Other parents talked specifically about the relevance of particular practices for individual children. For example, Laura Dunham said relevance was not an important issue for her daughter, a good student who would do whatever the teacher asked, but her son, who was a reluctant reader and writer, needed curriculum and methods with clear connections to the real world to motivate him. He "definitely needs writing to get him by in everyday life. . . . [H]e's going to need to know that if he ever had to write a business letter. . . . [H]e's going into business for himself."

Preserving Tradition

Despite the fact many people believe parents wish for "the good old days," only a few parents talked about doing things in school because "that's the way we did it." Sandra Manchester, for example, thought students should learn to do outlines "because they don't teach you how to put everything down on paper first the way we used to. . . .They just don't do that now." It wasn't clear why she felt this way. When asked why she thought that outlining was necessary, Sandra Manchester replied: "They simply don't do that, but I see

Janie writing everything down—she just writes—and she does very well too." Ms. Manchester did not give any reason for teaching students to outline other than the fact that because she and her husband always did outlines before writing their papers, her daughters should too—even though her daughter seemed to be doing well without making outlines.

Unlike Sandra Manchester, a few parents seemed to prefer the "old ways" because they didn't know of any better way. When Ronald Wallace was asked if students could learn punctuation rules better by doing exercises and worksheets or by correcting errors in their own writing, he said: "Probably the worksheets. [Why?] I don't know. . . . I think you can learn better by doing it out on a worksheet. Plus that's the way I can remember learning it." He went on to explain how difficult it was for him to learn, but it was clear from his comments that he had not experienced any method other than doing worksheets, and, in his case, the worksheets had not been effective.

What Might Explain Differences in Parents' Views?

Three factors seem to account for many of the differences in parents' views: whether they viewed students as having universal or individual needs and characteristics, how much they knew about many different ways of teaching, and whether they focused more on the *outcome* of learning than on the *process of learning* (*what* children learn rather than *how* they might best learn).

The parents who were most likely to favor nontraditional practices were those who (1) talked more about individual children rather than students in general or groups of students, (2) knew about more different practices, and (3) focused on the learning process more than its intended future outcome. Because these parents did not believe that all students could learn best if they were taught the same curriculum in the same manner, they would say that certain curricula or teaching practices were best for some students, but other students needed something different. As a result they talked about a greater number of practices and usually described them in greater detail. For example, the parents who talked about students in general could think of few ways other than discussion to help students understand a book they had read. On the other hand, Laura Dunham, whose son had "a visual connecting problem" that made reading difficult, suggested that he would benefit from "listening to a tape" or "watching it on the screen."

How did some parents acquire a greater knowledge than others? For most, the source was their own experiences or their children's experiences in school. Ronald Lancaster's preference for progressive practices came as a result of his children's positive experiences in the nontraditional ungraded elementary school in Eastland. Gary Mosher's recent experience in college business classes had introduced him to small-group discussion, which he now saw would also be beneficial for high school students. While some parents described problems with small-group work and opposed the practice, Sally Branigan's experience as an elementary teacher helped her see how problems with small groups could be resolved so she favored their use. Randall Cromwell's extensive experience as an educational administrator gave him knowledge not only of different practices but also of research in the field of education.

Parents also learned from having two children who were very different or one child for whom traditional methods had not worked, as was the case with Pat Wilson's daughters and Randall Cromwell's son. These parents had discovered from their children's school experiences that the same methods did not work equally well for all children. Teachers, then, would have to use many different methods to address their needs.

When parents focused more on the learning process rather than its intended outcome, they talked about the need for teachers to teach in different ways. Because they looked so closely at the process, they saw that individual children would not learn in exactly the same way as others. Differences among individual children's learning led them to see that teachers could not assume that "one size would fit all children."

Mental Models and Crosstalk

When educators do not have a full understanding about how parents (or teachers) form their opinions about new teaching and learning practices, the result is often crosstalk. This crosstalk—the lack of common language and understandings that causes people to talk "across" rather than "to" each other—creates more turbulent cross-currents and hinders meaningful discussion about educational goals and purposes. The challenge for all Americans—parents and educators—is to find a way to build a trusting relationship in order to uncover different mental models about what goes on in "good" high schools and classrooms and then begin to develop a common language for talking about the purposes of education.

Can parents and educators learn to talk more productively about these important questions? Can they develop a common language for discussing their perspectives? And if agreement is not possible, how might differing perspectives be accommodated in some way in a public school? To begin to answer these questions, we think readers would benefit from knowing more about parents' very individual and often idiosyncratic views. The following chapters explore parents' ideas on teaching and learning, what and how students should learn in English, mathematics, and social studies, and how best to evaluate this learning. We invite readers to keep this question in mind as they see what parents had to say: Is there any common ground?

PART TWO

Understanding Tensions Created by Different Opinions about Teaching and Testing

The tensions created by changing roles and relationships described in Part I is one reason parents and educators have difficulty working together toward common goals. Other tensions stem from the fact that people—both parents and teachers—have different opinions about what is important for students to learn, how they should be taught, and how their learning can be assessed. Parents, of course, always have been worried when their children were not doing well in school, but they may become more vocal and critical when this happens in high school classrooms that have adopted new practices. Parents of high schoolers may be even more concerned than parents of children in the lower grades because they want to be sure that their children are being prepared for admission to good colleges or for good jobs. For example, Eastland High School parents, believing that English and history should be two separate courses, were quick to blame their children's difficulty on the interdisciplinary American Studies course, and Grover's Corners parents were concerned that college admissions officers would not understand what was taught in the new math curriculum when the courses were renamed Math 1 and Math 2. But other tensions arise from basic differences in people's beliefs about the nature of the teaching-learning process.

The three chapters in this section provide a tapestry of parents' and educators' perspectives about teaching, learning, and assessment. As we have said before, neither parents nor teachers speak with one voice. Among both groups disagreement is likely because there will always be a range of philosophies leading to preferences for or opposition to certain practices. The perspectives of four parents profiled in Chapter 5 illustrate how such differences can be seen on a continuum—with a preference for a teacher-controlled class at one end and for a student-centered class at the other. Although these points along the continuum are described using parents' perspectives, teachers' perspectives and existing practices in any school also could be laid out in similar fashion.

Chapter 6 illustrates these differences of belief in terms of specific practices in the teaching of English/language arts, mathematics, and social studies. Even though both parents and teachers share the same goal—fostering students' learning and achievement—people have different ideas about the best way to do this in any subject.

Chapter 7 considers some issues underlying debates about assessment and grading. As more states and school districts adopt learning standards and "high-stakes" standardized testing, public debate will likely become more acrimonious. But parents also have concerns about changes in assessment practices within the schools. How, they wonder, can portfolios and exhibitions be better than tests to show what students know?

Even though educators are not of one mind on these kinds of changes, in most schools they have had the opportunity through workshops and meetings to discuss and develop new understandings. On the other hand, parents (and students), rarely included in the planning process, usually discover a change as the new program or practice is put into place.

So that readers can imagine how parents in their own communities may be thinking about changes adopted in local schools, for the most part we let the parents speak for themselves. When there are disagreements or misunderstandings among parents and teachers in any school, students are affected. When such tensions are public, students are caught in the middle. We believe that gaining a deeper understanding of differences—whatever they may be—is the first step in finding ways to resolve them. Students will be the ultimate beneficiaries if adults can find more common ground.

What Is Learning? What Is Teaching?

[A]s long as the teacher has set up the structure, the kids can be on their own. They learn the fact they have to do it themselves.

—Parent of a High School Student

You're not supposed to build a classroom around making children comfortable. It's not a required thing, but anything helps. If a child feels comfortable in the school, in the classroom, I think he works better.

—Parent of a High School Student

The teacher should explain the worksheet. This is the lesson. This is what we are going to cover. Are there any questions? Yes, no, maybe? Here's the worksheet. Just do what we went over. To me, that should be [the way the class is run].

—Parent of a High School Student

The differing mental models people—both parents and teachers—have developed lead them to construct very different ideas about the meanings of *learning* and *teaching*. Is the process one in which knowledge is transmitted from an expert teacher to novice students who memorize it? Or one in which the teacher serves as a guide or facilitator who introduces new knowledge and designs activities so that students can understand it in various ways and see how it connects to what they already know? Or is the process so personal and idiosyncratic that individual students should be at the center with the teacher serving as a resource to help them make decisions about what knowledge is important and how they can best learn it? Because these three perspectives are so different and contradictory, it is important to consider how people understand the very complex process of learning and teaching. Classrooms based on these various perspectives are very different from each other. In this case one size does not fit all.

How great might the differences of opinion be? The comments of Eastland parents provide an example of the range of views people have about the nature of teaching and learning. Their children were all enrolled in a required American Studies course, which was taught by two teachers (one history, one English). This course was atypical not only because two subject areas were combined but also because it was not "tracked"—students of all abilities were mixed together. Although the parents were asked to talk about what they thought would be the ideal curriculum and classroom practices for teaching and learning high school English, their responses provide a case for examining differences in people's beliefs about learning and teaching in any subject.

Parents were first shown a series of pictures of various classes— for example, a teacher in front of a class probably lecturing, or students working in small groups. They were asked to say which pictures seemed to show what they considered good ways for students to learn. Then they were asked to say what they thought students should learn in a high school English class and how they could best learn it. The profiles of parents included in this chapter represent the range of beliefs, from the most traditional to the most progressive; it is clear that people think very differently about the nature of teaching and learning. There were, however, some points of agreement that weren't always obvious at first. Further examination of these parents' responses reveal that just talking about teaching and learning would be very beneficial. When parents and teachers begin to understand each other's perspectives, points of disagreement may turn out to be misunderstandings, which might be resolved easily through participation in one-to-one conversations. And for almost half of the parents interviewed, the conversation itself was an occasion for learning new ways of thinking about learning and teaching.

How Did Parents Decide What Helps Students Learn?

As shown in Chapter 4, parents talked about their own experiences in school, the experiences of their own children, and/or what they thought would work best for students generally. Students learn best, these parents said, when: (1) what they are learning is interesting or engaging; (2) it meets their individual needs or personal characteristics; (3) it has real-world relevance; (4) they were taught in ways that were similar to their own memories of school; or (5) a combination of these criteria. Students, for example, would be more likely to be interested when a teaching practice meshed well with their learning styles.

Even though the parents used similar criteria for deciding whether they thought a particular practice was effective, they applied them in different ways. Some parents talked about students only in general terms, while others looked at differences among particular groups of students, such as college-bound or vocational, or specific individuals, such as their own children—with a learning disability or the tendency to be too social. As a result, some parents saw the need for the school or teachers to offer a greater variety of options. For example, the parents who talked about students in general could think of few ways other than discussion to help them understand a book they had read. On the other hand, Pat Wilson talked about "wonderful" projects, such as puppet shows, cooking, and fashion shows children had done in school.

Parents also differed in another important way. Some focused on the outcomes of learning—what students need for the future—while others talked much more about the process of learning in the "here and now." Ralph Jones, for example, was very concerned that students be prepared for the world of work. He talked about his current experience in the business world to show the negative consequences if students don't learn what they need to know to get and hold jobs in the future. These parents, who didn't seem to see the need for many different teaching methods and classroom practices, usually preferred a traditional type of classroom. On the other hand, the parents whose focus was more on the process of learning rather than its intended outcome, saw the need for a greater variety to meet the needs of different children, and they described them in more detail than did the parents who talked mostly about outcomes.

Given these differences in the ways parents discussed learning, how great were their differences overall? Profiles of parents' beliefs about the nature of teaching and learning presented in the next section were selected to show the range of views—from the most traditional idea of teaching and learning to the most progressive.

How Great Were the Differences among Parents?

In order to discover how parents seemed to think about the nature of teaching and learning, parents' views of effective practices for learning high school English were analyzed and rated using a framework created from six dilemmas about curriculum and classroom practice. These dilemmas, which came from a longer list developed by researchers Ann Berlak and Harold Berlak can be summarized as follows.[1]

1. *Teacher control vs. student control.* For example, who should decide what books students read or what topics they write about?
2. *Knowledge as content vs. knowledge as process.* Should students learn specific subject matter or is it more important for them to learn how to learn and think about any topic?
3. *Learning is molecular vs. learning is holistic.* Should students learn vocabulary words or punctuation rules in isolation, or should they learn words from their reading and rules by correcting errors in their writing?
4. *Children have shared characteristics vs. each child is unique.* Should courses or teaching practices be the same for all children or differentiated because students learn in different ways?
5. *Learning is individual vs. learning is social.* Do students learn best when they work on tasks by themselves or when they discuss and collaborate with other students?
6. *Differential allocation of resources vs. equal allocation of resources.* Do schools need to set up special classes for gifted students and those who have difficulty learning? Must they offer different programs for students planning on college and those who want to learn a trade?

TABLE 5.1

The Range of
Parents' Beliefs about Teaching and Learning

TEACHER-DIRECTED STRUCTURED LEARNING	TEACHER-MONITORED INTERACTIVE LEARNING	INTERACTIVE INDIVIDUALIZED INTEGRATED LEARNING	PERSONALIZED INTERDISCIPLINARY LEARNING IN CLASSROOM AND COMMUNITY
Lucille Farnum	Judy Johnson	Pat Wilson	Randall Cromwell
4 parents (16%)	10 parents (40%)	10 parents (40%)	1 parent (4%)

Parents' positions on these questions were rated first. Then the results were used to create four categories that show the range of the beliefs of this group of parents. Four were chosen to represent the views of others with similar ratings. The profiles, constructed from interview excerpts, show how descriptions of the ideal classrooms differ at various points along the continuum of beliefs about the nature of teaching and learning. A summary of the ratings and the range appears in Table 5.1.

On the left end of the continuum, parents described the ideal classroom as one in which students could learn best if the teacher directed most of the activities and children spent most of their time working individually or as a whole class. Students would have limited opportunities for choosing books to read or topics for writing and would work with other students in small groups only once in a while. Although these parents did not advocate a return to the good old days, their idea of teaching and learning was closer to the traditional classroom than those of other parents.

Moving from this end of the continuum toward the other end, parents held increasingly differentiated views of the learning process. They advocated giving students more choices and more time to work together with the teacher monitoring rather than directing their activities. The classroom becomes a much more interactive environment.

Farther over on the continuum parents began to express a more holistic and integrated view of learning. They believe that students can learn skills in context and that knowledge about American literature can be enhanced by studying history at the same time. Variety in activities and choice of assignments would be good not only to change the routine to keep students interested but also necessary because students do not all have the same needs, interests, and learning styles.

Placeholder Profiles

The four parents whose profiles follow were selected to mark four points on the continuum around which other parents with similar ratings cluster. Although some background information on the parents has been included to provide some context for their comments, this information does not suggest any relationship between placement on the continuum and parents' socioeconomic status or educational backgrounds. While these factors might be important to consider for other groups of parents, for this group they were not.

Teacher-Directed Structured Learning: Lucille Farnum

> The teacher has to have some input into everything they do, but I don't think she should stand over them and nag them.

Lucille Farnum, a married homemaker and mother of two children, was a high school graduate. Her husband also completed twelfth grade and worked as a warehouse manager. Norman, a junior at Eastland High, had no plans after graduation, and his school achievement was generally "poor" although his mother said it was "fair" in English. Norman had cerebral palsy and was scheduled for a "structured study hall" with the special education teacher. As Mrs. Farnum described it, learning and teaching are very much like what one would find in a traditional classroom.

Mrs. Farnum viewed learning primarily as a process of knowledge transmission that required memorization and practice. Slow to select a photo of a class she favored for her son, she finally pointed to one with students in a small group with the teacher and said: "I like the small group. One on one. Norman seems to absorb more." The photo of the teacher at the blackboard was "okay," but "kids are going to be really bored. Maybe they do absorb more than I think they do." The best way to learn vocabulary was "[m]emorization. Like we used to be given so many words per week, learned them and then had a test on them and did them over if we got them wrong." She did say that discussion with the whole class about a book would be good "if you got to one point you didn't understand. . . . It might help if you get [those parts] out in the open and everybody's discussing them."

Students need fairly close teacher supervision and direction and structured assignments. The teacher, Mrs. Farnum said, "has to have some input into everything they do, but I don't think she should stand over them and nag them." She liked the idea that her son has a "structured" study hall and recommended "quizzes" on "certain chapters" of a book to "make sure kids read that chapter." Students in small groups are likely to "just sit and discuss who's going with whom." Thus, even though she said small-group discussion "actually helps in some cases . . . even without the teacher" because "they can figure it out on their own," she also said students should work "mostly by themselves" and have "one group thing a month or sextile [six-week term]." Lucille Farnum appeared to favor what might be called controlled choice: "It's probably best [for the teacher to assign topics for writing]. I mean the teacher would say do an essay on a person and [her son would] choose which one." She recommended choosing books from a book list: "They could pick out the areas they liked." Unlike other parents with similar ratings, Mrs. Farnum did not specifically mention the need for classroom rules, but her comments suggested that she believed a structured classroom environment is best.

Like others, Mrs. Farnum emphasized the need for students to learn "the basics"—reading, writing, grammar, and spelling. For example, she said: "I don't think the school spends enough time on English grammar. . . . [Grammar is important] because if he ever got a business job where he had to speak to people, he could make them understand what he has to say." She did not believe her son had learned the basics and blamed the elementary school for "a senior in high school who can barely read." She thought that students could best learn vocabulary words and punctuation rules in isolation, such as by doing exercises or memorizing lists teachers give them. For example, "Spelling lists get the point across. Again it's the memorization."

While she thought students could benefit from writing drafts because the teacher can "write little notes all over it," she did not think other students would be of much help. Her son's friends "could care less" about school and "if he could go to a student who has all As, he'd feel inadequate." Process with regard to writing, however, was less important than product: "I don't see that it would make a difference as long as they got to the point of the right way or right answer." She expressed concern about teachers discouraging students by not praising them when they had made an effort or by returning a paper that "has nothing but red ink all over it." Even though she did not think every paper needed to be graded, "teachers should look at all [written work] and make some comments."

What students learn should be connected to real life and their future plans. Mrs. Farnum did not think everyone needs Shakespeare: "If kids aren't interested, they're not going to do it. What good is it later on? The school system doesn't seem to realize that not all kids are going to college. . . . I think you need to teach kids about life. . . . They don't have the common sense about basic everyday things like doing laundry and cooking meals." When they read a book, it would help to "put it in perspective as to what's happening now."

Like all other parents, Lucille Farnum believed that students learn best when they are interested and engaged. Her profile represents the category for one end of the continuum because her overall view can best be characterized as teacher-directed structured learning. In the next profile Judy Johnson described practices that are less tightly controlled by the teacher and more interactive.

Teacher-Monitored Interactive Learning: Judy Johnson

> I just think the groups of kids and being able to express their ideas between each other is very important, but having the teacher there . . . kind of keep[s] it together.

Judy Johnson, a single parent, graduated from Eastland High in 1973 and worked as a customer service rep for Medicare. She said her daughter Danielle, a junior, did "fair" in school and "good" in English and planned to attend college to study criminology. Mrs. Johnson viewed learning as a more interactive process than Lucille Farnum described.

Structure in the classroom is important, she believed, but students can work by themselves. Teachers should monitor what students are doing and encourage them, but direct and close supervision is not always needed. For example, the first photo she selected of a class she favored for her daughter showed a small group of students with a teacher: "I like this. I think it gives kids a chance to exchange ideas and get new ideas. They're coming up with them on their own yet the teacher is there—to step in every once in a while. I don't think that it would be as productive [without the teacher]. I think [that] gives [students] too much [room] to be able to wander, get off the track of what they're there for. . . ." [Looking at the photo with the couch in the classroom corner, she said] "I think there should be some sort of structure. I wouldn't be upset about [the couch] . . . , but you're not at home. . . . If you're sitting on the chair, you're going to have to concentrate on the things that are going to help you more when you get out in the business world." Referring to the photo of students outdoors, she said, "I wouldn't want it all the time, but sometimes changing your environment even for a short amount of time, it helps."

While she believed "the basics" are important, they should not be the main emphasis. She felt that in English students should learn "grammar, proper speaking, the use of words. Like you don't say like *ain't*." Learning the parts of speech and diagramming sentences is important because "it's a major means of expressing yourself, getting your point across to people and in some cases the only way to get your point across. The basics to me are spelling and reading, you know, being able to read, comprehending what you read."

Students, however, can learn skills both in context and in isolation. Like several parents, Mrs. Johnson said that when students first learned rules, it would help to do exercises, but they can learn best by correcting errors in their own writing. When asked the best way to learn mechanics, via worksheets or by correcting their own writing, she replied: "Probably the second, having to correct what you've done—I think the first part is important at the beginning to learn the basics and then the only way to learn them better is to work with them and to apply them to what you are doing." (Other parents with similar ratings sometimes suggested that a combination of exercises and correction of writing was best.) Vocabulary, she said, was best learned by looking words up: "I'm a firm believer in using the dictionary."

Even though her views on mechanics and vocabulary suggested a holistic idea of learning, Judy Johnson did not favor teaching English and history together. (Other parents with similar ratings either felt the same way or were uncertain.) Mrs. Johnson said: "I think history is one thing and English is another. . . . I think they [students] should be made aware of how they tie in together, but I think they should be separate. You really lose what each thing is."

She described a more process-oriented approach to the teaching of writing than did Lucille Farnum:

> I think drafts are okay, but I think you should write it, be graded on it, and have an opportunity to correct it. Say how would you correct it. See what it is that you've done incorrectly and why you did it incorrectly. . . . [In addition to the teacher] other kids could [give feedback], even parents. I think it comes down to the final result because everybody's an individual and how they get to a certain point is different. But I think you should be able to give them input and options for what they have to do. And let them, each individual pick which way they want to go about it. And if at the end, it's not a good result, then you discuss with them personally how it could have changed. [In the evaluation] both [content and mechanics] should be considered equally. . . .

The practices she cited for helping students understand books they have read were more interactive than the ones mentioned by Lucille Farnum, although Mrs. Johnson also raised questions about including works by Shakespeare.

> When you read something, you interpret it your own way. I think it's important for the teacher to say, to tell—what the general idea of it is, what the author was trying to put across, but how you interpret it is individual.

I think Shakespeare's plays are ridiculous in the classroom because I think it's just not applicable to everyday life. . . . I think they [students] should be told about them, and you know, have some knowledge of them, but I don't think it should be a full-blown subject. . . . [Performances, videos, acting scenes out] would be great, but to actually sit down and read it [Shakespeare], I don't think it has any meaning.

Judy Johnson was typical of other parents with similar ratings in that she favored more student choice—in her case, students would choose half of the topics for writing and one-third of the books they read. Like others, she would allocate class time about evenly among students working in small groups, meeting as a whole class, and working individually.

Mrs. Johnson's own words provide a good summary of the position on the continuum classified as teacher-monitored interactive learning: "I don't think it's necessary for a teacher to stand up in front of the class for English because I think English is one of the subjects where you constantly have to keep things moving to keep them interested. I just think [working in small groups with other] kids and being able to express their ideas is very important, but [it's also important to] hav[e] the teacher there to kind of keep it together."

Interactive Individualized Integrated Learning: Pat Wilson

[Y]ou can artistically and physically demonstrate your knowledge. . . . [Kids should be given opportunities to learn from each other] because if the teacher has been teaching the class for many, many years, they may get a little—not stale but repetitious . . . and kids can stimulate new ideas and discussion, avenues of discussion, and make it a whole new lesson.

Pat Wilson was a single mother who worked full time in customer service at a major local company. She had an A.A. degree from a college in Massachusetts, where she also attended high school. She said her older daughter, Martha, a junior, did very well in the arts and played sports, but in January she received failing grades in everything except chorus. In contrast, her sister, Tanya, who attended Eastland Middle School, was "an excellent student." Martha's short-term goal was to join "Up with People" (a performing group of young people) and, although she would like to be involved with the arts in some way, she probably would not attend "a traditional college." Her mother already had made arrangements for her to go to a private boarding school next year to repeat grade 11.

Mrs. Wilson also viewed learning as an interactive process that leads to greater understanding, but she and others with similar ratings tended to view knowledge more broadly than parents in the first two categories: They liked the idea of combining the study of history and English as American Studies. Pat Wilson said: "I think more classes should be combined—to see how they interrelate and I just think that they [students] can get something out of seeing how the real world relates to English. They can see why the particular writer wrote in that way because of the way things were going on at that time."

Students learn skills best in context. For example, Mrs. Wilson noted that at some point students need to learn "grammar, punctuation, the basic structure [because] it's a necessary skill, but I would hope by the high school level they'd have that type of skill under their belt and just reinforce it by saying "Please correct this." When asked whether students learn best from doing exercises or correcting their own writing, she replied: "I think their own writing. They'd care more about it. And I think that they're going to learn more from their own writing rather than worksheets that everybody else has that they copy off a friend." Later she said: "Just reading increases your vocabulary, period."

Like other parents with similar ratings, Pat Wilson often talked about a particular practice as being beneficial for one of her children but not the other because they have different needs and characteristics. "Martha definitely has the artistic and creative sides. . . . She has difficulty concentrating. She needs an individual presentation." When asked whether she felt the same for her other daughter, Mrs. Wilson said:

> No, they're totally different. Now this program right here [pointing to the photo of the student in front of the class], I think that would work for both of them, and I know Tanya has done that in her social studies

class. The teacher went to a conference recently and came back and had the kids teach the class. And Tanya thought that was fabulous. . . . I'm not sure Martha would do that. Tanya is just a really dedicated student. But she just thought it was great. And the other thing is that they worked in teams. Three of them would work as a team to prepare the test and to prepare the lesson. . . . Martha probably does well as far as the actual performance or presentation, but when it comes to the research, Martha's always the weak link. . . . [A]n independent study or anything like that, that's totally out of the picture for Martha because she just doesn't have the self-discipline.

Pat Wilson's comments also show another characteristic of parents' responses at this position on the continuum. A greater variety of practices was mentioned than in the first two categories. Learning for them was more holistic and process-centered. They believed that students can learn from each other. They can give each other helpful feedback on drafts because surface features, such as punctuation and spelling, are less important than the expression and analysis of ideas. While most of the parents with more traditional views emphasized discussion, Pat Wilson, along with others with more progressive beliefs than Lucille Farnum and Judy Johnson, suggested a number of other ways students can be helped to understand the books they read:

I know for Martha what helps a lot is that when she had a World Humanities class in tenth grade—the kids did wonderful working with the arts in their history lesson—and actually they do them in Latin class too. They do either fashion shows or cooking or—they made fabulous puppets, they put on puppet shows and performances together so they actually do something other than written. I don't think all of their work should be written because it shouldn't all rely on written presentation because you can artistically and physically demonstrate your knowledge.

Mrs. Wilson believed that children can learn from each other and that it is important to give them opportunity to do so, "because if the teacher has been teaching the class for many, many years, they may get a little—not stale but repetitive . . . and kids can stimulate new ideas and discussion, avenues of discussion, and make it a whole new lesson."

Pat Wilson and others with similar ratings favored letting students choose their own books, sometimes from within general categories, and their own topics for writing at least 50 percent of the time. They suggested that students spend at least 50 percent of their time in class working in small groups.

Parents at this position on the continuum talked about learning as a social process, but they also said it was important to adapt curriculum and classroom practices for individual students' different needs and interests. Pat Wilson is representative of others who hold what can be characterized as interactive individualized integrated learning.

Personalized Interdisciplinary Learning in Classroom and Community: Randall Cromwell

> [Ronnie's teachers] seem to understand more personally how he learns and [they] set up the independent study for him. . . . I think that should go for every kid.

Randall Cromwell, a former school administrator, was an executive director of a day nursery in a nearby city. Both he (M.Ed., C.A.S. [Certificate of Advanced Study]) and his wife (B.A.), an artist, attended high school and college in Massachusetts. Ronnie, their youngest child, was in grade 11. He had attended the traditional elementary school in Eastland. His father described his achievement overall and in English as "excellent." A highly gifted and talented student, he planned to pursue interests in art and writing at college.

Randall Cromwell's views always seemed to place him in a position shared by no other parent interviewed. Several factors may help to explain his anchor position at the far end of the continuum. Not only did he have many years of experience as a professional educator, he was the only parent interviewed who held an advanced degree. Moreover, one of his older children, now in his thirties, had needed special services for many years, and three others, also in their thirties, were excellent or good students who went on to college and professional training. His youngest son had been allowed to pursue a completely independent study rather than attend the regular American Studies class. Until he was given this option, he was almost failing.

After explaining how his son benefited from teachers who "seem to understand more personally how he learns and set up the independent study" for him, he said: "I think that should go for every kid." He viewed learning as a process that ideally stretches beyond the classroom into the community. He explained that students could develop necessary skills and knowledge by working on projects. For example, he described a project he favored in which students in Alaska actually sold salmon, talked about how valuable it was for some high school seniors to spend time in the day nursery working with two-and-a-half-year-olds, and mentioned the week his son spent in a nursing home when he was in a middle school home economics class.

Even if schools did not extend learning into the community, Mr. Cromwell thought teachers should give students more choices and "create an interesting learning environment in the whole school." He favored interdisciplinary courses, such as American Studies and global studies, because "students can see the relationships between parts . . . sciences, math, shop, and whatever else can be transferred into their learning." All kids, he said, need "a multisensory approach" and, while they should be exposed to "different for-mat[s]," their creativity should not be "stifled." By giving young students worksheets with "fill-in-the-blanks," teachers cause them to "function at a lower level" than they would if they were encouraged to build on the knowledge and skills they already have.

At the end of the interview, when asked if there was anything else he would like to add, Randall Cromwell said:

> The only thing I can think of that would be helpful is if they could almost like run a summer school-type program during the year for the kids who are behind and the ones who are ahead. In summer school you go for six weeks and what they do is try to figure out where you're at and then take you as far as you can go. So that they can intensify what they do. Like a kid who's behind in social studies because he can't do the reading. . . . Find the problem and fix it right

away. Over the years I've observed kids in summer school making gains in six weeks they couldn't make in thirty-six.

Mr. Cromwell's view of learning can best be described as personalized interdisciplinary learning in classroom and community. While the practices he cited were not so different in kind from those of other parents with ratings above the midpoint, such as Pat Wilson, they were different in degree. These practices, however, were light-years away from those of the few parents who clustered with Lucille Farnum at the other end of the continuum.

These four profiles—Lucille Farnum, Judy Johnson, Pat Wilson, and Randall Cromwell—illustrated the differences among parents with regard to the assumptions about the nature of teaching and learning that underlie the practices they cited as effective for a high school English class. Like an impressionistic painting, however, this portrait of parents as a group captures the essence of the beliefs landscape in broad brush strokes. Individual ratings were based entirely on what parents did say, but beliefs are like icebergs: Underneath the visible part exists a large mass of personal beliefs that are inaccessible and unknown to other people and sometimes even to the person who holds them.

Were There Points of Agreement among These Parents?

While parents generally agreed on the curriculum and methods that should be included in their ideal high school English class, they disagreed about how much certain curriculum or methods should be included or emphasized. Some parents believed small-group work would be okay only once in a while, for example, while others thought it should be used more. The range of opinions was greatest regarding the idea of knowledge as content or process. While the group leaned heavily toward the process end of the continuum, one parent who talked about "absorbing" and "memorizing" anchored the other end. There was also somewhat less agreement about the degree to which control should be shared between teacher and students. Seven parents favored more teacher control than the others. Parents as a group clearly leaned more toward conceptualizing learning as a social rather than as an individual process; only three parents viewed learning as mostly something students should do by themselves with the teacher's assistance rather than as something to do with help from classmates.

These parents expressed a clear difference of opinion about two issues: whether students should be heterogeneously or homogeneously grouped and the value of English as an interdisciplinary course. Heterogeneous grouping was favored by 56 percent of the parents, 28 percent preferred homogeneous grouping, and 16 percent were unsure. Forty-eight percent favored combining the study of English with history, 16 percent were opposed to this practice, and 36 percent were unsure. According to their comments, most parents had experienced neither heterogeneous grouping nor the combined study of English and history in the traditional classrooms they attended. The explanations given by those who spoke critically about American Studies suggested that their opposition may have been due in part to the way the course was being taught or their lack of knowledge about interdisciplinary courses, which were not offered when they were in school.

A Surprising and Perhaps Useful Finding from the Interviews

Parents talked about their ideal English class in three different ways. While some parents seemed quite uncertain or hesitant, others stated their views with certainty. But a third group of parents was very reflective. Their responses suggest that conversations among parents and educators may be a very good way for increasing parents' understanding and support for nontraditional programs and practices.

Some parents seemed uncertain about their preferences or unwilling or unable to say much about them. Although they answered the questions, they would not elaborate on their responses, even with some prompting. These parents tended to be less articulate and were much more difficult than others to interview. Perhaps they felt the interview was a "test" of their knowledge about schools. Their beliefs seemed to be hidden away in a closet that couldn't be opened. It was also possible that the parents themselves were not quite certain of what might be hidden there. Since they were so reluctant to speak, however, there is no way to know why this was so. For the most part, these parents were positioned around the middle and toward the traditional end of the assumptions continuum.

In contrast, a second group of parents, who spoke with certainty, were very articulate. Their views seemed relatively fixed. They were less likely than parents in the reflective category to say "I don't know," and they sometimes used voice volume and tone to emphasize how strongly they felt about a point they were making. For example, when Ralph Jones was asked how he felt about contemporary plays or poetry," he replied: "Like going to Portland for performing arts? I think that's a waste of the taxpayers' money. I really do." Throughout the interview, Mr. Jones expressed his point of view confidently and decisively. Unlike some other parents, he did not make new connections. For example, when he discussed some photos he was shown at the beginning of the interview, he talked enthusiastically about the benefits of small-group projects. Yet later, when talking about reading and writing, he said small-group discussions were not a good idea. In fact, he said he did not see any way that students were likely to benefit from being in small groups in an English class although it would be good for them to work together on projects in other subjects. He apparently could not envision any kind of project students might do for English. Even when he said, "I don't know," Mr. Jones followed that comment immediately with a definite statement. When asked if students could give each other feedback about the organization of their papers, for example, he said: "I don't know. I really think that should be the teacher's responsibility and not the students' because I don't feel the students are qualified."

Parents in this second group talked a great deal about their children needing to be prepared to go to college or succeed on the job. Randall Cromwell, for example, cited a study of chief executive officers to support his view that oral communication perhaps deserved more emphasis now than reading and writing. High school dropout Jane Conway stressed the importance of students learning in school what will be useful later. Her daughter would benefit from "writing letters," but she "doesn't see how she's going to use [the writing she is doing in class] when she gets out of school." More than once during the interview Sandra Manchester repeated her concern that the school was not doing enough to help her children learn the vocabulary they would need to do well on the Scholastic Aptitude Test (SAT).

For these parents, the outcome of the educational process seemed to be more important than the learning process itself. Randall Cromwell was something of an anomaly in this group of parents, but his interview indicated that, like the others, he held his beliefs with certainty, and even though he also sometimes talked about the process of learning as parents in the reflective category did, overall his comments reflected that what was most important to him was that school prepare students for the future. Except for Mr. Cromwell, these parents all occupied positions at the traditional end of the assumptions continuum. One way to explain how this category could include parents with such disparate philosophies was suggested by the different ways they believed the school should get students ready for the future. The parents with traditional views of teaching and learning tended to perceive school as *preparation* for the future, while Randall Cromwell advocated giving students *practice* in their future roles. For example, while Ralph Jones, Sandra Manchester, and Jane Conway favored school assignments and activities that would prepare students to write letters or speak at meetings in the future, Randall Cromwell suggested that students actually practice these skills as they were learning them by engaging in real-world projects.

The third group of parents, whose interviews can be described as reflective, was very articulate, but they expressed their views with much less certainty. These parents used the interview to reflect on and process new ideas. They said "I don't know" occasionally, sometimes they seemed to be thinking out loud, and some paused to think about questions before giving a definite answer. Catherine Tondreau, for example, asked to have the tape recorder turned off a few times so she could have time to think. Like other parents in this category, she expressed uncertainty or developed new understandings as she spoke, commenting several times that "I never thought about that before." These parents often seemed to be learning as they talked. Sometimes it appeared that they actually began to think about teaching and learning differently or in more depth as they considered and discussed the issues raised by the interview questions.

As some parents talked, what they said led them to a new idea or to reconsider their first response and take a slightly different position. Kurt Branigan provides an example of the latter case in his comments about whether students could help each other with writing. At first he seemed uncertain about the value of students giving feedback to each other, but in the end he suggested that sometimes students actually might give better feedback than the teacher.

> Yeah, I think that [student feedback] could be helpful. Not in all cases. I don't think it should replace the teacher's comments. It could be something to do occasionally . . . [because] they [teachers] have more expertise. It depends. I suppose you would want to pick a student that is also pretty good in writing if you wanted them to criticize your writing, but they could definitely help each other and it could be a more creative focus. Like a kid could have—might have some ideas a teacher might not have. She's apt to be more fixed in her ideas.

Alex Lamonte's comments about grouping students by ability provides another example to show how some parents moved away from their initial positions as they talked. At first he said that "it would probably be helpful" to put students all together in English, but he continued: "In some other courses, it would be a lot more difficult. Biology and chemistry, there you should group them. . . . No, I'll have to take that back. . . . The more I think about it, if you have a chemistry problem or a biology problem, they can stimulate each other. I know in Peter's case he really likes to help people. . . . He gets more satisfaction out of that than he does from a grade on a paper."

The major shift in Katie Pennell's thinking was not apparent to her until the end of the interview, although throughout she thoughtfully considered many aspects of teaching practices in relation to the complexities of the learning process. At first she was very critical of her son's American Studies class. At the end of the interview, however, she discovered that her view had changed. She seemed surprised at what she heard herself saying:

> They have a combination of groups. Right? . . . The assignments are different for each group. This [interview] is making me look at this

differently, you know. I've been anti-anti-this class and evaluating it. [*Laughs.*] This is wonderful! I think because they're combining the two classes, they get the movement, the change in activity. A more creative way of looking at the issues, you know, literature-wise.

These excerpts were representative of interviews with other parents in this category. The interview seemed to be an occasion for thinking and reflecting as well expressing their views. Sometimes they changed their initial positions and said, "I never thought or heard of that, but that's a good idea." While they also mentioned the outcomes they desired, their comments were much more focused on the learning process itself. They talked about specific ways students might reach the intended outcomes. These parents occupied places along the assumptions continuum from the midpoint toward the most progressive end.

Conflict or Conversation?

This wide range of parental perspectives can give school administrators headaches. Even though some parents might approve of certain practices, others adamantly object to them. What's an administrator to do? Whose voices should be listened to? Many times in schools the opinions of the politically powerful get heard while those of the less powerful are ignored. In fact, sometimes administrators decide not to introduce new practices because they anticipate resistance from these powerful parents. Conversations about teaching and learning practices among a wide spectrum of parents as well as between parents and educators are important, especially as high schools begin to introduce changes. Informal conversation can ensure that parents and educators are aware of the variety of opinions and create a climate of openness so that administrators don't feel compelled to censor innovations based on the loud objections of only a few parents or to forge ahead with an ill-conceived innovation.

It is also important, however, to recognize that teachers don't always agree about teaching and learning either. While some teachers have adopted more student-centered views, others continue to believe that the traditional teacher-centered practices are best. Although the media rarely carry stories about schools where parents have more progressive views than teachers do, some parents in fact do want more changes than teachers even were discussing. As explained in the preface, co-author Jean Konzal's efforts to influence teaching practices toward more student-centered practices in her son's schools met with little success perhaps because, like fish swimming upstream, parents who want more progressive practices were moving against the current of opinion. These parents feel frustrated by their inability to influence what goes on in schools.

As high schools have engaged in reform and restructuring, they have provided opportunities—workshops and visits to other schools, for example—for teachers with more traditional beliefs to learn about innovative practices. No one thinks to invite parents to participate. Scholar Michael Fullan, who argues that parent involvement is one of "the most powerful and least utilized instruments for educational reform," stresses that people need to develop their own meanings of change.[2] If anyone, parent or educator, wants to introduce new practices into a school, everyone needs opportunities to learn about them and to learn from each other.

What and How
Should Students Learn?

We are in the midst of an information age, and knowledge continues to explode. As writer Dr. Robert Hilliard points out, "By the time a child today graduates from college, the amount of knowledge will be four times as great [as it is now]. By the time that child is fifty years old, it will be thirty-two times as great and 97 percent of everything known in the world will have been learned since the time he was born."[1] Or, as the Washington editors of the *Kiplinger Newsletter* note: "Today, one single issue of the Sunday *New York Times* probably contains about as much information as a person was able to obtain during a lifetime back in the 1700s."[2] This dramatic change and others have forced Americans to question what they previously understood reality to be. In this constant state of flux and change, the process of making decisions about schools and classrooms becomes more and more complex and contentious.

Recent debates over the canon of important literature and over history standards attest to the difficulty of coming to common ground about curriculum issues. Should all students read Dickens and Shakespeare? Does a discussion of Columbus as a possible victimizer of Native Americans rather than a brave explorer who discovered a New World constitute a revision of history or provide a more complex knowledge of the past?

Debate also continues about the place of "drill and skill" in classrooms. Parents who grew up taking spelling tests and turning in only final drafts of essays to teachers are upset with teachers who write comments on children's papers but ignore spelling errors.

Many teachers have changed their classroom practices because they have had opportunities to learn about recent research on how students learn. As they seek to make students more active learners and engage them in activities that address the great variety of learning styles found in any group, parents are left in the dark—confused, concerned that their children are not learning what they need to know in the way they experienced and still expect.

Then, to add to the problem, parents may or may not know very much about what their children are learning in school. What they do know (or think they know) about curriculum and teaching methods comes primarily through the stories their children tell them. As researchers Michael Young and Patrick McGeeney point out, children can be very "unreliable informants."[3] Our studies indicated that some parents were clearly confused about or misunderstood what was actually happening in the classroom. Perhaps their children weren't very clear about what teachers were asking them to do and why. Most teachers don't explain to students why they have chosen certain books to read or decided to structure an assignment or activity in a certain way.

This chapter explains first what and how Eastland parents thought their children should learn in a high school English class and then provides the perspectives of parents in Grover's Corners about mathematics and social studies. Because we each conducted our studies independently, there are differences in the types of information presented, but, as will be seen, there are similar tensions. Some Eastland parents strongly opposed the introduction of an interdisciplinary course, and some parents in both communities—especially those of high-achieving students—were concerned about a shift from homogenous to heterogeneous grouping: How will their children learn enough to get into good colleges if they are placed in classes with less-able or less-motivated students?

Focus on English/Language Arts at Eastland High School

[In] the class that really got me going . . . the teacher . . . didn't sit in the front of the class and say "Plato said this and Plato said that." She would come up with a proposal and we would go back and forth with "What about this?" and "What about that?" To me that was true education.

—*Parent of a High School Student*

I don't think the school spends enough time on English grammar . . . spelling lists get the point across. Again it's the memorization.

—*Parent of a High School Student*

We try to integrate everything. We teach structure and usage in the context of students' own writing. We take the vocabulary words from the reading. When students read novels, they learn about the history at that time so they understand the works better.

—*High School American Studies Teacher*

The American Studies Class at Eastland High

The children of the parents interviewed in Eastland did not study English in a typical single-subject class. Instead, they were all enrolled in an interdisciplinary course called American Studies in which English and history were combined. The course was required for all grade 11 students, and passing it was necessary for graduation from high school. Course sections were heterogeneously grouped. However, because of the school's small size and of schedule limitations imposed by those students who were also enrolled in a vocational program, some sections were more homogeneous than others. Over the years the history and the English teacher had worked together to teach the course and had integrated both subjects to the point where students were given a combined syllabus. The teachers used the two-period time block quite flexibly. One teacher might work with the whole class for both periods, they might split the time evenly, or they might each work with smaller groups of students at the same time. All students in the course covered the same basic material, and the assignments usually required them to integrate English with history. Vocabulary study, for example, routinely included terms from history as well as other words. The teachers adapted the curriculum for some students, such as Randall Cromwell's academically talented son, who was allowed to work independently.

Occasionally other students who would find some of the American Studies assignments too challenging were given different ones or asked to do them in a different way, as was the case with "The Thirties Interview Paper." One version asked students to use their knowledge from reading *The Grapes of Wrath* to interview someone who lived in the 1930s, and to use other primary and secondary sources to investigate a topic, such as "The Dust Bowl" or "Yellow Journalism." This task was modified for some students to make it less demanding. Their assignment was to write a paper based on an interview with someone about work or family life in the 1930s. The emphasis in the course for all students, however, was on developing critical reading, writing, and thinking skills, and the work overall was quite demanding. According to an article in the newspaper about students enrolled in summer school because they failed the course, American Studies was known as a "killer course."

Only one of the two classrooms assigned to the American Studies teachers was regularly used for class meetings. The other functioned as kind of an office-conference room where small groups of students could meet or teachers could talk with individual students. For the past two years both teachers, plus teachers from other disciplines, had been involved in projects to integrate reading and writing in all subjects. Thus often students in grade 11 were asked to read critically and to write in science, math, foreign language, and other courses.

What Students Should Learn about Reading/Literature. Parents said that reading/literature should be an important part of an eleventh-grade English curriculum because reading was important for getting along in school and in the real world, especially as preparation for college or future employment.

A majority of parents (60 percent) believed that students should be given a wide variety of books to read, and 52 percent also said that the books students read or the way they are taught should help them see their connection with life today. Although parents generally agreed that students should read books by contemporary authors and that variety was important, they mentioned a wide range of other reading materials as examples, ranging from how-to books to magazine and newspaper articles. Several parents suggested biographies, historical novels, poetry, and nonfiction. Their views on the classics revealed which factors they generally believed should be considered in selecting books for students to read.

Kurt Branigan, one of six parents (24 percent) who said the classics were important, commented: "Maybe they should bring more classic stuff in. A little more Shakespeare or something like that. . . . There's a lot of richness there. I think we miss it."

Only two parents (8 percent) specifically said the classics should *not* be included at all. One, high school dropout Betty Horton, would give students "something newer, something they could get into." Noting that Stephen King was more appealing than Shakespeare, she said, "It should be up to them what they want to read."

Even though they favored including some classics, a few parents were critical of Shakespeare, but their explanations seemed to suggest that their negative reactions may have stemmed from the way his plays were taught. One parent, for example, said: "A good teacher will bring Shakespeare and make him up to date." As Nora Kendall's comments showed, though, that did not always happen: "Shakespeare I think is ridiculous. . . . What are they gonna need that for? I hated it when I was in high school. . . . Shakespeare doesn't even tell a story. . . . I read . . . *Les Miserables* when I was in high school and got a 100 on it because I loved it. It was a good book. . . . [H]uman stories are good for kids because I think it teaches them right from wrong, a lot of them."

Whether they favored including the classics or not, all parents said in one way or another that teachers must find ways to motivate students to read. Either the books should be interesting, or the teacher should find interesting ways for students to deal with them and, especially in the case of the classics, make them relevant to students. Another option for increasing students' interest would be to let them choose some books to read.

For these parents, student interest was a very important factor— perhaps more than anything else—in determining what the curriculum in literature should be.

What Students Should Learn about Writing. Parents also believed writing was important and should be emphasized. Students should have the opportunity to do a variety of types of writing, including some practical and personal writing as well as research and other formal academic writing, and be given some choice of topics.

When asked to list the writing practices that worked well—and some listed more than one—the largest number of parents (44 percent) said that a variety of types of writing was best. Many parents (40 percent) said that students should write papers about the books they read; maybe this response came to mind because they had just been discussing literature. For some this meant writing only their opinions about a book. Gary Mosher, who admitted he was not an "avid writer," said it was "important to get their ideas and viewpoints on it." Others, like Paul Harlow, said that students should do "analytical" writing; they should "be able to critique something they have read."

Quite a few parents (36 percent) mentioned research papers in some form, perhaps because their children were then enrolled in the American Studies course and had a number of research papers to write. Some parents were concerned about the difficulties their children had in finding information. For example, although Mary Andrews believed this type of assignment was valuable, she was critical of the specific requirements: "[W]e've gone to [college] libraries looking for materials . . . and it shouldn't be that way. It should be that they could get the stuff they needed in the school library or the town library."

Seven parents (28 percent) said that students should also do some creative writing or "fantasy," "fiction," "short story," and "poetry." Randall Cromwell, whose son was a gifted writer, agreed: "Ronnie has been stifled this year mainly because there's room, but not as much room, for creative writing." He went on to explain that "free thinking and creative thinking is stifled" from early childhood and said students "should be exposed to different formats, but they should cultivate their own at some point."

Personal writing—students choosing topics of interest to them and related to their own lives—was favored both by parents of good students and poor students. Practical and personal writing, they believed, would be more likely to motivate students to work more on their writing than, for example, writing about literature or a research paper. In response to a question about the ideal writing class, Katie Pennell described an assignment her son, usually a reluctant writer, had done the previous year. The task, a combination of practical and personal writing, captured his interest: "[The teacher] said, 'I want you to write to a person and tell them what you think. . . . ' For Joey it was the right to bear arms, to buy guns. He ran home and got on his computer and went crazy. Wrote and wrote and wrote. . . . He wrote to a congressman to give his opinion. He learned a lot." The assignment was effective, she said, because "[o]ne of the most common things we do is write letters, but because of his poor abilities in English, he doesn't ever do that. . . . It's part of everyday living, a real-life situation."

The idea that writing can be integrated across the curriculum was mentioned by Kurt and Sally Branigan, who talked very positively about the opportunity their daughter had to write in subjects other than English, something they both believed was important. Mr. Branigan said: "Writing skills are being developed throughout the whole curriculum, not just in English class. . . . A holistic approach. Rather than just somebody hen-scratching multiple choice, they're writing whole papers in other classes."

Randall Cromwell carried the idea of integration a bit further. The only parent who talked about personal writing as a means of reflection, he cited a recent example of integrated writing that went beyond the school. After first talking about the value of the senior independent projects students did at Eastland High, he commented on four "jocks" from a parochial high school who did school projects at his day nursery: "[T]hey had to work with two-and-a-half-year-olds and they wrote reflection papers on what they discovered about themselves."

Computer Use/Literacy. Parents were uniformly positive about the idea of students learning to use computers. Computers give students an opportunity for "hands-on" learning, and all agreed that the computer was a necessary tool in today's classrooms. Several commented that more computers should be available to students in the classroom because their children had no access to a computer at home.

Most talked about the need for students to learn to use computers in order to be prepared for the job market or the world today. Only a few parents talked specifically about how computers can be helpful in writing. Learning to use the computer was also important to some parents as a way for students to access information in the electronic age, a skill they thought should be taught in school. Some parents acknowledged that their children knew more about computers than they did; a few parents said that they had asked their children for help.

On the other hand, even though parents believed computer literacy was essential, four expressed some concerns about computer dependency. Gary Mosher's comments were representative: "Although I think computers are good, I think students are basing too much on machinery and not enough on the basics. . . . [A word processor] is fine as long as they understand the principle of what they are trying to learn."

What parents believe students should learn is shaped by their own and their children's school experiences as well as what they believe students—all, some, or individual children—need now or in the future. Although it isn't clear how schools could better accommodate such a variety of student differences, these parents seem to believe that one required curriculum will not suit everyone.

How Students Should Be Taught

Just as parents have different ideas about the ideal curriculum, they also do not agree about how their children should be taught. The "how" includes teaching methods, the structure of the course (in this instance, an interdisciplinary course), and the grouping of students— homogeneous (e.g., college, vocational, general, and honors classes) or heterogeneous (mixed-ability classes). Parents' views of the teaching of writing—and how it should differ from the teaching of reading/ literature—suggests another question: What should be the role of the teacher?

When asked to describe an ideal class in which students would be dealing with writing, many parents paused longer and were more likely to say they were not sure than they did when asked the same question about reading/literature. Most recalled only classes in which the teacher assigned the topic for papers that students wrote by themselves and handed in; the teacher then marked all of the errors in red ink, graded them, and handed them back. Because of these limited experiences, many did not seem familiar with the process approach to teaching writing, where students choose topics, write several drafts, and share these drafts with peers to get feedback for improving them.

When asked specifically to comment on a newer practice, such as students sharing drafts in a small group, some said that it would help, but many could not explain why.

One way to understand differences in parents' views about teaching writing is to consider the degree to which they emphasized product in relation to process. Another way is to consider the value they placed on feedback and help students can get from the teacher in relation to that which they might get from other students.

About 40 percent of parents had a rather traditional idea of teaching writing: What the student writes (the product) is more important than the process; the teacher, not other students, should give help and feedback. On the other hand, 46 percent thought product and process were at least of equal importance and students could give help to each other. The range of parents' views, can be seen in the comments of Gary Mosher and Alex Lamonte. Mr. Mosher had a very traditional view of teaching writing. He was the only parent who did not see some value in drafts. The final product would be graded by the teacher; feedback on it would come only from her. On the other hand, Mr. Lamonte's description of the ideal writing class was very close to the process approach used by many teachers today. He and others with similar views emphasized the process of writing and the importance of students working with each other. In some cases these parents said students might give even better feedback than the teacher.

Randall Cromwell, whose view of learning extended beyond the classroom and school into the community, was once again in a category all by himself. For him, writing and other skills can best be developed as students work on real-world, interdisciplinary projects. When he talked about writing in terms of his own son, he said the process approach was not good for him because Ronnie preferred to work on his own in his own way. Mr. Cromwell believed that worksheets in the lower grades often stifled students' writing and thinking. He noted, for example, that "some kids already come to school knowing how to do inventive writing," but then "they're asked to function at a lower level . . . and [they] write 'Spot is black.'"

Parents expressed the most uncertainty about the value of student feedback, and they seemed to think small-group work was less desirable for writing than for reading.

A large majority of parents believed the teacher's feedback on writing was best. Perhaps because most parents had not had the opportunity to write drafts and then meet in small groups to get feedback from other students, they were not sure whether student feedback would be helpful. Thus for them the teacher was the one with expert knowledge who could best help students improve their writing. Parents gave several reasons for having students get feedback from the teacher. The Branigans illustrate the two most common responses. Kurt Branigan said it was important because "they have more expertise." His wife, Sally, agreed and added, "And they know what they want." Teacher feedback was important on drafts because teachers knew best, especially when it came to correcting errors in punctuation and usage, and, since they would assign the final grade, students would benefit from knowing what specific changes to make in order to earn better grades.

Some parents, however, did believe that students could benefit from getting peer feedback. Nora Kendall, a high school dropout, explained how discouraged she was as a student when her papers came back with "all kinds of red marks everywhere." Her teachers did not allow her to get help from anyone else, a practice she would like to see changed. "Kids explain things better than adults do. . . . [I]f a child knows more than another child and they're friendly enough and they want to help each other, I think that's great." She noted that help can come from other sources too: "[W]hen they're writing out something, they should be able to ask questions of their parents or their peers."

Fourth-grade dropout Roland Foster saw feedback from classmates as cheating. "I don't think they should [help each other] because . . . Let's say I'm doing something. Why should I get it corrected before I turn it in? Well, why not just have that person turn it in? . . . It's like a test. If you've got to take a test, there's nobody going to be helping you. Right? . . . [T]he end results, what you did there, that's it. The bottom line." Because the practice of sharing drafts with peers was not something Mr. Foster experienced in the few years he spent in school, it was not surprising that his first reaction was to think of students helping each other as cheating.

The major differences in the role of the teacher suggested by parents' beliefs about best practices for reading/literature and for writing could be seen in their views about the value of students working in small groups with each other. Parents seemed to think teacher expertise or knowledge was more important in the writing classroom. Technical knowledge that students might not have was required for correcting errors in sentence structure and punctuation. Thus students lacked the background to give each other much help with writing. On the other hand, because no parent believed that a book had only one meaning, students could develop a better understanding of something they had read by sharing their own views with each other.

In the writing classroom the teacher was the authority, the expert—the one who knew the correct way to punctuate a sentence. In the reading classroom the teacher's role was different. She would function more as a monitor or facilitator, the one who kept students on task or asked questions that led them to look at things differently. She may have more knowledge about literature, but her view of a book was just another opinion.

Parents' differing perceptions of the teacher's role may be related to their lack of knowledge about the process approach to writing. Even though no parent would give more weight to mechanics than to content on the final grade for a paper, many parents talked about the importance of correct spelling and punctuation and said that teacher feedback was essential on these technical matters. Perhaps, then, they did not understand the draft as an intermediate step in the writing process in the way many teachers do. Teachers often have students work in groups to comment on content matters, such as organization and development, as preparation for revising their papers. They do not want students to deal with editing matters, such as spelling and punctuation, until later in the process. Because parents often talked about both content and mechanics simultaneously, they may not have been able to envision the possibility of students dealing first only with content and then later with mechanics.

Teaching methods are just one aspect of how students should be taught; whether the curriculum and courses should be structured in ways that connect rather than separate subjects is another.

English as an Interdisciplinary Course

Almost half of the parents (48 percent) believed students would benefit from studying English in combination with history. However, parents' views on this topic were less clear than on any other topic discussed during the interviews, in part because some parents did not know much about or were confused about their children's American Studies class. Many were unable to separate the idea of interdisciplinary study from the specific requirements and demands of the class in which their children were enrolled. Some students had a very difficult time meeting the demanding requirements of the course, especially the independent research.

Typical of other parents who liked the idea of American Studies, Alex Lamonte said: "I think it makes a lot of sense. . . . [S]ome of the great literature is about history and so why not tie things together? . . . American history and English are a good combination."

Several parents expressed concerns, however, about the amount and difficulty of the work students had been assigned in the class. Kurt Branigan said that because students had not been prepared in previous years, the workload in the class hit students "like a ton of bricks." He suggested that "maybe [the work] could be spread more evenly through the high school years because the American Studies course is quite an intensive program as it is, and if they put anything else in there, they could blow the kids away." His wife agreed and said "it would be nice if they could choose one book" and do some "creative writing," but "it is an excellent program and should be continued."

Most parents of children who were doing well in English spoke positively about the American Studies program. Ralph Jones, however, was very critical. Even though he described his daughter's achievement in English as "excellent," he expressed a view that was typical of parents whose children were *not* doing well in English. And what may give educators some pause to think about the effects of back-fence and beauty-shop gossip is the fact that several of these critical parents said, as Ralph Jones did, that they had discussed the course with other parents. No parent who spoke positively about the class mentioned similar discussions. Parents who spoke negatively also talked about students not being at a college level yet and liked the idea of keeping

English and history separate because that is the way it was when they went to school. Ralph Jones could have been speaking for the other parents who held negative views: "I doubt very seriously it's like [my ideal class] from what I've heard from Janie and, talking to other parents, I don't feel it's like that at all. I think they are trying to go on too much a higher level the way it is right now. It's fine to prepare them for college, but don't make it a college course, particularly at eleventh grade."

When asked whether he would like the idea of combining history and English if it were done right, Mr. Jones replied: "I go along with the old school. That's the way I did it. Why change it? Those were two separate courses." He saw no advantages from combining the subjects.

Parents whose children were not doing well often seemed unable to separate the problems their children had in the American Studies course from the idea of its interdisciplinary nature. Pam Sloan, who said her son's achievement overall and in English was "poor," commented: "It seems as though [it's] a lot just reading and writing. . . . I think they miss a lot of the history part by concentrating so much on the writing. I'd like to see history as a history course and English or literature as an English course. . . . Carl just gets so overwhelmed because there seems to be so much for him to do and so much expected of him and he just slips behind."

Of course, confusion about the course also leads to other opinions. High school dropout Betty Horton was very critical of American Studies, and her comments indicated much confusion about her son's team-taught class. "It's the world history that he says that totally blows him because he's had one teacher one day and the next day will be a totally different teacher with a totally different subject." When asked whether she was referring to the American Studies class, Mrs. Horton said: "The one that every junior takes. Whatever it is. . . . You know, one day you get something to do and then whatever they do the next class, it's just totally off the wall. It's nothing [like] what they had Monday." Anyone familiar with the actual course at Eastland High would not recognize it from Mrs. Horton's comments.

Finally, some parents were uncertain about the value of the course. Sometimes they said they were not sure exactly what their children were doing in class, but they felt the workload was too heavy and students did not have enough choice about assignments. If their children were doing well, some said the class must be okay, but they were not sure whether combining history and English was a good idea.

There seemed to be two main reasons that a majority of parents was either uncertain or critical of the American Studies course. First, their children were not doing well: The expectations, the workload, or both were too high; students had not been prepared well enough for this class; or they were not being given enough individual help. Second, parents were confused about what was actually happening at school: They did not understand the purpose of the interdisciplinary course, some of the assignments their children had to do, or the nature of team teaching. Parents wanted their children to be successful. When they were not, the parents looked for causes. It was easy to lay the blame on an innovation, such as an interdisciplinary course, which, because they had never experienced it, they may not have understood.

Grouping: Heterogeneous or Homogeneous?

Surprisingly, grouping did not seem to be an issue for most of these parents as long as their children got an appropriate curriculum and enough individual attention so that they could learn. Even though most parents interviewed (68 percent) said they knew that the American Studies class in which their children were then enrolled was heterogeneously grouped, no parent—even those who preferred homogeneously grouped classes—mentioned grouping as a problem with the course. However, many did express concern about the amount and level of the work assigned.

Parents who favored assigning students of all levels to the same classes said that the slower students would benefit by not being labeled and/or by having the opportunity to learn directly or indirectly from the more able learners. Ralph Jones's explanation was typical of others: "I believe it will help the morale of the child that's a little bit slower. A child can mean well and be trying 200 percent—if this child . . . gets grouped with a group that's 'Here, you're the slow one. You're over here in this corner,' I really think you're destroying the morale of this child. . . . I don't think it's going to slow [the others] down. They're going to work at their own pace. . . . Number one, you're not hurting the morale of individual children . . . and number two they can learn from each other." Mr. Jones further explained his view by talking about his daughter. Janie, who learned to read earlier than many of her classmates, benefited from being the teacher's helper in first grade.

Many of those who favored mixed grouping qualified their answers, however, by saying that in a mixed class, it was important for the teacher to address in some way the needs of students who learned more quickly or more slowly than others. Like Ralph Jones, several suggested that the more able students could help the ones who were having difficulty. Betty Horton put it this way: "I'd see a couple smart ones in with the slow group to help them, to explain. They'd do great. I think it'd be a good chance for the smart ones to teach the slow ones because I've seen it in . . . fourth and fifth grades. They get along great. They have respect. . . . They love it. I think it gives them you know like 'I'm the teacher. I'm helping these kids.'" Others qualified their responses by saying that mixed classes were best as long as students were all interested in learning.

The seven parents (28 percent) who believed that students learned best when they were grouped in separate classes on the basis of ability or achievement most often said that slower students would feel frustrated or inadequate and the more able students would get bored if they were placed in the same class. Several of these parents seemed less sure of their opinions than others; some appeared to be deciding what they thought as they talked. Mary Andrews, for example, said the students "in level 1 might not be able to do the work in level 3" and might hold the level 3 kids back or the kids in level 3 might go "so fast that kids in level 1 couldn't catch up." At the same time, however, she noted that an advantage of having students all together was that "then you're not putting them into little cliques. . . . 'We won't talk with him because he's not on the same level that we are.'" Finally the balance for her tipped in favor of separate classes because "it can be very frustrating catching up with what everybody else is doing." Other examples, though, suggested that in some cases parents may be quite willing to consider new ideas and change their opinions when they have an opportunity to discuss them in a nonthreatening situation.

Explanations by some parents to support their preference for separate classes seemed to have more to do with matching the curriculum to students' different interests and/or future plans than with their ability or achievement. Lucille Farnum, whose son received special education services because he had cerebral palsy, talked about "the need to teach the kids about life" and said: "I wish they would go back to like it was when I was in school. They had courses for college, commercial for business, and general." Asked why that was better, she replied: "Academic had chemistry, algebra. If a kid's going to work in a gas station, he doesn't need that." Ronald Lancaster, who believed that, given a choice, "kids will migrate to their ability group" anyway, said: "I think you do better with people who have something in common with you. Kids at PRVTC [vocational school] are going to be talking about repairing a car and the English and math are going to be tied to what they are going to do."

Unlike the other parents in the category of mixed responses to the grouping question, Randall Cromwell differentiated between what might be best for students generally and what he preferred for his own child. The parent of a gifted child, he waffled at first. It took a few minutes of probing to get to his bottom line, perhaps in part because, as an educator, he knew that it was fashionable in professional circles to favor heterogeneously grouped classes. He talked about the difficulty of scheduling a single section of a course, the number of his son's friends who had left Eastland High to attend private schools, and the importance of training teachers to teach heterogeneously grouped classes effectively. Finally he said: "I think if I were really altruistic, I would say, yeah, kids ought to be heterogeneously grouped and teachers ought to be trained to deal with those kinds of issues . . . [but] ideally if I had to do it all over again, I would insist that Ronnie be with nothing but top kids."

A majority of these parents thought that students could learn best in mixed classes; even some who preferred that students be separated on the basis of ability, achievement, interests, or future plans said that there might be some benefits for students in mixed classes. As will be seen, Grover's Corners parents felt somewhat differently about grouping, but parents in both communities are like parents everywhere in one respect: Their greatest concern is that their own children's needs be met. If something is working for their kids, it is probably okay. If teachers can provide individual attention or differentiate assignments/

curriculum for students who learn more slowly or more rapidly than others, then parents may see no problem with their children being placed in mixed classes. Eastland parents wanted classes, no matter how they are grouped, where bright students will be challenged and interested and other students, especially those who have difficulty learning, will feel comfortable, accepted, and successful.

Focus on Mathematics and on
Social Studies at Grover's Corners High School

I was real concerned about the new math curriculum because I didn't know how this would go on the college transcripts.

—Parent of a High School Student

I don't think a lot of people in this country are that up on politics and I don't think they are up on policymaking. I think if they get exposure to it young that's wonderful.

—Parent of a High School Student

There is plenty of evidence to suggest that differences of opinion are apparent when parents anywhere talk about changes in subjects other than English. For example, an article in *USA Today* headlined "Critics say the latest math methods do not compute," criticized the new math standards developed by the National Council of Teachers of Mathematics: "Pick your favorite derogatory nickname for the math showing up in textbooks across the country: new-new math, fuzzy math—even 'rain-forest math.'" The writer goes on to explain that, because the focus is now on the process of problem solving, "students could arrive at the right answer the 'wrong way' and get marked lower [on a test] than students who arrive at the wrong answer the 'right way.'"[4]

Like Eastland parents, Grover's Corners parents had many different mental models of good schools and classrooms. As a result, they held a wide range of opinions about the new practices that had been introduced at Grover's Corners High School. Here we show what parents thought about changes in the ways mathematics and social studies were taught.

Grover's Corners High School reflected the town's struggle between the values of the old and new residents. The town voted support for a bond issue for a $10 million addition to the high school at a time when the state economy was weak and state aid, stagnant. Yet the following summer the town voted to recall both the town and the school budget. Why then did the town vote to totally renovate the building and add a large new addition?

One explanation given by both educators and parents was that the high school bond issue passed because both old and new residents could see their values embodied in this new building (even though there is still nostalgia for the old building among some parents and faculty). Old Grover's Corners people prided themselves on caring about their young people and recognized that the old building was totally inadequate. Additionally, as in many rural communities, strong support for sports activities was deeply rooted in this town. Because the new building included a new gymnasium and outdoor track facility, the sports booster clubs were active supporters of the bond issue. New Grover's Corners people, more typically those who were living in the new homes built on the edge of town, supported the bond issue because they were looking for educational facilities that more closely matched their mental images of educational facilities in the towns from which they came.

Although the new high school addition showed how both old and new values can be accommodated simultaneously, the changes going on within the walls of the school continued to test this uneasy marriage of values for both faculty and parents. The effort to adapt curriculum, teaching strategies, and school structures to the realities of the 1990s and beyond became a struggle to re-create the heart and soul of the school, to decide which of the old ways should be maintained and which should be replaced. Changes did come, but they were initiated by the faculty, not parents.

Because faculty members were active members of a newly formed school/university partnership, they participated in discussions about curriculum issues with other high school educators from the region. One group formed an informal discussion group that met after school to talk about their vision of education:

We would stay late—none of us were married and we'd stay late and we would talk education. We'd just bang ideas left and right. And we'd look up and it would be like seven o'clock and say, "Geez, we need to [get] pizza or something." It would be during the week. So we'd go to the corner pizza place and we'd keep talking 'till like eight or nine at night. We were doing this . . . on a regular basis, like every night almost. And one time we were there talking and a parent came in and the term the parent used was "this is a formidable group of educators" because they had seen us there all the time. I'm sure they caught pieces of our conversation.

These conversations were catalysts for two major new curriculum thrusts: one in social studies and the other in math.

The New Math Curriculum

When one of the teachers who created the new math curriculum presented a workshop for math teachers from around the state, he moved confidently around the room demonstrating, explaining, and answering questions. As he described his project-based integrated curriculum ideas, the buzz of excitement and enthusiasm that filled the air confirmed for him that his professional colleagues were impressed with his work.

Other teachers who became more active and reflective about curriculum and teaching decisions also received public recognition from their peers. Unfortunately, there were downsides to this new role as well. Whereas in the past, teachers could redirect critical questions about curriculum to the principal, now they were asked to answer these questions themselves. After all, if they designed and developed the curriculum, who else could answer questions about it? The developers of the new math curriculum at Grover's Corners discovered that parents did not all respond as positively as professional colleagues.

The new math curriculum was introduced to Grover's Corners High School freshmen in 1992. The two math teachers who developed the curriculum were influenced by the new math standards published by the National Council of Teachers of Mathematics and encouraged by a grant from a local corporate partner. They designed a curriculum that was integrated, grouped by mixed ability, and project-based. The four-year integrated math sequence incorporated all of the various disciplines of secondary mathematics—algebra, geometry, probability, statistics, calculus, topology—and wove them throughout the curriculum. And the courses were renamed: Math 1 replaced Algebra I, Basic Math, and Consumer Math; Math 2 replaced Geometry; Math 3 and 3A replaced Algebra II; and Math 4 replaced College Review Math. Precalculus and Calculus were still offered.

To design the Math 1 curriculum, the teachers began by asking the following question: If students could take only one year of high school mathematics, what would be most important for them to know and be able to do? The curriculum consisted of five interrelated units, each with identified core skills and concepts. These core skills built on and extended knowledge students got in the kindergarten to grade 8 curriculum.

The teachers were excited about the new design. Parents, however, were not so enthusiastic. One of the major concerns was the change of the course names. Parents were afraid that when colleges saw "Math 1, 2, 3, or 4" on a transcript, they would not know what it meant. For instance, Annie Jefferson, a single mother who struggled to get her own college education and was not about to let anything stand in the way of her daughter's college education, said:

> The math scares me. The school math concept of Math 1, 2, 3, and 4 absolutely scares me to death and I guess Marcia's class is going to be the first class that has graduated with the whole Math 1, 2, 3, and 4. I just don't know. Going back to when I was in school you really had to conquer Algebra I, Algebra II; and each one was a building block onto the next. How they can group them together and expand on that is just beyond me! I can't believe it. Also, I don't know how colleges are going to look at Math 1, 2, 3, and 4 and say, "Oh, okay." That scares me.

Another concern, expressed over and over again in many different contexts, was that, although the idea was sound, the way the school implemented the program was flawed: The reality didn't match the rhetoric. How much really did change? Austin Halliwell, a parent who was also a teacher in another district, explained: "The problem was they didn't know where they were going. They were totally unfocused. What has really happened, from what I can see, is that Math 1, 2, 3, and 4 are Algebra I, Geometry, Algebra II, and then . . . I think it's become more traditional recently. I think it's slid back to where it used to be."

Cooperative Learning. Parents did not agree about students doing classwork in cooperative learning groups. They expressed a wide range of views. Some—primarily parents from working-class backgrounds who grew up in the town and whose children were not high achievers—really liked the idea of students working together in cooperative groups. They thought students could help other students learn better than teachers could. Mary Reidy, who grew up in town and worked as a clerk in a local retail store, said:

> I think if I was going to try to figure something out with my pals as opposed to having a teacher try to teach it, I might learn it better. Sometimes you get kids that are more on your level. Maybe another kid can come up with just such a simple way to show you how to do something that you would remember how to do it. My son did a little bit last year. He doesn't say too much about school at all. But I think he enjoyed it.

Other parents, like some parents in Eastland, liked the idea of cooperative group work because it prepared students for "real life." One such parent was Barbara Gleason, who grew up "on the wrong side of the tracks" and who worked as a clerk in an office. Her son was in special education classes. "I think that working in a group would be good because I think that helps kids to learn to work as a group. When they get out into the world, they have to work with different people and be able to discuss things with them."

Even though Tom Ballard, a tradesman in town and a graduate of a technical college, also liked the concept of cooperative group work for the same reasons as Mrs. Reidy and Mrs. Gleason, he was concerned about the school's implementation of the approach:

I like the idea of it, but what I don't like—and I noticed it with my youngest son because he repeatedly tells me about this—that if there's three people or four people doing a project, many of them end up lugging at least one person. That's one thing I don't really care for. I talked to people that worked for a big company in town and other places and asked, "What do you do about it?" And they said, "Well, if we've got a project and there's five of us on the project and there's one person that's not doing their job, the next time there's a project and his name comes up, the other four of us flat out say 'No way, we're not going to have that person work with us or we won't do that project.'" That's how they're doing it at the workplace. And it eventually ends up so that nobody wants to work with that person. You've got to have everybody with different abilities—but everybody needs to pull their own weight.

Mr. Ballard's concerns were interesting because he took the educator's arguments for cooperative group work—preparation for the workplace—and explored them more in depth. His insights would have made a good starting place for important discussions about how cooperative group work should be structured, but, because he was viewed as a "problem parent" by the school—one who was against change—his views were not listened to. This was another missed opportunity for dialogue.

Other parents—primarily those whose children excelled in individual work—objected to cooperative group work because they believed the practice would hold their children back. Edna MacFarland, a college graduate who grew up in a nearby town, explained:

I had a problem with it when they had three and four kids in a work study group in the classroom and they always put one of the smarter kids with the lesser kids, which is all right, but that is slowing my daughter down. She used to complain about that. She used to come home and say, "Geez, I couldn't get all my work done because I was helping so and so." Geez, you should be doing your own work first and then helping. And it seemed like that is what the teacher should have been doing.

Grouping: Heterogeneous or Homogeneous? In addition to the coop-erative-group class work, the new math curriculum was the first attempt at Grover's Corners High School to do away with tracking. Instead of being grouped together on the basis of their ability and achievement levels, all freshmen were placed together in a Math 1 class regardless of ability. The first three years the classes were heteroge-neously grouped; teachers tried to meet individual differences by grouping within the class as an elementary teacher would do. Parents had mixed reactions to the idea of mixed-ability groupings. Some, like Mr. Ballard, had learned very well the lessons taught by schools for years: Classes are best taught when children are grouped in like-ability groups. This is what he expected for his children.

> I've told my son all his life, when you get to high school they'll have different levels of math that you can take and you'll be in with a bunch of kids of your own ability and you'll be able to go. And he got to high school and math and—NO—there's just one Math 1 for every single kid in that high school and a Math 2 for every single kid in the high school. And it's just knocked the stuffing right out of him. He just wants to graduate and that's it. He was totally turned off. If he had been brought in in his freshman year and had got in with a grade level of students of his own ability, I'm sure he'd go right on. But after two years of just sitting there with every single kid in the high school in your class, every grade . . . he just gave up.

Some parents, like Sandra Lacey, a nurse who opposed mixed-ability groupings, did so based on their children's negative experiences in these classes. "My finding with our son was he always got in with a group that seemed to be covering the same things semester after semester after semester and he was bored."

Jane Amberson, a parent of a student at Grover's Corners High School and a teacher in another school district, saw some benefits of heterogeneous grouping—but not for all children: "It's good for the wide middle but not for those very high kids and those very low kids. Especially the top kids, if the teacher is cognizant of what they're supposed to be doing with these kids and stretching them, then they'll do fine. But if they're not, then they're just biding their time. And that's what I was afraid of for the math."

Eventually the program evolved into a hybrid of heterogeneous and homogeneous grouping. Two teachers taught Math 1 or Math 2 during the same period. Students were initially grouped heterogeneously for the introduction of a unit. After a time they were tested on the unit material. Those who demonstrated mastery at an 80 percent level were regrouped into an enrichment group with one teacher, while those who did not demonstrate mastery were assigned to the other teacher for further instruction. This process of grouping and regrouping was repeated for each unit. The underlying principle was that the groups didn't remain static. Many students would be in the enrichment group for some units and in the additional help group for other units. In reality, however, some students were always assigned to the enrichment group or to the review group; only some students in the middle moved from one group to the other depending on the topic. And it was possible to get an honors designation for their work if students were in the enrichment groups for a majority of time during the course.

Parents who knew how the approach had changed, such as Peg Halliwell, a parent and a teacher in another school district, thought it was a good idea.

> I have a daughter who is a freshman this year and her math program is far different from the one my first daughter went through when they first introduced the program. Sometimes a large group of kids receives instruction and at times the group is broken up and maybe the kids who need a little more time, work with this teacher, and kids who are ready to keep moving ahead work with another teacher. It seems to change with each unit so it's not punitive. It ebbs and flows and then they come back again and they reshuffle and that's really kind of neat. So some of the time they are with kids of their own ability and other times they are with the whole group. I like that.

Unfortunately, most of the parents interviewed for this study were unaware of this new approach.

High Standards for All? Recently a new concern emerged from some parents of special-needs students: How relevant was the curriculum for their children? As one teacher from outside the math department put it: "It's a Catch-22 situation. [I want] to see . . . students leave here with something that they will be able to use. The kids . . . will definitely pass Math 1, but what's it going to gain? In the long run I don't know. But I don't want to provide special ed math for all . . . students either, because that's going away from the inclusion effort." Yet math teachers and the principal believed the Math 1 curriculum was relevant for all students because "one of the focuses of the course is not just the algebra and the geometry and the statistics . . . it's the teamwork and the group problem-solving skills, the individual problem-solving skills, the thinking processes that take place [when] do[ing] algebra or solv[ing] problems or work[ing] in a group." As both math teachers reiterated, "You don't get math credit for doing arithmetic anymore."

This issue was not nearly as volatile as the original parental concerns, possibly because the parents who were concerned this time were not representative of the town's powerful parents. Parents met with the math teachers, the special education teachers, and the principal. Unlike teachers in many schools who want students put in separate special classes, these math teachers argued to keep special needs students in their classes; special educators advocated taking them out. Finally everyone agreed to remove some students from the class and provide others with additional help within the class.

While reasoned conversation in the case of the children with special needs led to reaching a compromise that seemed to diffuse the situation, some parents (and perhaps also some teachers) continued to doubt whether what was taught in the new math classes was relevant to their children's needs: Who would teach a child to balance a checkbook? Parents argued that the goal of higher expectations for all children needs to be tempered by attending to the individual needs of each child. These parents thought that balancing a checkbook was more important than algebra for their children. This tension between high standards and individual needs is one of many that parents and teachers struggle with as they try to understand each other's views in the process of change.

Results of the New Math Curriculum. With the introduction of Math 4 during the 1993-94 school year, the phase-in of the new math curriculum was completed. Math 1 had been taught for many years, and educators pointed with pride to results that seemed to indicate that this new curriculum had a positive impact on student learning. Scores on the statewide testing of eleventh graders in mathematics showed significant improvement for the classes of 1993 and 1994 over their eighth-grade scores; SAT math scores were on the rise (even as language scores dropped); and more students than ever before were taking advanced math classes. Educators believed that what parents cared about most were results, and that, when the school showed results, debate over the changes diminished. As one administrator said:

> The point I'm trying to make is I think and I continue to think that parents are becoming increasingly concerned with results, increasingly concerned with being able to know that there are results . . . quantifiable, visible results. I want to know that my kid can read. I want to know that my kid can think mathematically and I want to see it on test scores. And they're willing . . . to look at exhibitions as well and have conferences where they really look at a portfolio that has real work in it.

Some educators at Grover's Corners High School believed strongly that the planned changes in curriculum, instruction, and assessment would lead to the results parents wanted to see. As a result they argued they should forge ahead with the changes whether or not parents joined in the planning or initially supported the change: They believed that time was of the essence and that waiting for parental consensus would slow down their forward momentum. When talking about the poor attendance at a parent forum, one administrator said, "See, I'm getting back to the time issue again, I'm . . . going to continue to promote involvement with the community . . . [but] I'm sure that time is involved here and that results speed up people's willingness to accept change." As the next section shows, parents also were asked to accept changes in another curriculum area.

The New Social Studies Curriculum

Changes in the social studies curriculum at the school also bypassed parental participation in the planning stages. The social studies course, designed by teachers, was an example of a results-driven curriculum. Although parents weren't involved in its conception, the teachers said they learned a lot from what happened with the math curriculum and made some strategic decisions they hoped would defuse parental concerns.

According to the *Grover's Corners Social Studies Curriculum Guide*, the new social studies course was "a two-year required course that studies the interrelationships between the State . . . , the U.S. and the world, past and present . . . the course includes much more than history and is better described as an integrated social studies course . . . designed to help students learn the essential concepts, information, and skills they will need as responsible and prosperous citizens in the 21st century."[5] The three social studies teachers responsible for the new course were leaders in the school's restructuring efforts and had born the brunt of internal faculty struggles over the long years of debate about the shape reform would take. Attending to parental concerns, while not the primary driving force behind the design of the course, did influence the way teachers crafted it. One teacher explained:

> We have made some modifications that we felt didn't compromise the goals and objective of quality learning in ways that would not create unnecessary anxiety in parents. A specific example would be that . . . parents grew up getting a test every three weeks on Friday or whatever. We don't go by any set schedule, we get there when we get there, but we do some core content - type testing. We feel that's a confidence builder for the parents—that they know that that's a part of the curriculum and that gives them a sense of confidence . . . even if there are some other things in the class that don't seem quite like the way they were when they were in school. This is one that gives us some credibility to have some freedom to do some other things. And gives them some comfort and confidence that the kids aren't just doing a completely "process-oriented" or "values-oriented" curriculum that's criticized as "mush" and so forth.

The teachers wrote their own textbook, distilling American history, sociology and anthropology, political science, and economics to core concepts that they thought every student should know. They required all students to master this knowledge at an 85 percent level. Students who had difficulty attaining this mastery of the core knowledge were required to attend academic coaching after school. Students had to write and orally present a monologue in the voice of a historical character and a public policy position paper. Students were asked to take a much more active role in their education. Teachers also incorporated a variety of instructional strategies, such as video discs, lectures, and games, to try to meet individual students' styles and pace of learning.

High Standards for All? Parents expressed mixed feelings about the 85 percent passing standard. Some, especially those parents who had not done well in school themselves and who had children who were also not doing well, didn't think it was a good idea. For instance, Mary Reidy said: "Hmmm. With an 85? Boy, that would be kind of steep for some kids. That really could be. Um, I would even go along with like a 78 or something like that, but an 85 is really pushing for some kids." Similarly Barbara Gleason explained:

> No, I don't like such a high requirement because it's not fair to children that do struggle. You know, everybody's different. I don't think anybody should be made to take it over because they didn't make an 85 average. I figure if a child is really struggling and trying to make a 70 or a 75 that they should be allowed to pass because they're going to find something out in the world to do that's at their level. It's not fair to hold somebody else back and make them look foolish in their friends' eyes.

Other parents—generally those who did well in school themselves and whose children did well—liked the idea of setting a standard. Annie Jefferson did not think the standard was unreasonable: "I don't think kids are pushed enough. I think kids can probably work up to what they are expected to do. Not that every child in that class can probably get an 85 percent, but if they don't think they have to try, they won't. And I don't think there is anything wrong with that." Peg Halliwell also favored setting a standard:

> I liked the fact that the standards were clearly articulated. I would like to see more of that carried over. I'm known in my school as "the criteria lady" because I've taught every seventh grader what criteria are, how you use them in schools, [and] how kids can generate criteria for product forms and for work that they do. So it was very exciting for me to have somebody else do it. But I don't think it's spread throughout the school yet.

In the beginning the new social studies course was tracked into two levels. Later, the course was grouped heterogeneously. Students had an opportunity to earn an honors designation based on mastering the core content tests the first time they took them. The new approach to social studies did not raise any parental concerns—a much different scenario than when math was introduced with mixed-ability groupings. Some people suggested this was because the honors designation was built into the new approach from the beginning. Others thought the reason was that the change in social studies was introduced with much less fanfare than had been the case with math.

Public Presentations. Assessment of student learning in the social studies course combined traditional multiple-choice teacher-made tests for the core knowledge with a more innovative performance-based assessment of research, analysis, and public presentation skills. Sophomores presented dramatic monologues written by the student in the voice of a figure in American history. The junior presentations were public policy papers on issues of the students' choosing. On the whole, most parents really liked the idea of presentations, primarily because they could see the real-life application of this work. Mrs. Jefferson commented: "My daughter's doing that on gun control. She called all of the candidates and got their opinions and wrote a paper. I think that was wonderful. I don't think a lot of people in this country are that up on politics and I don't think they are up on policymaking. I think if they get exposure to it young, that's wonderful." And Mary Reidy:

That's great. That is great because at least she can get up in front of people and speak. I mean, I remember when I got up at one of our regular town meetings where we were talking about recalling the taxes. There were a lot of things that I really wanted to emphasize to the town council. I got up and I started out fine, but the further I went, the more I could feel myself getting really, really hot. You know, like pulling-at-the-shirt hot. And my legs started to shake and it's like, "Shut it off right now, dearie, because if you don't, you are going to pass out right here on the floor." So I think that public presentation is definitely a good experience for my daughter. Hopefully she'll never do what I did.

Of course, there were also parents who, even though they liked the idea of the public policy presentations, questioned their execution. And, as before, parents who had some concerns were those whose children excelled in school. Marie Lorenzo talks about her perception of the presentations:

I don't think the forum at the end was as nice as I would have liked, but the concept was great and there was a lot of effort put into that, a lot of skills—time management, knowledge, reading, writing. But my daughter had hoped to learn a lot about American history. She might have learned a little bit about specific history regarding her two topics that she chose but when she goes off to college and has written down that she has had American history, she's going to have to do a lot of reading on her own to augment what she learned there.

Bill Amberson worried that some students didn't do enough work.

The teachers in their quest to provide as much independent learning for kids may not always put enough pressure on some of the kids to do a certain amount of work. They might need to assess some of the laggards who need some push. I think their philosophy is this: "There's all this learning out there, we'll give you the tools to do it and you go do it." That's not enough for some kids.

A small minority of parents—those who viewed themselves as traditionalists—questioned the idea of public presentations if students did not have the basics. John Stanford said:

> Since the 1960s they [educators] have been guilty of increasingly taking their eye off the drills and skills. I sat through some student presentations (not the social studies class, but another class) and I was absolutely appalled. You don't expect a sophomore to put up a poster which has five spelling mistakes on it—not even corrected spelling mistakes. Therefore, I lose interest in the reasoning behind organizing the presentation. All I see is spelling mistakes that a kid of fifteen makes—why doesn't this kid know how to spell? The response I get is "Oh, well, that's less important than what they're trying to say." Not to me it isn't!

Grover's Corners Teachers' Perspectives

Just as parents have different mental models of what goes on in "good" schools, so do teachers. And while it is true that teachers have more of an opportunity—especially in schools where changes are taking place— to examine their mental models and to revise them, certain teachers adamantly stick to the mental models they grew up with. While many teachers in Grover's Corners High School supported the changes in the math curriculum, their support was by no means universal. For instance, there was no universal agreement on the benefit of mixed-ability groupings. Many teachers did support the notion of mixed-ability groups, but fourteen (47 percent) of the thirty classroom teachers who taught heterogeneously grouped classes most of the time did not support mixed groups. As with the parents, there was a range of opinions within the faculty, from strong support to strong opposition.

Teachers who supported mixed-ability groupings did so for a number of reasons. Some thought that this approach was beneficial for those students who have struggled in school:

> I think the kids on "the bottom" . . . are doing a lot more, they're not being dismissed as "You don't really have to do this because you're

not very bright anyway." I think these people who are college bound or honors are sitting in classrooms now with some kids [lower achievers] who have some profound thoughts, and who feel comfortable about voicing them, and some of these people are looking at them suddenly as if "Wow, where did that come from?" . . . I think it's a good experience.

Others liked mixed groups because they helped students to learn to interact with others who were different from themselves. Some liked the way the honors designation in the mixed-ability courses forced students to take responsibility for their learning: "They don't get an honors designation until the work is done at the end of the year. In the tracking system, they're tracked into a class that's called 'college prep.' That's it; once they're in, they're in. . . . I like this way because they have to make the effort, they have to come and talk with us, they have to take the responsibility of choosing [what to do]."

Teachers expressed concerns similar to those of parents. One thought that such groupings would be a problem both for students who excelled and students who struggled. For other teachers, mixed-ability groups created an impossible teaching task: "[M]aybe there are people who can teach all ends in the same class. I can't do it. I can't do justice to either group because the ones who are lower academically, they know when the other kids are using words they can't understand. They know they're going to sound ignorant if they question it . . . I couldn't teach both groups together and I don't think most teachers can."

Finally, there was one teacher who opposed mixed-ability groupings but didn't necessarily argue for like-ability groupings either. He was more concerned about students' aspirations and suggested groupings based on what a student wanted to do after high school:

> I definitely think people ought to be grouped, tracked, or whatever else you want to call it. And the reason I believe that is because people have different aspirations. I don't necessarily think that they ought to be grouped by ability level, but everybody who wants to try to get into Harvard or some other institution has to be grouped in classes that lead you there. It doesn't matter if they have a 50 IQ or

a 150 IQ. Everybody who wants to be an auto mechanic probably ought to take courses that direct you there.

There's nothing wrong with tracking as long as every track leads to a destination. People here say everybody can do quality work. No, they can't. Not in Shakespeare. Not in a lot of things. Some kids read on a fourth-grade level because they're learning disabled. You're never going to fix that in some people. They will never do a quality essay in written form. I will never dunk a basketball. I learned to live with the limitations. They've got to learn to live with the limitations. So what do you do? You focus on what they can do and you direct them in a direction that takes them somewhere. They may be a very, very fine machinist and we might have to give them coping skills to read blueprints and number of other things. Including them in an English class that doesn't meet their needs while they hold back the people who want to go to a four-year institution in my view makes no sense.

Unfortunately, in the past this view has led to tracking students (and therefore influencing aspirations) based on socioeconomic status or on race, ethnicity, and gender. In order to deal with this problem, some educators now suggest that high schools provide the same core curriculum for all students through grade 10, offer career counseling free of bias, and offer specialized programs depending on a student's aspirations in grades 11 and 12.

Parent/School Tensions at Grover's Corner High School

Even though parents and teachers held varied opinions about these new practices at Grover's Corners High School, the teachers who supported the practices prevailed in the school, and the parents with the most vocal opposition were heard most often. Both the new math and the new social studies curricula generated opposition. However, opposition to the math curriculum was much more intense and resulted in lasting bad feelings between parents and teachers.

Parent/school tensions about the new math curriculum erupted in the spring of 1991. Parents were not consulted or informed about the curriculum change, and when it was first announced at an eighth-grade high school orientation meeting—after it actually had been taught for a year without the formal name change—parents erupted with anger. There were questions about the integrated curriculum, about the titles of the courses, and especially about the heterogeneous grouping. These concerns continued to surface throughout the first two years of the program. Finally, in response to these concerns, in 1993 the revised grouping process was introduced. Some educators pointed to this new grouping process as evidence that parents' concerns were listened to and that they learned about working with parents from this experience. One administrator said:

> We learned a lot about listening to parents. We learned about having a . . . genuine conversation with parents as opposed to bringing them in and telling them . . . and just sending them on their way. This was a real confrontation that went on for several months . . . we'd take their suggestions down and we'd go back. One of the . . . major issues that came up that led us to think, to make some significant improvements in the program, had to do with . . . the kids that could go faster . . . that's where the whole idea for grouping and regrouping came up.

Some educators saw this process as a positive learning experience, but for others it demonstrated a lack of respect for the teacher-as-a-professional—the tension discussed in an earlier chapter—as well as parental distrust of teachers' motives. One teacher said:

> I guess that's that trust thing for me . . . I felt at times like . . . they didn't respect my professional judgment. . . . I don't mind if people disagree with me, that happens. I disagree with other people too, but not . . . [dis]respectfully. I got the feeling that they thought we were experimenting or willy nilly just making changes without really much thought . . . .That's when I think that trust does break down, and you lose that ability to work cooperatively when . . . it gets into that mode. . . . I think it was [that way] for a period of time.

Many of the parents interviewed whose children were involved in the new math program in its first years still feel frustrated by the experience. They were not aware of the changes that were made as a result of the concerns they had expressed.

The new social studies curriculum also met with some parental opposition, especially when parents thought the 85 percent mastery level was too high. As one parent exclaimed: "The law says that 65 percent is passing!" But, unlike that surrounding the math curriculum, the resistance quickly disappeared, for several reasons.

First, the school board was firmly and unanimously in support of the social studies curriculum change. On the other hand, the math curriculum change was heatedly debated at weekend parties frequented by board members.

A second factor was the difference in the ways the programs were first implemented. Excited by their new ideas, the math teachers put them into practice and then, prompted by parental concerns, worked to fine-tune them. In the social studies program, the teachers worked hard to ensure that most students were successful in the course the first time around. The teachers planned after-school tutoring and mentoring sessions that students were required to attend if they did not reach the 85 percent mastery level on a core knowledge test. They proudly pointed out that not one special education student who followed through with the help offered failed their course. One parent who complained to the school board rescinded her complaint after one social studies teacher worked diligently with her child after school and the student did well on her tests.

A third reason is that social studies teachers had the advantage of learning from the experience of the math program. The teachers said they presented the social studies curriculum to parents based on what they heard parents say about the math program. They went out of their way to carefully explain what they were doing and why in long (some parents said too long) letters home.

And a final reason may be that the people of Grover's Corners valued math more than they did social studies. As one of the "basics," parents viewed math as more important for children to learn than social studies. Thus they were less willing to tamper with what worked well for them and for their children. In many parents' minds math was a much more "real-world" subject than was history. They felt that their children's future success in college and in the workforce demanded strong math skills. They didn't want to take a chance that the new math curriculum would not prepare their children adequately for college and for work.

Lessons to Learn from Eastland and Grover's Corners

What can we learn from the experiences in Eastland and Grover's Corners? There are, we think, three lessons. The first is that what parents say at first may not tell the whole story. When parents were asked to explain something they objected to, their reasons were personal and complex. Sometimes it turned out that they were not opposed to the curriculum or to the teaching method per se but rather to the way it was being implemented in their child's particular class. In other instances parents who objected to changes in their child's classes—perhaps because they did not fully understand them—had surprisingly innovative ideas about curriculum and teaching practices they would like to see in classrooms. But how would teachers know this without any positive, two-way conversations with parents? One woman in Eastland, a high school dropout, who was very opposed to American Studies (probably because her son was in danger of failing it) had never talked to her son's teachers! Yet she spoke very positively about the nontraditional practices her daughter was experiencing in middle school, probably because she had met with the girl's teachers on many occasions and had even visited the school when students were in class.

The second lesson is that parents' concerns must be taken into account when planning innovations. Had the Grover's Corners math teachers talked with parents about their plans early on and gained an understanding of what parents wanted for their children, perhaps the later rendition of the math program might have been developed in the first place—without all the animosity that surrounded the eventual development of the new plan. Likewise, if Eastland High School teachers had understood parents' concerns about the amount and difficulty of the work students had to do in the American Studies course and addressed those concerns, the parents might not have demanded that the school board ax the program.

The third lesson is that thoughtful implementation of new teaching and learning practices matters. Parents are more likely to support new practices when their children are successful with them. They don't want to see teachers struggling to become skilled with these new practices while their children flounder. Many parents we interviewed implored the schools not to treat their children as guinea pigs. The Grover's Corner social studies teachers planned and implemented their program based in part on what they understood parent concerns to be and provided alternative strategies—including after school tutorials—to help all students succeed. Perhaps this is why the initial concerns of some parents were quickly allayed.

In hindsight, many of the teachers we interviewed would probably agree that they could have done a better job of preparing parents for these changes. Afer examining parent views about assessment in Chapter 7, Chapters 8 and 9 will examine a variety of ways that other high schools have involved parents and suggest other ways to initiate conversations about new teaching and learning practices and to invite parents to work with educators as they consider changes in teaching and learning practices.

SEVEN

How Should Student Learning Be Assessed?

I think [grading] should be up to the teacher. If I had to grade myself, I'd give myself a better grade than I deserved. . . . [Grading] is the teacher's duty.

—*Parent of a High School Student*

I was concerned about exhibitions because I thought it was going to be something teachers hide behind. Then at one meeting they had rubrics. That was a key thing to me that built my confidence back up because the rubric spells out everything the child needs to do so the teacher, the child, and the parents can see exactly what the child can and cannot do. I like that.

—*Parent of a High School Student*

Even if everyone agreed on what and how students should be taught— which, as previous chapters show, is certainly not the case—there is a more essential question: What do students *learn?* Of course, students are always learning something, but not necessarily from the teacher and many times not what adults want them to learn. Take, for example, what teens learn about sex from their peers. In terms of the curriculum, student learning is—or should be—the ultimate goal of any school. But given everything that goes on in schools, too often learning gets overlooked.

Teachers, worried about keeping students interested, may spend more time trying to find activities they will enjoy rather than analyzing the results of the latest tests. They may notice only how many students did well or poorly—and fail to take the next logical step: finding out what and why individual students did not learn and how they might help them learn. Parents, concerned that their children will do well enough to get into college or to land a good job, may focus on grades and standardized test scores and not think much about the knowledge and skills their children actually have acquired. In both cases, *learning* gets little or no attention.

This chapter discusses three ways of thinking about student learning: setting standards for learning, traditional and innovative means for measuring learning, and, the subject of the most interest to many of the parents interviewed, grading, which is a way of reporting—not measuring—progress.

Understanding Assessment

The topic of assessment is more complex than it might seem at first. For example, when many people hear the word *assessment,* they immediately think of tests, but tests can range from large-scale assessments, such as the Scholastic Aptitude Test (SAT), to a classroom quiz over the concepts covered in one chapter of a textbook. Sometimes the purpose of a test is not to report on the performance of an individual student. Tests, such as the National Assessment of Educational Progress (NAEP) and the Maine Educational Assessment (as well as similar assessments in other states), administered to all fourth, eighth, and eleventh graders, originally were designed to get a sense of how schools or groups of students perform rather than to determine the achievement of individual students. In fact, on assessments of this type, students usually don't all get the same questions. The information desired can be gained by sampling the responses of some students rather than assessing everyone who takes the test.

Another complication to a productive discussion about the assessment of learning arises because of the different ways people use the word *assessment* itself. Some use *assessment* to mean a measurement of progress. Others, however, use it to refer to the judgement of how well someone performed, as would be the case when a college uses test scores to make admission decisions or a teacher averages test scores to determine whether students pass a course. Also, because paper-and-pencil tests traditionally have been the most common way to assess learning for large national groups as well as for students in a classroom, most parents have no experience with or little knowledge of alternative forms of assessments, such as the use of portfolios and exhibitions in many high schools today.

And if these differences were not enough to muddy the waters, some teachers are beginning to make another distinction theorists have considered for years, that is, the difference between *formative* assessment and *summative* assessment. Formative assessment often doesn't "count" and may be very informal. Its purpose is to let students know where they are, not to judge how well they have done. In the process of learning, some teachers now expect students to assess their own work as well as that of their classmates, although the intent is not to "grade" or "evaluate" anyone. Instead, the idea is that students can learn—and thereby improve their own final product—by getting feedback on their work from classmates and the teacher and by giving feedback to other students on theirs. The feedback may take the form of comments or questions.

Formative assessment is always in-process. Summative assessment comes at the end of the process when a judgment is made about the quality of the final product. Increasingly, teachers are finding ways to make the products of student learning available to a larger audience so in some classes the summative assessment may take new forms. In addition to grades from the teacher, students may get comments from people who read their work published in a school newsletter or who attend an event featuring students presenting their work in a semipublic forum.

As more schools expand the concept of assessment of student learning to introduce new and unfamiliar ways to find out what students have learned, some parents and teachers are likely to ask whether these changes are in the best interests of their children/ students. For example, parents in a mid-Atlantic state were asked to talk about their perceptions of a ninth-grade program that included a public presentation—an exhibition—of research projects they had done. This presentation counted for 20 percent of the grade—even though most parents didn't know this. They thought it carried much more weight, and they also had other concerns. One parent said, "[T]his has just blown my mind! There were no final exams. They have to start taking final exams. Are teachers testing students to see if they learn anything?" Another parent pointed out, "They will need to do that [take finals] when they get to college." A third parent was concerned about the grading: "Objectivity! [There's no objectivity in grading these exhibitions. Tests are better because] there's either a right answer or a wrong answer. There are concrete answers and essay answers. Objectivity versus subjectivity, an important criteria for grading."

Portfolios as a means of assessment fare no better than exhibitions with some teachers and parents, as was apparent among parents in Grover's Corners. A high school teacher (and parent) who had been a human resources manager prior to becoming a teacher doubted whether employers would really be interested or have the time to review a candidate's portfolio—especially for entry-level jobs:

> The big thing right now is portfolios. And these people are going out telling kids that people want to read their portfolios. Nobody gives a tinker's damn about a high school kid's portfolio. Because everybody in the business world knows that when you do things in high school, high school teachers help you do it. Now, a nice, well put together résumé, that's worth doing. A high school English paper that you wrote, I could care less. For one thing I don't have the time to see everybody's portfolio—particularly at an entry level.

Clearly, some parents and some teachers are not convinced that the new approaches to assessment are better than the ones they are replacing. Others worry that the new ways will put students at a disadvantage, for example, by not preparing them for what they will face in college. Many people also have concerns about the movement to set standards for student learning.

Setting Standards for Student Learning

Recently the push to set standards for learning has become a hot topic in discussions about improving education at every level. And it makes sense. Americans are all paying for schools to teach children, so people want to know what they are getting for their tax dollars. It is interesting to note that almost all those who call for improving schools agree that raising standards is an important ingredient in the process of school reform even when they disagree about other aspects. For example, at one point both the former U.S. Secretary of Education, Lamar Alexander, who called for all schools to be charter schools, and the leadership of the American Federation of Teachers (AFT), which adamantly opposed charter schools, agreed on the need to set higher standards.

That some unlikely individuals and groups agree, however, does not mean everyone does. A few years ago standards were referred to as "outcomes." Some of the outcomes lists developed as goals for schools and students included nonacademic outcomes, such as raising students' self-esteem or developing interpersonal skills. Some people believed that the schools were trying to take over the roles of parents or, even worse, to countermand the values that parents were teaching at home. They opposed what they perceived as the latest trend to make schools more "touchy-feely" by teaching values and ignoring the "basics." (Read "three Rs" here.) They let their voices be heard loud and clear, and the result was conflict. As educator William Spady said, "This is a clash of world views." [1]

So educators backed off and changed their approach; now there is talk about standards rather than outcomes. One of the most public skirmishes around "outcomes-based education" occurred in Pennsylvania, where there was a well-orchestrated political campaign against outcomes—or, as was believed, against teaching values. The result was the state reversing its support for outcomes and moving to a set of academic standards. There are still many people opposed to the idea of schools going in this new direction: Conservatives in many places have made valiant efforts to block the passage of standards-setting legislation. Even so, a majority of states, such as Pennsylvania, and many local districts already have adopted or are in the process of adopting learning standards in nearly every subject area. In some states these standards are enforced by the states through testing of all students, but that is not the case in all. Legislation in Maine, for instance, gives much more control to local districts. Each district is required to develop its own means for demonstrating that its students meet the state standards. The Maine Educational Assessment, a state-administered test, has been redesigned to align with these new standards, which are called "Learning Results," and will be only one measure for these standards. Professional organizations representing teachers of various disciplines, such as the National Council for Teachers of Mathematics and the National Council of Teachers of English, also have published and are widely publicizing standards in their subject areas.

One reason why the standards movement has reached nearly all schools in the nation so quickly is the public's interest in making sure that American children are prepared to compete in the global economy. Many people see setting standards as a way of ensuring that children in the United States will score higher on international comparisons. For many reasons American students have not done so well in the past. For example, countries with higher scores often have national curricula, fewer teenage students from the general population still in school, or a family and social culture that fosters school achievement in a more focused way than in the United States. Many reformers pay little attention to factors such as these and believe that setting standards and introducing high-stakes assessment to measure them will make schools accountable for learning. The end result, they hope, will be higher scores by U.S. students on these international measures.

Teachers' and Parents' Views on Standards

Many teachers and parents doubt whether it is possible to hold all children to the same high standards. Many Grover's Corners administrators, teachers, and a few parents are working to develop "learning results" (another term for standards) for all of their students. The superintendent said: "I think the difference in this particular wave of reform is that the conversation is focusing around results. . . . We're trying to say to each other and to the community . . . that improving means that we'll be able to show results and that's [why] this focus on assessment, the focus on outcomes, the focus on raising standards . . . I think that's . . . very different."

Studies such as *American's Views on Standards: An Assessment by Public Agenda* conclude that "support for standards is nearly universal. Americans of different ages, income groups, and racial and ethnic backgrounds express strong support for standards."[2] However, what this study (and others like it) sometimes doesn't ask is how these community members—including parents—define standards. For instance, in this study the parents and other community members surveyed were not asked to talk about what they mean when they say "set higher standards than are now required" or "require students in the public schools in your community to meet higher standards than are now required."[3]

Our experience is that parents and educators may mean very different things when they talk about standards. For instance, take the issue of spelling. For some parents interviewed, the clearest indicator of higher standards is correct spelling. Poor spelling often is cited as an important reason for raising standards because good spelling is essential. Higher-order thinking skills and critical thinking are all well and good, but proper spelling is so important that, without it, the other standards can't be met. The issue of good spelling may be a symbolic issue—one related to people's mental models of an educated person. From their earliest school days people remember having it drummed into their heads that proper spelling is absolutely imperative. They wonder, "How can educators speak of raising standards when our children can't even spell correctly?" Educators don't mean to ignore poor spelling, but it may seem that they don't place the same value on it that the public does. It may be less important than critical thinking or writing a well-thought-out argument. Or, teachers tell students not to worry about correct spelling when they are doing informal writing ("talking on paper") or early drafts of a paper—although they do expect correct spelling on final draft. Although parents and educators say the same words ("Raise standards!"), they assign very different meanings to them.

Another complication is that, while agreeing with standards in the abstract is easy, parents may have more difficulty supporting standards when they actually are implemented. When the new higher standards are applied to their children and they come up short, parents complain. That's what happened in one of the first districts in the country to try to raise standards and to make it a high-stakes process: Students who didn't meet the higher standards would not be allowed to graduate. As seen earlier, when some parents saw that their children might not graduate, they rebelled—and they won. The school board rescinded the new standards and the curriculum and assessments related to these standards were revised.

As was shown in Chapter 6, the social studies curriculum at Grover's Corners High School was revised to include higher standards for all students. They were required to pass the core knowledge tests at the 85 percent level instead of the traditional 65 percent. Even though teachers felt knowledge of this core curriculum was essential for future success in their course and they worked hard to meet the needs of all children through extensive after-school tutoring and mentoring sessions, this did not stop parents from complaining, or as one said: "The law says that 65 percent is passing!"

Concerns about higher standards also were raised by teachers and parents who participated in focus groups for a study conducted by the Education Commission of the States (ECS). A core group endorsed the idea of setting high expectations and had faith that students could learn at high levels if they were provided with the right resources. On the other hand, many participants wondered whether it was realistic or desirable to hold such high expectations for all students. Their concerns included the fact that some students might not be able to learn at these high levels, too much pressure would be put on students, or, because all students must achieve the standards, they would be set too low. In this study researchers also found that educators in focus groups expressed skepticism about the possibility of actually achieving such high standards."[4]

Even though some reformers repeatedly state "All children can learn," surveys and focus groups conducted with parents and teachers in the ECS study strongly suggest that both groups are more inclined to support a goal of "improving success for all students" rather than buying into the notion that "all children can learn at high levels." Or, as the authors of this report put it, "Higher standards for all students receives more support than high standards for all."[5]

Because the standards movement is so new, however, much of the data about parents' and teachers' views comes before the fact: The standards have not yet been implemented in many places. The assessments are not completely developed, and teachers must be helped to change their expectations and teaching methods so that all children will have a chance to meet these higher standards. Conflict is likely once assessment of the standards begins, as has already been seen in some states that have introduced high-stakes assessment tied to high school graduation.

When many students fail, educators—and sometimes legislators—have to scramble to deal both with the problematic situation and with an unhappy, grumbling public. Some conflict will arise from clumsy implementation practices in schools. For instance, in the mid-Atlantic high school mentioned earlier, many parents said that they were not against the new practices, they were against the way in which they were being implemented. Perhaps they had a right to be concerned. The teachers—while well intentioned—were having a difficult time during the first year figuring out how to make the changes work, and it showed in their classes. And there will surely be conflict if many children fail to meet these new higher standards.

Traditional Ways of Assessing Learning

Everyone is familiar with standardized tests, such as the SAT, and achievement tests, like the Iowa Test of Basic Skills. It is not so clear, however, that parents—and some teachers—actually understand the scores students get. For example, scores are sometimes reported as grade equivalents. Thus when a child in fifth grade gets a score of 7.2, a parent may think the child should be moved up to the seventh grade. This grade-equivalent score is just another way of reporting how much above the average (say, 5.0) a student's achievement is. It has nothing to do with what grade a child should be in. These tests do not measure a student's knowledge of the curriculum taught in a particular grade. Educators already have a lot of work to do to educate parents about the meaning of the printouts they get of their children's test scores. If scores on the new assessments are reported in a different way from other tests students take, this job will become even more difficult.

At the classroom level, parents know and understand the traditional ways of assessing learning, such as a test at the end of a unit in social studies, perhaps with some multiple-choice and fill-in-the-blank questions along with short-answer essay questions, or a paper on a book read in an English class.

Having knowledge does not always mean agreement, however. Eastland parents did not believe that these traditional ways were always best, as their responses to questions about the ideal approaches for assessing student work in a high school English class show.

How Students' Understanding of Books Can Best Be Evaluated

Eastland High School parents suggested a number of different ways to evaluate students' understanding of books they have read. The most common response, given by 10 parents (40 percent) was a formal paper, perhaps because such papers had been assigned quite frequently in their children's present class. However, they also would like to see a variety of other means used to allow students to demonstrate their knowledge of the books they had read, such as discussions, role playing, book reports, and homework and quizzes.

Of the six Eastland High School parents (24 percent) who said a test was the best way to evaluate students' understanding, three specified further that essay tests were better than short answer. While Pam Sloan believed that multiple choice was okay for "factual things," essays were necessary for "opinions." High school dropout Betty Horton favored only essay questions so that students could "express their ideas, what was in the story. . . . Multiple choice would be too easy." Even when it came to tests, parents believed it was important for students to have the opportunity to express themselves.

Many Eastland High School parents were critical of tests. Laura Dunham perhaps was thinking of her son, who had trouble with reading and writing, when she said, "I don't think that [a test] is the correct way. Some students test well, and some people don't." Gary

Mosher, who said "a comprehensive outline" of the book would be a test, commented negatively on teacher-made tests:

> [T]hey're kind of useless. Because then you're basically back to the old idea of teaching when you go in and you're learning phrases, dates, and different events, but the student spends so much time trying to learn those that he really doesn't understand what the book is about. . . . He's just so boggled up with learning times and dates and phrases and quotations, I just don't think the student would get to enjoy the book the way a book should be enjoyed.

While parents differed about the best ways to evaluate students' understanding of books, they all said in one way or another that the methods used must be fair and allow students to really show what they know. Not even one-third of them said that tests met these criteria. Because students differed in the ways they could best express themselves, it was sometimes necessary or desirable to choose different methods of evaluation for some students.

How Students' Writing Should Be Evaluated

Parents as a group believed teachers should note errors, make comments, and grade student papers. For the most part, they thought that students were not able to evaluate their own work. Ralph Jones mentioned the two reasons most often cited by others: "They're more biased to themselves. The benefit of the doubt is going to go in their favor and I think the teacher is more qualified to make that evaluation. And we pay a lot of money and put a lot of faith in teachers. Let's use them."

Even though teacher evaluation was always needed, Ronald Lancaster and a few other Eastland parents felt students could evaluate their own work: "[My son] does it anyway. . . . You have a combination of what the kid thinks he did and what he really did. He has an idea of how he felt he did, and it might be altogether wrong. If they discuss it, he can see how this teacher grades. . . . 'I thought I did the greatest paper ever. Was I just so excited about it that I didn't do the grammar right or what is it?'"

Unlike other parents, former school administrator Randall Cromwell believed his son was a tougher critic of his work than his teachers were. He also raised more complex questions about the connection of evaluation standards to the degree of control students have of their learning environment. His son, Ronnie, a highly gifted writer and artist, "has set very high standards for himself and when he works well, he creates his best and if you don't like the product, that's tough. . . . And his preference is that if he didn't think it was his best work, he'd prefer not to turn it in and take a zero." Randall Cromwell acknowledged, though, that other students "don't hold up such high expectations of themselves."

Most parents (72 percent) believed that content and mechanics should be given equal weight in the grade on a final paper. To further clarify the difference between the ideas students express and the way they express them, some said two separate grades should be given. The rest (28 percent) would like to see content given more weight. No parent thought surface features, such as punctuation or spelling, should be counted more than the expression of ideas.

Some parents gave qualified responses. Laura Dunham explained that "it depends on what grade level. If high school, then I'd go content 75 percent, and 25 percent for mechanics. In lower grades, I'd say equal. . . .If they've had to put a lot of time into a big subject or writing a long paper, I would say more emphasis on content." Because Alex Lamonte had a daughter in middle school who is deaf, he may have been more sensitive to the problem some children might have with mechanics. He would set priorities for evaluation that begin with content and move down to sentence structure: "[T]hen the last thing would be spelling and punctuation." He said that "it's been an interesting adventure having a deaf child because you approach things completely differently."

Some parents noted that students should be given an opportunity to correct their work and turn it in again after it has been graded and to have time in class to discuss their papers with the teacher. For example, another parent explained: "The teacher said, 'We're here after school. . . .' Well, my daughter has softball . . . field hockey . . . work, and this and that and just can't do it. I think it's really too bad that they don't set aside some time if they have a problem with the way a paper was graded to talk it over. More time should be allotted during the school day."

Regardless of the manner in which teachers evaluated student writing, parents again said that it was important for teachers to encourage rather than discourage students in the process. Some parents related painful experiences their children had, for example, when a child worked very hard on a paper and then got it back covered with red-inked errors.

A few of these parents may be quite open to the introduction of nontraditional means of assessing learning, but others likely will resist some of the assessment strategies described in the next section.

Newer Ways of Assessing Learning

In addition to higher standards, many educators are in favor of assessing what students have learned in different ways. These new assessments—portfolios, exhibitions, and performances—ask students to demonstrate what they have learned. Students may collect examples of their work; make presentations to other students, their parents, and other community members; or demonstrate their learning through performances. Each of these is then evaluated by the teacher—and sometimes by the student or a panel of adults—based on a predetermined set of criteria (sometimes developed with the help of students) called *rubrics*. Even though some parents appreciate the use of rubrics to clarify how students' work will be assessed, many still want to see the results of standardized tests so that they will know how their children compare to other children and/or how their schools rate when compared to schools nationwide. Parents of college-bound students think it is important to know how their children are likely to fare in stiff competition for college admission.

When parents and teachers in the ECS study mentioned earlier were asked, "Which of these three ways is the best way to measure learning?" they responded as follows: 33 percent favored portfolios; 32 percent felt standardized tests were best; 31 percent chose public displays of student work; and 4 percent didn't know or refused to answer. Is the public stalemated on the issue? Perhaps not. The study concludes that this is not an "either-or" question of traditional standardized tests versus newer ways to evaluate children's knowledge and abilities. Participants in the surveys and focus groups made it clear that they favor a combination.[6]

There is a good reason for this preference for both types of assessment. Results from large-scale quantitative standardized tests, which are more efficient, less costly, and more easily scored than newer types of assessment, are useful for comparisons. Parents and teachers can see how an individual student, school, or school district ranks with regard to state, national, and international norms. But to get a more personal, meaningful, and fair assessment, students are best served by qualitative assessment means, such as portfolios or exhibitions.

There is no one solution; issues remain to be resolved. Writers of the ECS study note that while parents and teachers understand the need for holding educators accountable for student learning, they also have questions about the means for doing so. One major concern—and the one that is most difficult, perhaps even impossible, to address—is the belief of focus group participants that "there are too many factors outside educators' control to hold teachers fully responsible for student achievement."[7] In fact, these groups recognize the importance of also holding parents and students themselves responsible for what is learned in school.

Experiences with Exhibitions in Two High Schools

Even when schools adopt the same innovations, they do not have the same experiences. Two high schools, Grover's Corners High School and New High School (a school in a mid-Atlantic state), that introduced exhibitions as one way of assessing student learning had different results, in part because of differences in their community and school contexts.

The first high school, Grover's Corners, had a long history of reform efforts, as explained earlier. Teachers were encouraged to develop new courses based on the latest research. Two of these courses incorporated exhibitions. The first (described in Chapter 6) was a two-year United States history course developed by three social studies teachers. Its centerpiece was a public policy paper each student was required to research, write, and present orally to a panel of teachers, students, and community members. Some parents—mostly of students who had not yet taken the course—worried that their children would have a hard time making an oral presentation and wondered whether it was fair to require all children to do this. Because these parents often prefaced their remarks by saying that they themselves would never be able to get up in front of a panel to make this type of presentation, perhaps they were projecting their own fears on to their children. (This fear of public speaking may be universal: Eastland parents felt the same way.)

One teacher, concerned about meeting the varied needs of different children, worried about requiring all children to make public presentations of their work:

> What are we preparing kids for that we have to have them be able to do this? Does every person in a democratic society always stand up in a public meeting and present a public position? Does the president do all of his own research? I don't think so. . . . So when I ask a question about "Well, what does this requirement mean in terms of what I have learned and know about pedagogy?" I'm not sure that it meets the needs of all the kids. . . . The stars [top students] liked it because it was something they could do well. I saw some special education students do some wonderful work and I think it was great. But I didn't know what that had to do with the kid that was going to auto body mechanics vocational school for two years after high school.

On the other hand, many of the parents interviewed whose children had taken the course—parents of the stars and of children in the middle—were enthusiastic about having their children research public policy issues and make public presentations about what they found out.

Yet some parents were not equally enthusiastic about the exhibition. Barbara Arthur, a parent and a substitute teacher at the high school, had much to say, and part of the problem was the audience:

> My daughter picked the endangered species, which she was very into at the time. I sat in on one of the . . . presentations, and the teachers were there that day and whoever they could grab from the outside

was on the panel, and the children stood up in front of us on the podium and read their public policy papers. They were very nervous. One of the gentlemen beside me kept coughing and yawning and tapping all through it and I was very aggravated with him and wanted to say something.

I could see the little girl getting extremely nervous and looking up at him [and thinking] . . . "What did I do wrong?" She started stuttering and stuff and I kept thinking "Why don't they let these students have visual aids to take the audience away from them for a while, to see graphs, or an overhead projection or something, some sort of aid just to remove it from them so we can scan that and give them a little breather?" I was really frustrated. I mentioned it to the teacher and she said they would be willing to implement that next year.

I think it's good for them [the oral presentation], but I think it would be more valuable to me as a person on the panel to see a visual aid. . . . So I think it's a good part to have but they need to make some adjustments.

In a mixed-ability sophomore English class at the same school, two English teachers developed a course in which students were required to make oral presentations to an audience of their parents and teachers. Parents and teachers, for the most part, were pleased with the presentations. One of the teachers said:

Overall, I was pleased. It was our first time through it and what we'd hoped was that there would be a chance to make that good work great; to make excellent work awesome; or to make horrible work decent. And we had done . . . the presentations in class once and given them a lot of feedback from each other and from ourselves as teachers. And we wanted to have them have to stand up—kind of face the music before the community. . . . [T]here were four [sessions]—two in the afternoon and two in the evening. Overall the kids did better [in the afternoon], but there wasn't a real sense of audience.

We certainly learned some things about what to do next time. We . . . [need to make] a few of the requirements more explicit. We wanted to tie in more literature and make sure they used more outside sources, both in terms of text sources and people sources, because we thought some of the research was a little thin. In terms of presentation skills though, they were about what we hoped and definitely they improved them.

The parents that were there were all very positive. There was one man who was not very positive who was not a parent [of a sophomore—although he is a parent of two high school students].

The parent referred to was John Stanford from Chapter 6. As a parent interested in the basic skills, he was annoyed when spelling errors marred the presentation.

The second high school had less success with exhibitions. Unlike Grover's Corners High School, this school was new to reform, and, although some teachers were integral to planning the new program, many of the teachers who were actually teaching in it had not been part of the planning process. This new ninth-grade program consisted of a number of interrelated changes. Students were grouped in mixed-ability groups and stayed with these groups for all of their classes. The teachers planned two major interdisciplinary units for the year. Students were expected to work in groups on these projects and to make public presentations (exhibitions) to their classmates and teachers.

Most parents who participated in focus groups expressed concerns about these presentations, many of them centering on the "fairness" of group presentations and group grades. One parent explained:

> Those [students] who don't want to work scrape by on the work of others. I have problems with grading of individual work versus group work. On my daughter's individual work, she got grades of 97 to 99 percent. On group work, solid Cs even though she did her part of the group work. My daughter did a lot of extra credit work to earn bonus points to bring her grade up to compensate for group grades. My daughter [became] resentful. [She developed the attitude] "you don't want to share your work with other students."

Other parents worried that the students were not prepared to make oral presentations and questioned the value of requiring the entire class to sit through presentations by about fifty students over two weeks.

> It was a very frustrating experience. As I heard one kid put it, "It was like sweating bullets." My son had never been prepared to do what he had to do for the final exhibition in any class. The afternoon after his final exhibition presentation, he collapsed in a reclining chair at home and was actually shaking from the experience.
>
> I know that everyone in some time in his life will have to go through a public presentation. However, there were two major problems with this final exhibition: the nature of the topic was too complex. My son had the topic of the effects of acid rain on soil. You would have to be a chemist to understand some of the stuff, and there was a lack of thoughtful, coherent preparation for the experience on the part of the teachers.

A father explained, "My son was tired of listening to boring presentations, so he changed his whole presentation the night before to a TV-type show and put humor in it to make it more interesting to the audience and different from the other presentations."

Two parents talked about the problematic behavior of the students in the audience, who had been asked to use a checklist to assess the performance of student presenters. One said: "My daughter was nervous about getting up in front of others to present. With her last name beginning with V, she was near the end of the alphabet and had already heard the jeers of students toward other students giving reports before her." And the other reported: "My daughter said 'You have to be perfect, right down to the nylons.' You're judged by your appearance only, not by the presentation. She said 'It was tough' after giving the report."

A few parents did think the experience was good for their children. Despite having some criticisms of the program, one said, "My son was looking forward to the project. He was happy with his presentation, and it was a good experience for him. He didn't seem to be nervous, and he was prepared. He did some practicing at home in front of the mirror." And another parent noted: "This was one of the few opportunities for them to take responsibility during the whole year."

Many of these parents were critical of much of this new ninth-grade program. Even though every effort was made to get a representative sample of parents, those who chose to participate in the focus groups may have been those who had very strong negative feelings about the program. Perhaps satisfied parents felt no need to discuss the program. In any event, it is difficult to determine whether these particular parents were more upset with the actual use of exhibitions or with the way they were being implemented during the new program's first year.

Grading: Issues and Concerns

Grading is a topic of perhaps greatest interest to parents because all parents, of course, want their children to do well in school. Traditionally, schools have communicated student progress to parents through grades. First and foremost, parents want grading to be fair. Many parents don't see the value of teaching students to evaluate their own and each other's learning because not only are teachers the ones who have the responsibility—and the ability—to be fair, they are the only ones with enough knowledge and expertise to judge students' progress accurately. Parents in both Grover's Corners and Eastland objected to cooperative learning because they thought that group grades weren't fair. Above all, parents wanted teachers to grade all students equitably, but, just as important, they wanted teachers to consider the special needs of the individual child—their child who had difficulty learning and needed encouragement more than criticism and correction.

Parents' Perspectives on Grading

As explained earlier, the Eastland children were all enrolled in a required interdisciplinary course, with mostly heterogeneous grouping, in which they learned American literature (English) together with American history (social studies). The following comments about grading and related issues reveal that the parents had varied perspectives about grading.

Judy Johnson liked the idea of students working in groups, but thought this work should not be graded. Although her daughter worked best independently, she saw the value of group learning: "I think they [students] should be made to work in classroom . . . groups—to expose them to that, as far as grading purposes, if they work better as individuals, they should be able to work that way." Groups would be fine for "general" learning when no grades would be given, but it is important for her daughter to do her own work and "to be responsible for herself. And in the group it's more general . . . and there's less accountability."

According to Jane Conway, grades are necessary for motivating students. The teacher is the one to decide on grades, and grading should be more consistent from school to school. When asked what would happen after a student completed writing a draft of a paper, she replied: "Rewrite the paper and give [it] to the teacher. The teacher would grade it." When asked if teachers should mark every error, Mrs. Conway replied:

> Could they learn anything if teacher didn't correct? How will they know what they did wrong? If they get a D and nothing was written, how would they know? . . . Students shouldn't do something for nothing. A lot of students would feel if I'm not getting a grade, why do it? It's not going to hurt if I don't do it. It's important to get a credit or grade.

When asked if students could be involved in the evaluation process, Mrs. Conway said:

> Maybe certain things like a quiz could be passed to another person. You correct theirs. . . . One thing that bothers me about schools in general—There's no one set of grades. 93 to 100 [is an] A, B [is] 92 to 80, and it's not statewide. That bothers me. Take a student from EHS [Eastland, her daughter's high school] who wants to make the honor roll. An EHS student has to have a higher average to make the honor roll than a student [at another area high school].

Although self-evaluation wouldn't replace grades, Gary Mosher, in contrast to other parents, said it would be a good idea for students to evaluate themselves "if you can get them to evaluate honestly . . . they would be better able to understand themselves, their own problem area and their high points."

But can students help each other? Ralph Jones wasn't so sure, and his comments raise another issue, that students don't have the expertise or won't be as fair as the teacher when it comes to grading. "I really don't have an answer for that [students grading each other's work]. There may be something that they would have some information on [but] . . . I really think that should be the teacher's responsibility and not the students' because I don't feel maybe the other students are qualified. That teacher's there for a reason and I think she should have the final say—correct it or give feedback or whatever." When asked if he ever worked with other students on writing when he was in school, he replied: "I did. I can't remember—that was thirty-five years ago. At the time I don't think that I got as much out of it because I don't think the other kids were that interested."

Asked how much weight should be given to content and mechanics on an essay, Mr. Jones said:

> I think they're both equally important, but I do think it can be taken a little bit too far and I won't go into specifics, but there's a teacher in Eastland who was a professor at Bowdoin [a highly selective liberal arts college] and for whatever reasons left the college level and is now teaching high school but still feels that she is in college level and at times can be overly strict and overbearing on the kids. I've seen cases where Janie has put the word "many" in a report and had the whole entire thing voided because the instructor says I think you should have put "varied" instead of "many"—that particular word, and missed the whole entire question because of one word. And to me "many" and "varied" could loosely mean the same thing.

For Ronald Lancaster, grades were important as an indication of achievement, but there were other effects of grading to consider: "I think that [a grade] is the only way the kids can see achievement. Kids always say, 'I got this on that.' It's a psychological thing. If they got an A, they're happy and they'll do it again. If they flunked it, they'll get discouraged. I think a paper should be red-marked and turned in again with the changes. Kids get red marks and they never go back and find out what they did wrong."

Betty Horton, who was worried about encouraging rather than discouraging students, offered a different perspective on red marks:

> [My daughter] wrote a story and it was just like one whole thing. It had no paragraphs, no periods, no nothing. And she had a lot of red lines and I went to the school and asked them because she was upset—it took her three whole days to do it. I said you know my daughter has a lot of problems. She can't spell right. I said why don't you take her aside and explain to her what you really wanted instead of writing "You know you need to have periods and paragraphs . . ."? It was [too much for her all at once]. . . . She could say her ABCs but she didn't know what—I mean, if you pointed at one of them [a letter], she didn't know what it was. And I tried to explain that to the teachers. I said . . . I know what my daughter's going through. . . . [S]he works three days on this paper by herself and then she thinks she's [done] something great and then it comes back with red marks because she didn't put in her periods. She just messed it all up. And you know you really hurt her feelings.

Husband and wife Kurt and Sally Branigan (an elementary teacher) worry about motivation, standards, grades—and fairness. Their comments also show how complex this whole topic is. According to Mrs. Branigan:

> Maybe they [students] should be motivated first. Maybe there's something wrong. I think there is something wrong. One thing I think is wrong is we have a floating standard and kids that don't try as hard, they still pass through, they still get the diploma. They still get good grades even though they probably don't deserve them. A lot of kids that don't work as hard as [our children] and they get just as good grades. And perhaps—I think there's a tendency to push the kid through.

Mr. Branigan, who was worried about differences among students, said:

Well, you're always thinking like, in the groups: This kid will work hard. This kid won't. This kid won't. This kid won't. So this other kid gets all overloaded, but these other kids are just riding along and they're all going to pass just as well. Maybe this kid will get an A and these kids might get Cs or Bs, even though they're not trying as hard. I think a lot of them are there because they have to be there and I don't think that's—if you're trying to figure out schemes to force them to do things—are they really going to learn as well as if they wanted to do those things? I don't think so.

Mrs. Branigan believed some of the differences among students could be traced to their families:

I think that a lot of it depends on who you have—if you have parents backing you. If you have a parent that is interested and wants to know what you're doing, I think your child's going to do a whole lot better than if you have a parent [who isn't]. . . . [P]arents need to be involved in their education, not just in K through sixth grade, [but] . . . all the way up through high school. They need to know what [their children] are doing. They need to know [more than just their grades]. . . . [R]ead their papers, show them that you're interested in what they are doing. And I don't think that can stop in high school. It needs to continue all the way through college.

These parents wanted teachers to be fair and to encourage children. They often recalled instances when teachers discouraged children with red marks or negative comments. Most parents would probably agree with Lucille Farnum, whose son was a special education student, when she said: "[T]eachers need to encourage the work kids do more than they do rather than discourage what they do. . . . There have been cases where Norman did his homework and passed it in. It may be wrong, but she doesn't say, 'Good effort.' He'll think, 'Why bother, Norman? You blew it this time.' They need more encouragement when they do it. If in fact the kid actually makes an attempt to do it, that's good."

Grading is an important topic for parents first and foremost because they want their children to be treated fairly, they want them to do well, and they want them to be motivated to continue working in school. Grades can help, but they also can hurt. Sally Branigan also suggests another complicating aspect of grades: They may be linked to family background and status. Her comments also hinted that grading in a heterogeneously grouped class may result in a child not being sufficiently rewarded for work because the standards for grades may either be too low or too high. Thus parents' concerns about grading raise questions about other aspects of the school, such as the practice of tracking and its impact on students with different backgrounds.

What Should High Schools Do About Assessment?

Assessment of student learning is a complex and problematic aspect of education because there are many perspectives, many calls for reform, and a lack of knowledge about what schools are doing and what parents and the public know and understand. Policymakers and reformers (often from the public sector) demand more accountability in the form of higher standards and high-stakes assessment at the same time parents want their children to be treated more personally and fairly.

Educators may be caught in the middle—forced to adopt new practices they do not fully understand or support. Some are worried about the possible implications for their futures if students do not do well, because some school districts have begun to include student test scores as a factor in the evaluations of teachers. Then there are other complicating factors. For example, vast differences in students' socio-economic background and inequities in the resources available to schools in different communities may make it more difficult for some schools to help all students reach these higher standards. Parents, on the other hand, also may be caught in a bind. For some, the new practices clearly clash with their mental models of what good assessment practices are—individual work evaluated through pencil-and-paper tests with grades that they understand: As, Bs, and Cs. Even parents who do not object to an innovative practice, such as an exhibition, have concerns about its implementation. It's the old dilemma of change: "How do you keep the plane flying while you are redesigning it?" The first few times a new program is introduced, teachers are still learning what works and what doesn't. Parents of students in new programs may feel that their children are being shortchanged or treated as guinea pigs in a untested experiment.

When high-stakes assessment based on standards is introduced, important questions arise. Can all children really be helped to meet these standards? What happens to students in special education classes? Should the less-able students be left out to improve a school's scores? When scores are reported in the media and schools are compared against each other, will there be too much pressure on schools and teachers to get good numbers? Recently one elementary principal was forced to resign when, after having bowed to these pressures, investigators found that the answers on tests from his school had been changed so student scores would be better. In order for real estate values in his affluent suburban community to remain high, his school and others had to maintain levels of student achievement much better than average.

Parents, of course, are most concerned about what happens to their own children, but all children are not the same. One-size assessment will not fit all. How can assessment, standards setting, and grading be fair to one at the same time they are fair to all? How might parents and educators share perspectives and negotiate differences? Can they work together to develop new understandings about effective ways to measure student achievement?

As changes in assessment of student learning go beyond the classroom and the stakes get higher, however, the number of interested stakeholders likely will grow. Educators and parents should not be the only ones to discuss assessment. Others in the larger community should be invited to join in. What schools do should matter to everyone because all Americans will reap the benefits of educating all students well—or deal with the consequences if they fail.

Building Bridges to Parents and the Community

The first two sections of this book presented some reasons why the relationship between parents and educators is so often problematic. The following questions summarize the most important challenges:

- What is the primary purpose of education and the goal of schools? Can parents and educators learn to talk more productively about these important questions?
- Given the lessons of the past, what vision of schools should people have for the future? Can they create a twenty-first century version of the nineteenth-century common school? Can Americans implement positive change in schools and make it last?
- How can parents and educators rethink their roles and relationships so that the expertise of both groups is valued and respected? Can they avoid crosstalk by developing a common language for discussing their perspectives? Can they develop common understandings about such specifics as the nature of the teaching-learning process, the ideal high school curriculum, classroom practices, and standards for measuring and reporting student achievement?

- But if agreement is not possible, how might differing perspectives be accommodated in some way in a public school?

There are no "right" answers to these essential questions. Central to the creation of a democratic school community is the idea that parents and educators must work together to develop their own responses. Thus the following chapters offer not answers but some approaches that will help educators and parents discuss these questions in the context of their own situations.

Schools, of course, should find ways to involve parents, but involvement alone is not enough. What matters more is building relationships, and sometimes programs are not helpful in this respect. For example, researcher Mary Henry explains the contradictions between the goals of parental involvement and proposed formal processes, such as site-based management councils. In the first case, schools are like "corporations." And, like stockholders, stakeholders have a right to know what is happening in the school, but professionals have control of its operation. The school in this instance is somewhat bureaucratic, and professional teachers keep a distance from "clients" (parents/lay people). In the other case, the focus is on developing "common feelings, traditions and goodwill that bond people . . . together." This school can be viewed as a microcosm of the larger society, and daily life in school should be extended into and connected to the wider social context. Here relationships matter— "between teacher and student, teacher and teacher, teacher and principal, principal and parent, parent and teacher, and so on."[1]

Henry believes that "authentic parent involvement" and "community-building" cannot rely on bureaucratic structures, such as a mandated decision-making council, but rather must develop as a result of caring, responsive relationships—best developed through informal rather than formal interactions. Or, as researchers put it: "[P]rograms are implemented; partnerships are developed. . . . By their very nature, most programs have steps, elements, or procedures that become static. A program cannot constantly reinvent itself, change each year."[2]

EIGHT

Parents as Learners: Four Profiles

The previous chapters show the importance of including parents as learners. If educators truly believe that high schools should be communities of learning, then schools must invite parents to join with teachers and students in developing new understandings about teaching and learning to guide the process of school improvement and reform.

Although all schools ask parents to attend informational meetings and conferences, few invite parents to participate actively in extended and engaging activities. This chapter profiles four projects that have seriously addressed the idea of parents as learners. What they have in common is the recognition that learning communities inclusive of parents must be built on a foundation of trust and respect, that time must be spent building this bond, and that both teachers and parents are important members of the school community.

In each case, parents were invited to participate in ways that validated them as learners and as valuable members of the school community. Many jumped at the chance. Their comments indicate just how excited they were to be given a chance to participate in meaningful and substantive ways. In reading the profiles of programs that follow, readers may think of other ways to involve parents as partners and learners in their own communities.

UCLA Parent Curriculum Project

As readers will see in this profile, the collaboration between a university and an urban school district allowed parents to learn together through curriculum workshops, action research, and role playing with readers' theater scripts.

Program Beginnings

Lois N. André Bechely has two children who have attended schools in the Los Angeles Unified School District (LAUSD). Before returning to the University of California at Los Angeles (UCLA) for her doctorate in education, as a teacher in the district she participated in the California Subject Matter Projects. These intensive professional development programs, modeled after the Bay Area Writing Project, bring teachers together to share their practices with each other during three-week summer institutes.[1] Lois found this involvement empowering and transforming for her work as a teacher. As a parent, Lois also attended meetings at which educators told parents about new practices the local school or district planned to introduce. She saw that, unlike teachers in the summer projects, parents had no way to actively engage with these new ideas. In fact, there was limited time—and, on occasion, no time—for them even to ask questions. Lois was concerned that parents were not engaged in substantive and meaningful ways about issues of curriculum and instructional practice. Why were parents as learners treated differently than teachers as learners?

She wondered why, if we want parents to understand and support new practices, teachers don't share what they have learned about "good" teaching and learning practices. Shouldn't parents have an opportunity to think about, talk about, and debate these new ideas just as teachers do? Her research at UCLA in educational policy studies, which centered on issues of parents and schooling, seemed to support a need for new models of parent education. How could schools better prepare parents for a seat at the table in shared school governance and at the same time help them to support education for social justice?

The UCLA Parent Curriculum Project, designed to address the upper end of Joyce Epstein's six types of parent involvement (discussed in Chapter 3) with the added emphasis on issues of equity, addresses some of Lois's concerns.[2]

The Program

In 1995 the Los Angeles Unified School District began to move decision making from the central office to the schools and began to include parents on decision-making councils. When it became apparent that parents would need support in their new roles, the UCLA Parent Curriculum Project was born. With the support of Jeannie Oakes, director of Center X in the Graduate School of Education & Information Studies, and Stuart Bernstein, a cluster administrator for the school district, the University of California at Los Angeles and the district were able to provide parents with new knowledge about schooling.

Typically parent participation is limited on school decision-making councils because parents don't have the same knowledge as do the educators on the council. Since they don't have the same understandings or language, they may be reluctant to speak. And even when they do get up the nerve to say something in the council, parents usually do not exert much influence. Lois and her colleagues wanted to change this imbalance. By giving parents the same knowledge base as educators, they believed parents could participate more fully in council decisions about teaching and learning practices.

Since its inception the UCLA Parent Curriculum Project has worked with more than 150 parents who had children in kindergarten through the twelfth grade and who represented a diversity of ethnic and socioeconomic backgrounds. All parents, poor and well off, from more privileged racial and ethnic groups and from more marginalized ones, say they have benefited from this experience. Parents feel knowledge about school reforms is important not just for their children but for all children. One Latina high school parent said, "When it gets down to the nitty gritty, I am not doing this for my child. I am doing it for everybody. When I go to the school and I represent the school, I represent everyone. . . . My children are doing fine and sometimes I take it for granted that they get straight As and Bs and I don't have to worry about it. But I know there are other children out there whose parents are not interested, and those are the ones I work for."

More recently, as a result of California's vote against affirmative action, the UCLA Parent Curriculum Project has begun another collaborative effort with the Los Angeles school district. Because the University of California has been forced to seek other ways to ensure that minority students have access to the university system, there is now an extensive outreach program to school districts serving kindergarten through grade 12. The goals of this collaborative effort are to ensure that all students are prepared for a variety of postsecondary education options and to increase the number of students who can compete for entrance to University of California schools, including the most selective campuses, UCLA and Berkeley, where the numbers of minority students have decreased dramatically.

Rather than attempt to have the parents play catch-up to the educators who would participate, the UCLA project included a Parent Education and Involvement Task Force. This collaboration built strong relationships with the teachers and principals right from the start. During the spring and the summer of 1998, twenty-seven parents—mostly Latino/Latina and African American—participated along with principals and teachers in this newer version of the Parent Curriculum Project. In this, as well as in previous versions, parents were involved in curriculum workshops, action research, and role playing.

Curriculum Workshops. The workshops involved parents in learning by experiencing the same kind of activities their children did in class: Parents became students. To learn about teaching writing, they wrote. To learn about experiential science, they set up and conducted experiments and went outdoors and collected samples. To learn about cooperative learning, they participated in cooperative groups. Because the curriculum workshops were taught by the same outstanding teachers who offered the teacher workshops, parents were impressed. They said, "You mean our [kids'] teachers are getting the same kinds of workshops we're getting? Are they going to be making these kinds of changes in our children's classrooms? We're really excited to know this is going on at our school."

And parents recognized the power of good teaching and learning practices. A frequent comment heard from parents during the sessions said it all: "If only I had teachers like this when I was in school."

A key principle of this program is the bonding that results from a diverse group of people working intensely on common tasks. Such a tight-knit group can address difficult issues together. And so they did. For example, parents discussed and debated the use of Ebonics (the African American language, or dialect, depending on one's perspective) in schools, tracking, and the disparate educational achievement for children from different ethnic groups. The idea of such a diverse group of parents struggling with such difficult issues is powerful. Parents whose children benefited from tracking, a practice that held other children back, were confronted by parents who wanted their children to have their fair share. The affluent white parent who hears a working-class African American parent say, "I want my kid to have the same opportunities as your children," gains a new perspective. This project offered a rich opportunity for sharing different views about education and helped parents realize that what is good for their child should be good for *all* children.

At the end of the program each parent developed an action plan to show how he or she would share what had been learned with other parents. This project was a far cry from the traditional way most schools inform parents about new practices—talking at them in large auditoriums. Parents appreciated being treated with respect and getting important information about what their children were doing in school, as the following comments of some participants show. A Latina high school parent said:

> Lo que más me interesó de la presentación, fue la participación de cada uno de nosostros. Cada quien en su equipo hizo lo mejor que pudo y todos contentos nos olvidamos por un rato de los conflictos que han acontecido. [What interested me the most was the participation of each one of us. Everyone in their team did the best they could and all of us happily forgot for a moment the conflicts that had taken place.]

An African American high school mother related:

> We had teamwork, we had the chance to deal with prejudice, we had a chance to share [round robin], to say what we understood about

what we read. Could it be possible to have all teachers do and practice the same procedures?

Another Latina high school parent talked about her response to the low achievement scores for minority students:

> Es muy importante ver cifras reales. Pero es traumante ver por medio de estas cifras tal nivel de "racismo" o "discriminación" o no sé cómo llamarlo. ¿Por qué no es la misma enseñanza para todos, que todos salgan de H.S. [high school] con la opción de asistir a la universidad? [Very important to see real figures. It is traumatic to see through these figures such level of "racism" or "discrimination" or I don't know what to call it. Why isn't it the same education for everyone, everyone to graduate from high school with the option to attend college?]

An African American mother of a middle school student said:

> I feel as if I'm experiencing the world of a child. I am more in touch with the child's perspective on education. I just keep feeling like yelling out. I want to tell teachers, children, and community members how we feel as parents. I want the children to know how much we care. I want teachers to know how concerned we are and how much we care about the education of our children. I want EVERYONE to hear!

What school wouldn't love to have such enthusiastic and engaged parents?

Parents Seek Answers through Action Research. Following the curriculum workshops, an advanced seminar for interested parents was offered. This seminar, comprised of two full-day sessions and eight evening sessions focused on leadership for change in schools.

Parents were encouraged to plan a research project based on their own questions about schools, such as, "How can we provide resources for disadvantaged parents?" "How can we create a special program at the neighborhood school without making the program elitist?" "What are the grouping practices in elementary schools that lead to tracking in secondary schools?" "What can be done about the large number of substitute teachers at a low-achieving middle school?" Other topics included the role played by paraprofessionals in classrooms, bilingual education, and the different ways that schools invite—or don't invite—parents to be involved.

Parents conducted their research through interviews, observations, and reading. At the seminar's evening meetings they met and shared their writing with each other. In the end, although some parents didn't write lengthy reports, they all shared what they had learned about their questions with the group.

What did these research projects teach parents? According to Lois André Bechely of UCLA and Stu Bernstein of the school district, parents began to understand the complexity of schooling issues: They began to rethink what is "best" in schools, to appreciate diversity, and to recognize the importance of working for equity in the school community.

Readers' Theater Role Playing: A Safe Way to Share Different Perspectives.
In addition to the hands-on activities, parents, teachers, and administrators participated in an unusual exercise. They enacted two readers' theater scripts constructed from the interviews with Grover's Corners High School parents. The scripts demonstrate the diversity of opinions among parents about school change. Because the original scripts were written in English, Spanish translations were provided to ensure that Spanish-speaking parents could participate. The mental picture of urban parents and educators in California reading in English and Spanish the words of parents and educators from New England is remarkable.

Some people might wonder if the experiences of an all-white community in small-town New England can translate to the experiences of Latino/Latina and African American parents in an inner-city environment. Yet they do. Parents, no matter who they are or where they live, seem to have the same hopes and dreams for their children and the same concerns about their schooling.

Before the theater session began, teachers said they felt a little defensive about the scripts because some parts seemed "anti-teacher."

Their feelings changed once the reading began. Teachers and administrators (many of whom were also parents), were all assigned parent roles. They said that the script helped them to remember what it was like when they advocated for their own children. For example, one teacher said: "When I put on my parent hat, I feel that same way. I want my children in courses that will prepare them academically."

The scripts opened a dialogue between parents and educators who would be working together. Reading the scripts helped raise some of the difficult issues related to change without pointing fingers. Rather than talking about *their* schools, teachers, and administrators in scripts, parents and educators could talk instead about the schools, teachers, and administrators in Grover's Corners. Readers' theater gave them a safe and less personal way to confront some of the thorny issues of concern in their community.

A Model for Other Communities

The UCLA Parent Curriculum Project is a rare example of how parents and educators might learn to confront their differences and to begin to talk openly about what goes on in good schools and classrooms. Such honest dialogue can occur only when there is a climate of trust and a commitment to learning from each other. Even though this program served parents in city schools, it suggests a powerful model for districts or individual schools anywhere.

Gwinnett County (Georgia) Standards-Setting Project

Setting standards for student learning can generate conflict, but a public school system in Georgia demonstrated that inviting parents to learn about standards-setting can instead be a positive and productive experience for everyone.

Program Beginnings

Kate Kirby-Linton, the student assessment coordinator for the Gwinnett County (Georgia) Public Schools in the early 1990s, with colleagues Nancy Lyle, the district's language arts coordinator, and Susan White, an assistant principal in a district elementary school, initiated and coordinated a writing standards-setting project. Parents were invited to learn and to work side by side with the district's teachers. Reflecting on this project in a recent conversation, Kate said, "The memory of this project still makes me smile. It's the best thing I have ever done in my career."

When the nation was engaged in a debate about outcomes-based education (described in Chapter 7), some parents argued against this approach because they thought it usurped their role in teaching values to their children. Many educators, however, viewed outcomes-based education as a means of focusing on what students should know and be able to do when they finished school. Because the term "outcomes-based education" seemed so inflammatory, reformers shifted the discussion to talk about standards and standards setting instead.

The debate about outcomes-based education had created problems in the suburban Atlanta school district that served 70,000 students, leaving it in turmoil and some parents very unhappy. When Georgia turned its attention to setting standards for writing, standards that all high school students would be required to meet in order to graduate, the Gwinnett county school district, which was proud of being a leader in the state, wanted not only to meet but also to surpass state standards. The district decided to create its own writing standards.

The story of how this district involved both teachers and parents in the standards-setting process is another example of authentic parental involvement. It shows how parents—even those who may be unhappy with the system—can come to better understand what schools are about.[3]

The Program

During the summer of 1994, thirty teachers and fifty parents came together for a two-week workshop. The teachers represented all grades (kindergarten through grade 12) in the district as well as the different disciplines. After a letter was distributed to all parents by each school, 125 parents applied to participate in the project. Of those, fifty were chosen to represent all grades; many of them had children of high school age. While mostly mothers applied, there were also five or six fathers. Participants were also selected to represent both the district's different geographic regions and the distribution of the different socioeconomic groups. The group included participants with college educations and others who hadn't graduated from high school. Some parents who had expressed anger about outcomes-based education came to the project feeling that they were going "to set the schools right." Teachers and parents alike were paid a stipend of $75 per day to participate in the work.

Their task was to read through over 3,500 pieces of student writing—gathered from each school and grade level in the district—to identify papers that exemplified different levels of writing for each grade level. These "anchor" papers then would be used by schools as "standards" of what students in each grade level were capable of producing.

Parents and teachers were taught how to assess writing holistically and what qualities of good writing to look for in children's writing samples. Each week a different group of twenty-five parents attended the workshop for three days—working side by side with teachers, many of whom were also parents in the district. Because each paper had to be rated by three people with some agreement, they read, discussed, and negotiated the scoring of each paper. As the groups worked, it was difficult to differentiate between teacher and parent: They had a common task and worked together to complete it.

At break times parents and teachers often sat out under the trees, involved in animated conversations. This opportunity for parents and teachers to talk informally is rare and yet essential for trust building. And the common task gave teachers and parents something to talk about; as they moved from talking about their work to other topics, over time, they began to form closer relationships.

Once parents became immersed in reading the papers, they began to view writing differently, sometimes expressing amazement and pleasure at the level of writing that children were able to produce. They began to look beyond surface features, such as spelling and punctuation, and focus more on content, organization, and language use. They saw that "invented" spelling helped children in the early grades express their ideas and be more creative. For example, one parent wrote in her evaluation of the project:

It is amazing how the invented spelling that children use at this age can allow the creative process to flow without interruption. At first invented spelling was a sore spot with me. I questioned its possible effects on the students. Now I can clearly see how much more these young students can convey on paper than we could when we were in third grade. By the time spelling becomes a necessity, the creative process is set.

Kate Kirby-Linton believes that the reason the project worked so well was that parents were treated as valuable resources. "They felt important and they *were* important to this process. Parents with advanced degrees as well as parents who didn't graduate from high school successfully participated in this process. Parents learned a lot and teachers saw parents in a different light." Parents—along with teachers—learned what good writing is. They were able to see how children's writing progressed through the grades.

The responses of four parents, who reflected on their experience in the project, confirm the value of this work.

If the county decided to fund this kind of project again, I would suggest that the parents be treated the way they were treated here— very respectfully and professionally. The expectations for the task were clear, and parents and teachers were very similar in using the clear criteria to rate the papers.

The most important benefit of this collaborative experience to me was to see the fantastic level of cooperation and commitment from parents and teachers alike in selecting anchors that will have a direct practical benefit in every classroom for all teachers, students, and parents.

My interest in working on the Literacy Standards Project was to be sure a high level of quality writing is expected in Gwinnett schools. I wanted to help high-achieving students have a measurable level of excellence available in the classroom.

Let more parents know about the opportunity to work with you. I have mentioned this project to twelve to fifteen parents, and the majority would like to participate. Well-planned and executed effort. I really appreciated the opportunity to meet and work with teachers from the county's schools. An impressive group!

At the end of the first three-day session, the first group of twenty-five parents was so enthusiastic about the project that they wanted to continue working. Although this wasn't possible, they were invited back on the last day of the two-week workshop to read each of the anchor papers that everyone had agreed upon. And that was quite an experience. Close to one hundred people sat in the room reading the chosen papers. People were laughing and crying as they read what the children had written. "You've got to read this one" or "Look at this" could be heard as they shared papers with each other. It was impossible from looking at the group to tell who were the parents and who were the teachers.

As a result of this experience, one parent, formerly one of the severest critics of the district during the outcomes-based education brouhaha, became one of the strongest supporters of this process. She helped get the collection of anchor papers into each of the county's public libraries. She also made presentations with Kate about the project to the school board and at Georgia State University. Now many of the district's elementary schools and one of its middle schools continue to hold similar workshops for their parents and teachers. Unfortunately, to our knowledge, none of the high schools has followed suit. While we are disappointed, we are not surprised. It is just one more example of a lost opportunity for a high school to invite parents into the school community.

Vermont Parents and Teachers Engage in Action Research

Another example of involving parents through action research demonstrates the value of parents and teachers learning together. The Vermont project began as a result of the state's effort to assess student learning through portfolios.

Program Beginnings

In 1992 "The Partnerships for Achievement in Learning Project" at the University of Vermont collaborated with the Franklin Northeast Supervisory Union (the local school district) to "describe the impact of the Vermont Portfolio Assessment system on our families, especially the families of children with disabilities."[4] Pam Kay, the project coordinator, developed a process of Parent-Teacher Action Research (PTAR) in response to a need expressed by parents who were working as members of the research team on a project funded by the United States Department of Education. As Pam explained, "Our parent liaisons were not content with merely gathering information about the impact of school reform and helping us analyze it. They wanted to make improvements in their schools with the knowledge they had acquired. They also wanted to get more teachers interested in encouraging parent involvement."

"We believed that teachers were more likely to change their practices as the result of their own action research than as the result of presentations by parents and researchers," Pam said, "and we wanted them to learn to work collaboratively with parents, across both general and special education domains. Parent-Teacher Action Research provided a model and structure for collaboration among equal practitioners, parents and teachers, while allowing each team to develop and explore its own research questions and come to its own conclusions." Pam went on to explain: "Our guidelines were that each team had to have parents of children both with and without disabilities, as well as both general and special educators, and that their research questions needed to focus on improving home-school collaboration. Even though our funding allowed us to provide small stipends for those who participated (in equal amounts for parents and teachers), recruitment was not easy. Our parent liaisons worked hard to find people in each school, often needing several contacts to convince the principal to distribute the information to teachers."[5]

The Program

Teaming parents with teachers to do action research is not a practice commonly found in schools. And when it is found, it is more likely to be found in elementary schools or in middle schools. That's why the Partnerships for Achievement in Learning Project is so interesting. It demonstrates how high school parents and teachers can come together to examine issues important to both groups.

Action research allows teachers and, in this case, parents, to identify a problem they want to study, plan a way to study it, collect data about it, analyze the data, decide on a course of action, implement that action, and then to evaluate the results and start the planning process all over again. This is the process that seven teams in elementary, middle, and high schools in the Franklin Northeast Supervisory Union followed, but, as the two high school projects reveal, the teams developed their own designs.

Enosburg Falls High School parents and teachers raised the question of communication about grading. They wondered "if parents and students were satisfied with the methods of obtaining information on grading methods, general classroom expectations, etc." The high school team interviewed students, teachers, and parents to find out what each group knew about the curriculum objectives, the teaching methods teachers used to reach those objectives, how students were graded, and how parents can communicate with teachers about school issues.

Their research results seemed to suggest that, although teachers and students were able to talk knowledgeably about course objectives and teaching methods, parents were mostly in the dark about them. In addition, parents had little idea about how to contact teachers about curriculum and grading issues.

The research team concluded that parents needed to know how to get more information about the curriculum and grading practices from teachers. They suggested a variety of ways that the school might solve this problem: better phone accessibility for teachers, parent liaisons to answer questions, a variety of smaller parent-teacher gatherings, workshops for parents, and student and faculty handbooks placed in the public library.

The Richford Junior-Senior High School team decided to examine how the school staff and community members viewed community participation. The research team developed a questionnaire about involvement with the school, awareness of school events, and perceptions of the school in general. Then team members interviewed the school staff and conducted a telephone interview of thirty randomly chosen community members. The results of the study showed that teachers wanted more community involvement in the school, but they didn't have the time personally to invite that participation. Community members, on the other hand, said that they would be more likely to participate in the school if they were personally invited or contacted.

Based on these findings, the action research team brainstormed a list of possible actions: asking the school to share the results of the community survey with the staff; creating a list of school needs and a community resource bank based on these needs; using a "phone tree" to solicit help; holding open house earlier in the year; increasing school activities in the community; developing a community service student group; developing a public relations club; attaching personal invitations to school mailings, such as report cards and progress reports; and asking for support from the existing parent support group. Of these, the team focused on increasing personal contact with the community by using "personal touch," creating a resource bank, and extending more school activities into the community.

What did parents and teachers gain from participation in these action research teams? One teacher said: "It certainly is a true beginning in bridging the gap between school and community." A parent commented: "I learned that parents and teachers share a lot of the same concerns about communication between home and school." And one team wrote this in its final report: "Doing the research gave us a sense of involvement and connectivity that will have an effect and influence on us for a time to come."[6]

Roosevelt High School:
Building a Culture of Conversation

Every school can benefit from involving parents, but perhaps the neediest schools have the least to lose and the most to gain, as this Texas high school profile shows.

Program Beginnings

When Melvin Traylor was named principal of Roosevelt High School (RHS) in Dallas, Texas, the school was in disrepair. It seemed to fit all of the public's stereotypes of an inner-city school: poor student performance and attendance, rowdy students and sometimes dangerous hallways and classrooms, a mostly demoralized staff, and meager parental involvement. Over the course of the ten years that Mr. Traylor was principal, the school made a remarkable turn around. Student achievement was dramatically raised: In 1996-97 the school missed achieving a state evaluation of "Recognized Achievement"—the next to the highest rating—by only two percentage points. Attendance increased, order was restored, teachers were energized, and parents and community members became part of the school community in record numbers.

Brenda Shell was one of those community members. When her son's elementary school teacher told her that he was doing fine in school, she was furious: she knew that her son couldn't read. She had to learn on her own how to get through to teachers who thought that "parents don't know anything about their own kids." When her church, which is located in the Roosevelt High School community, called for volunteers to work with RHS parents, Brenda was anxious to volunteer to help other parents learn about how they could make themselves heard in schools. Melvin Traylor and Brenda Shell are but two of the many educators, parents, students, community members, and church members who banded together with the help of the Dallas Area Interfaith (DAI, a member of the Texas Industrial Areas Foundation, headed by Ernesto Cortes, Jr.) to create a "culture of conversation" in Roosevelt High School. What follows is their story.[7]

The Program

Upon his arrival at RHS in 1987, Melvin Traylor identified three fundamental problems that needed immediate attention. The first was the abundance of remedial classes and a dearth of advanced classes. One of his first acts was to eliminate many of these remedial classes and to add advanced placement classes.

The second problem was a demoralized staff in need of opportunities to develop professionally. That first year he spent a lot of time listening to his staff, building a trusting relationship with them, and seeking and finding grant money from the Texas Education Agency to provide high-quality professional development opportunities for them. He knew that without a committed, energized, and knowledgeable staff he was powerless. While building the morale of his existing staff, he also focused on recruiting high-quality new staff to fill vacant positions. He got an idea from thinking about the way football teams draft new players—the worst team in the league last year gets first pick of the college players the next year. Why, he wondered, wasn't that the case in schools? Shouldn't the schools in the most difficulty get the best of the incoming teachers each year? He pitched this plan to the superintendent of schools, Martin Edwards, and his assistant, Lois Harrison-Jones. The result was that in the future, schools such as RHS, would get first pick of the incoming teachers to replenish their staffs. And, for the first time, principals would be able to interview and pick their teachers rather than having them assigned by the central office.

The third problem was the very limited parental involvement and presence in the schools. He began reaching out to parents in a variety of ways. For instance, when teachers expressed frustration that so few parents came to school to collect their children's report cards, he asked what could they do about this. Together the teachers and principal came up with the idea of hand delivering the report cards to the parents. So on the next report card day, teachers, accompanied by the school's football players, fanned out in the community delivering report cards. It is easy to imagine the surprise on parent's faces when these teachers came knocking. Some parents were so taken aback that they cried. Never before had teachers demonstrated concern about their children in such a way.

Things began to stabilize in the school as parents' initial concerns (that eliminating remedial classes would hurt their children) were allayed by the concurrent rise in student achievement and expectations and as teacher morale began to rise. At the same time the need for more sustained conversation between and among teachers, parents, and community members took center stage. Thanks to the DAI and a grant from the Texas Education Agency, there was help for strengthening relationships among parents, teachers, and community members.

Working through neighborhood groups and especially through community churches, synagogues, and mosques, the DAI's purpose is to "teach families how to become engaged in the public life of their communities."[8] Brenda Shell was one of the volunteers recruited to work with schools to improve education for their children. Early in the process when Roosevelt High School went to neighborhood churches to begin to build a relationship, Brenda Shell volunteered to help organize and mobilize parents. She now works hard with groups of parents to teach them what their rights are and how to act together to advocate not only for their children, but for all of the children in the community. She knows that many voices are more powerful than one and she knows who to go to to get things done. She shares this knowledge with other parents.

One of the tenets of the DAI approach is that of building a "culture of conversation." The school, with the help of the community/school organizer assigned to them by DAI, sought to engage teachers, students, parents, and community members in conversations about what they thought about Roosevelt High School and how they thought it could be improved. They set out to listen. Organizer Leonora Friend met with each teacher individually to find out what they perceived to be the greatest needs and strengths of the school and how they wanted to be involved. Two other efforts quickly followed: Community Walks and House Meetings, both of which have since become routine activities in the RHS community.

The Community Walks involved teams of parents, community volunteers (many of whom are from the area's houses of worship), teachers, and students spreading out throughout the community on a Saturday morning, stopping passers-by, shoppers, and others to talk with them about school. "What do you know about RHS?" "What would you like to know?" "What do you think about the school?" "What do you think needs to be changed/improved at the school?" "How would you like to help?" The first time this happened, residents, of course, were stunned. "You mean you're actually coming out and asking *me* what I think?" This was certainly a new experience for most. That first walk helped the school to realize the changing nature of the community: Many Latino families who didn't speak English had moved into the area. One of the major requests from these new residents was for adult English classes. As a result, the school tapped into a partnership with the local community college to offer parents classes in the evening. The demand for these classes was so great that not all of the parents could be accommodated. Because these efforts reflected a sincere desire on the part of the school for parental and community involvement, parents and community members began to say, "We want to be a part of RHS. We want to help." Everyone has come to expect and to look forward to the Community Walks that are now held twice a year.

A second approach to encourage conversation was the initiation of House Meetings, small groups of parents and teachers who met in parents' homes. Teachers were there to hear what parents had to say about the school and to listen to their ideas for improvement. It was just one more way for the school to demonstrate its commitment to bringing parents into the conversation about schooling. These meetings also have become a regular part of the way RHS does business. Small groups of teachers, parents, and students getting together to talk with each other about mutual concerns is now a common expectation of the RHS school community.

Unfortunately Melvin Traylor had to leave Roosevelt High in 1997, when a newly appointed superintendent decided to rotate over one hundred principals of the Dallas schools. A new principal from outside the school district was assigned to Roosevelt High School. The transition for the school and for the new principal was difficult because Mel Traylor was a hard act to follow. He had built strong relationships with teachers, students, parents, local churches, and community members, who would miss him sorely. His replacement, working for a superintendent who did not understand the importance of building relationships, made a number of missteps that further upset teachers, parents, and community members. Mary Beth Larkin, an organizer from DAI now working with the school, said, "A bureaucratic culture collided with a relational culture and resulted in an interruption of the culture at Roosevelt High School that had been so carefully constructed to build trust with parents and community members."[9]

The school spent a year in turmoil as the new principal tried to get her bearings. The 1998-99 school year, however, started out better. The superintendent was replaced, and the principal, recognizing the need to rebuild strained relationships, worked with teachers, parents, and community members to restore the "culture of conversation" that had been so painstakingly developed in the past ten years.

Parents-as-Outsiders or Parents-as-Learners?

These four profiles suggest ways that parents can be included as learners in school communities. However, rarely are programs like these found in high schools today. What is more typical? Parents may find themselves in one of the two following situations. In both they may feel like outsiders looking in.

In the first situation, parents have children who attend schools where teachers are involved in active learning communities. In these schools teachers and administrators have taken seriously the call for a more professional approach to their work and now take time together to talk about and study their teaching practices. Yet even though the importance of parent involvement in school decision making may be acknowledged in these schools, teachers sometimes respond defensively when a parent questions new teaching and learning practices. When parents are not part of the school's learning community, they experience the "dark side" of communities. Being excluded can be a very painful experience. As outsiders who are not involved in the formal and informal opportunities teachers have to interact, parents do not have the chance to learn about or debate new teaching practices. No one, therefore, should be surprised later if parents object to something new.

In the second situation parents have children in a school in which teachers are not yet involved in such conversations. These teachers spend their days isolated from each other, laboring to do the best they can without support from colleagues, with the boss/worker mentality of management and union—and bureaucratic procedures and red tape—grinding them down little by little every day. Here too parents are excluded; in fact, they are often seen as the enemy. Teachers are likely to say "If only parents would support us, our job would be a lot easier." To these teachers, the best parental involvement means supporting what they do without question.

A third situation—the one suggested by the profiles—occurs when parents, teachers, and students are members of an energetic and inclusive community of learners. In these schools everyone regularly and actively participates in learning with and from each other. We believe such communities of learners should exist in all schools and hope that the programs profiled in this chapter offer some new ways to think about how to invite parents in. However, each community must decide on an approach to meet their own unique needs.

Where can a school begin? Chapter 9 provides more information about parent involvement as well as snapshots and suggestions of other ways to open doors to parents and community members.

NINE

Opening Doors to Parents and Community Members: Snapshots and Suggestions

The profiles in Chapter 8 indicated how rich and productive parent participation can be, but few districts or schools have done as much to involve parents. In most cases parents have been left out of the conversations about new practices that educators—teachers, administrators, researchers, and teacher educators—have engaged in for more than a decade. Even though many schools across the nation call themselves "communities of learners," these "communities" usually do not include parents.

At the very least parents want more information. Columnist Robert J. Samuelson writes in *Newsweek* that the "true 'inputs' to education are students' hard work, quality teaching, rigorous standards and parental engagement. When these are missing, money and reorganization can't compensate." He argues that people are deluding themselves by thinking that "the school" can do it all. Parents must do their part, but Samuelson's gripe with the school—one probably shared by many other parents across the country—is that "it doesn't tell parents what's expected of students, or how, exactly, parents can help."[1]

Because parents often do not know exactly what is really happening in schools, their criticism may be the result of a misunderstanding. One reason parents of high school students may be misinformed or uninformed is that high schools traditionally have had lower levels of parental involvement and communication than is common in elementary schools. High school teachers say that most parents don't care or don't want to be bothered by the school unless it is necessary and that students want to be "on their own" and do not want their parents to know much about their school lives.

This chapter first looks more closely at the general topic of involvement. Then it offers a variety of snapshots (examples of what some schools and school districts have already done), strategies, and suggestions for opening school doors to parents and community members in four loosely-constructed and overlapping categories: improving communication, engaging stakeholders in discussions about public education, creating and fostering opportunities for everyone to learn, and involving more people in making decisions about schools and about learning and teaching. These categories move from the least engaging to the most engaging. We would like to see more high schools involve parents and community members at the highest levels (as learners and decision makers), but, as Samuelson points out, many people would be happy just to know more about schools. Every effort counts, no matter how small.

Teachers' and Students' Views on Parent Involvement

How do teachers and students really feel about parent involvement with schools? To answer that question, Louis Harris and Associates surveyed a total of 1,306 students in grades seven to twelve and 1,035 teachers for a Metropolitan Life survey, which examined issues similar to those included in a survey of parents and teachers a decade ago. The following were some of the major findings.[2]

- Many teachers today have higher expectations of parents than they did a decade ago, and many still feel, as they did in 1987, that parents can do more to support their children's education both at school and at home.
- Students welcome and are generally satisfied with parents' involvement in their school lives. Overall, most students

feel that their parents are actively involved and supportive of their education both at home and at school.

- [There is a] strong and consistent association between students' ability to succeed academically and the extent to which they feel their parents take an interest in and support their academic and personal aspirations.

- Teachers today are as likely or more likely than they were ten years ago to feel that parents are a valuable asset to schools. . . . They are generally satisfied with the frequency of contact with parents.

- However, most teachers still believe, as they did in 1987, that it is more appropriate that parents be informed, but not actively consulted about changes in class curriculum and homework policies. . . . [Yet] most students believe parents should have some, but not a lot of say, in these types of decisions.

- Urban teachers are less likely than others [suburban and rural teachers] to feel that parents are sufficiently involved in their children's education and they are more likely to believe that parent-teacher relationships in their schools are fair or poor.

The report concludes that teachers see more value today than they did ten years ago in working with parents to improve public education.

Although many people believe that high school students do not want their parents involved with school, this survey shows that "a majority of students in each grade level feel that parent involvement is a good idea." More surprising, perhaps, is the fact that more high school students (75 percent) think so than do seventh or eighth graders (67 percent). And, even more telling, "more than half (55 percent) of students whose parents are not very or not at all involved with their education think that [parent involvement] is a good idea."[3]

Of course, there are good reasons that high schools are less likely than elementary schools to work closely with parents. Students have five or six teachers rather than one. Both teenagers and their parents expect older children to be more independent. Yet studies show that students who do well in school are more likely to have involved parents than less-successful students. So it is in everyone's best interests for high school educators to find ways to encourage parents to stay or get more involved with schools even as the children grow closer to adulthood.

The School as a Community of Learners

High schools that are in the process of making significant changes must create opportunities for parents to learn about new teaching and learning practices along with teachers, for, as researcher Michael Fullan argues, everyone needs to develop his or her own meanings of change.[4] As has been seen in previous chapters, many parents oppose changes they do not understand. Including parents as learners will not only help them understand why schools want to introduce new practices; by doing so, educators also will learn how parents think about teaching and learning, as they did in the programs profiled in Chapter 8.

Mutual understanding of each other's thinking—of each other's mental models—is the first step to coming to consensus about what is best for students. And disagreement might be positive. Scholar and author Sarah Lawrence Lightfoot points out that "conflict is potentially constructive . . . [in] resolving differences."[5]

It is ironic that some schools that pride themselves on involving their students in active learning experiences do just the opposite when they introduce new practices to parents. As we have noted throughout this book, they sit them down in a large auditorium and talk at them for a long time. Then they expect parents not only to understand the new approaches but also to support the school's decisions—decisions they had no say in making! We don't think adults—any more than children or adolescents—learn new concepts this way. All learners need to be personally engaged in order to process and internalize new information or ideas.

Good classrooms and good learning communities offer their members many different ways to participate. Different students, different parents, different teachers have their own learning styles, preferences, and needs. We don't expect that the ideas suggested in the

Chapter 8 profiles or in the snapshots and suggestions in this chapter will be right for every community, but we are certain that the wider the variety of opportunities for involvement, the greater the likelihood that more people will become involved.

Getting parents to come to the school only for what Lightfoot calls "ritualistic" contacts, such as formal parent conferences or parent-teacher association (PTA) meetings, may serve merely to keep "boundaries" between home and school in place. If schools want to get and keep parents involved, then they need to pay attention to building bridges between home and school and developing and maintaining relationships between parents and educators. Thus it is important to have informal as well as formal opportunities for parents and teachers to come together. Informality fosters community building as people get to know each other as individuals and learn to trust and care about each other.

Community-building opportunities can be embedded in more formal learning activities, as was done in the Gwinnett County Writing Standards Project. In that project, the best times for forming personal relationships turned out to be the informal down times: lunch and breaks. Schools also can plan separate activities specifically designed to build community. For instance, one Maine high school holds a late-afternoon barbecue every September for teachers and incoming ninth graders. If a school isn't too large (or is divided into houses), this back-to-school picnic, which might be set up as a "potluck," could include parents as well. Such an informal gathering at the beginning of the year can go a long way toward building a school's community spirit.

In order to build a school learning community that includes parents, schools first must take an honest look at their current relationships with parents. Do parents feel welcomed in the school? Do they feel teachers and administrators are responsive to their concerns? Do parents come to school only when called or to complain? How many times in the past year have teachers and administrators had an opportunity to talk informally with parents? Do teachers feel threatened by parents? Do they keep parents at arm's length? How are parents involved in the school? How do parents want to be involved?

Once a school understands—and acknowledges—its current status with parents, it can begin to create a climate where parent/teacher relationships are genuine, open, caring, responsive, and honest. Parents will be invited, intentionally and sincerely, to be part of the school community. After this commitment to a more inclusive school community is made, then a plan for involving parents as learners can be developed. One model for doing this is suggested by the PTA. We, of course, would urge schools to add community building and specific opportunities for learning to the planning process outlined by the PTA.

Developing a Plan for Parent Involvement

The PTA's standards for increasing effective family involvement with schools build on Joyce Epstein's six types of parental involvement (discussed in more detail in Chapter 3). The PTA standards include (1) regular communication between home and school, (2) support in parenting skills, (3) an emphasis on assisting student learning, (4) the promotion of volunteering at school, (5) parent involvement in school decision making and advocacy, and (6) collaborations with the community to provide needed resources.[6]

The PTA makes several recommendations for working with parents. First, schools should create an action team comprised of administrators, teachers, and parents to set goals and guide the process. Surveys can be used to examine current practices with regard to parent involvement. Using this information, the school should develop an improvement plan and a written policy on parent and family involvement. Stakeholders should be kept informed of the progress, and necessary financial resources must be found to implement the plan. The PTA emphasizes the need to provide professional development for the school staff. Finally, by regularly evaluating and revising the parent involvement plan, the school commits itself to the long-term goal of continuously improving parent and family involvement.[7]

Schools joining the National Network of Partnership Schools follow a planning process very similar to the one just described. Under the direction of Joyce Epstein, the partnership was established in 1996 at Johns Hopkins University by the Center on Families, Communities, Schools & Children's Learning. The goal is to bring together schools, districts, and states that are committed to developing and maintaining strong school-family-community partnerships. Epstein and her colleagues have worked closely with teachers, parents, and administrators in Maryland, helping them plan partnership initiatives.[8]

Readers of Chapter 8 may have thought, "This is great, but it can't be done here." Perhaps that is true, perhaps not. In any case, every school or community can do more than it is now doing. The following snapshots and suggestions can be starting points for thinking and action. Readers who want more participation in and support for schools may have to work to get changes made locally.

Improving Communication

Parents of high school students have fewer contacts with and know less about the school than parents of elementary students. The best communication is two way, but too often high schools don't even do a good job of one-way communication. People in the community who have no school-age children may know only how the high school teams fare in athletic competition or what they hear around town. Everyone—not just parents—needs to know more about what is really happening in the local high school. Otherwise, they will likely believe every negative rumor or exaggerated crisis as presented by local media. Even if a school is not involved in change, the more "good things" about the school people know, the more likely they will be to support budgets and bond issues.

Making New Connections with the Internet

Many schools and school districts now have Web sites to inform parents and others about school events and programs, but Wauwatosa, Wisconsin; Palo Alto, California; and many other school districts also are using computers to get data, find experts, and make connections beyond their local communities. Parents on their own also are creating Web sites—many times to offer views contrary to those of the schools. Reporter Andrew Trotter, writing in *Education Week*, says some school officials are worried "that the use of the Internet could distort their communication with the public because Internet users are drawn disproportionately from the ranks of the affluent." Furthermore, "'[W]eb sites can conceal the real dimensions of a group's strength,' said Liz Whitaker, the technology coordinator of the Tucson, Arizona, schools, where a local group has a Web site that is critical of the district's curriculum. 'You can't tell when you look at a home page if there are 1,000 people behind it or one.'"⁹

Parent groups opposed to some school changes already have recognized the power of the Internet. For example, in Wauwatosa, Wisconsin, the president of PRESS (Parents Raising Educational Standards in Schools), said she "has received e-mail from people in 40 states and was stunned to receive a check from a math professor in Switzerland who had seen the group's Web site." Another example is Palo Alto's HOLD (Honest Open Logical Debate on Curricular Reform), which "seeks to influence the teaching of mathematics and reading in the Palo Alto school district." It sponsors a Web site that is a "one-stop shop for academic research and newspaper articles that support its view that recent curricular reforms have been mis-guided." Even though this group has not been successful in achiev-ing its objectives (and the district's acting superintendent said, "We're not interested in the larger community [on the Internet]; they don't influence our decision making"), a member of HOLD's steering committee thinks the site has been valuable: "One of the great pooling effects of the Internet is that scattered people who don't know each other can exchange information. . . . We gain from work other people have done."¹⁰

Finally, the Plano, Texas, schools have an official Web site, but a parent runs the "Unofficial Plano Independent School District site, which rivals . . . [the official one] in quality and thoroughness." Tim Williams and some other parents set up the site to "oppose a series of school bond proposals they believed were excessive and poorly explained." Because the local newspaper did not adequately explain the complex proposal and few people would go to the district office and photocopy the details, Williams put the full text on the Internet. Even though the bonds passed, he saw the 1,000-plus visits to his site as a "vote of confidence" and decided to continue it because it "offers local parents the only independent view of the Plano district's management and performance." Williams's site, which posts data not offered on the official site, such as budget information and state ratings, includes a link to the district's official home page, but the reverse is not true.[11]

The reality is that Internet communication is here to stay, so how can schools make the most of it? We believe that if parents felt they were included in the school community and that their views were heard and respected, there would be no need for antagonistic Web sites. Both school- and parent-initiated Web sites could represent a way of holding civil and respectful discussions about different points of view.

Reinvigorating the PTA: Mt. Vernon (VA) High School

Thanks to the determined efforts of its president, the PTA meetings at Mt. Vernon High School in Virginia grew from a dismal turnout of eight to twenty members to 100 percent of teachers and a dramatic increase in parent and student participation. The president reorganized the PTA, created a new mission statement, established a parent council in each grade, and developed community resource teams to distribute monthly newsletters and to gather support from the entire community.[12]

School Hot Lines Inform Parents and Students

As part of a national effort begun in 1995 with funding from the business community known as the Bridge Project, 102 high schools across the country established "hot lines." By calling the school's voice mail, parents can find out what homework their children have to do. Teachers also "have used the hot line to give parents tips on helping their children with schoolwork or to talk about the day's lessons." Some systems were set up so that parents could leave messages for teachers.[13]

The principal of Stonewall Jackson High School in Manassas, Virginia, said, "I've had several parents tell me it's become a daily car-phone ritual to call up and find out what students are studying that day and then to have a conversation about it at dinner." He also has used the system to leave messages for all parents about upcoming meetings, noting that "attendance at the school's annual January orientation for incoming freshmen increased to 1,000 from 50 the previous year."[14]

Researchers evaluating the program confirm that the hot line has increased parent involvement: For example, in a survey of employees of sponsoring corporations, 43 percent of parents reported "using the system regularly," and "half said they were more involved in their children's schooling and that their children did more homework."[15]

Personal Phones Increase Teacher-Parent Communication

There are many reasons that teachers make so few phone calls to parents. Unlike nonschool people and administrators who work in offices where phones are taken for granted, many teachers work in schools with only one or two phones available for their use. Often these phones are in semipublic places, such as a teachers' workroom, making private conversations difficult if not impossible. One Maine high school solved the lack-of-privacy problem by installing a London-type phone booth inside the teachers' room, but this is still the only phone for faculty use. Many teachers do not live in the communities in which they teach, and that means that calls to parents from their homes may be at long-distance rates.

Teachers at Grover's Corners High School were looking forward to the completion of their new school because for the first time they would have telephones in their classrooms. This access will improve communication. In another high school, in Portland, Maine, thanks to a donation of twenty-five wireless phones from Sprint, teachers can call parents from their classrooms as well as their cars. One teacher said, "I love my phone. The first three days I just went nonstop on parents. I called five the first day and six the next . . . making all the calls I should have made but couldn't [before having the wireless phone]." Because teachers have distributed numbers to the phones, parents can call with questions. And that's a big help because, as one parent commented, "It's been very difficult to contact teachers . . . on the telephone. I've actually had [to leave work] to go down to the school and try to hunt them down."[16]

Creating and Sharing Information about a School

To pass school district budgets and bond issues in most communities today, it isn't enough to have the support only of people with children in school. Others, such as senior citizens, also must be reached and convinced of the need for funding. But even if funding approval isn't a problem, people in the larger community should know what's happening in the schools. Educators should be good PR (public relations) people.

To communicate with people outside the school, it is important to avoid using jargon or educationese! In all printed materials (and parent conferences or special-education team meetings) the language should be clear and direct; the tone, friendly and conversational. To make certain that what has been written is appropriate for an audience of noneducators, educators should ask some parents or businesspeople to read a draft and provide feedback before the final copy is printed for distribution.

So that speaking to a civic group or responding to a request for information will be easier for anyone who does it, each school should consider developing some of the following materials:

- Videos about the school showing students and teachers in action.
- Videos about school change.
- Fact sheet, profile, or brochure that describes the school. It might include demographic data, test scores, faculty and their accomplishments or awards, special programs— anything that presents the school in a positive light.
- Schedule or calendar of school or school district activities, including special events as well as regularly scheduled board meetings.
- Directory that includes the names and phone numbers of key school and district people, committees, and elected officials.
- Speakers' list: the names and topics of people who are available to speak to civic groups, such as Rotary or other clubs. (Some students might be included on this list as well.)

- School scrapbook of newspaper clippings of stories about the school. (Keep the stories in plastic sleeves so they can be removed, if needed, to make copies for special purposes.)
- Bookmarks (or posters or stickers) with the school's name, logo, and mission statement to distribute within the community.
- Collections of samples of students' work. Keep them in three-ring binders organized by grade levels or subjects or mounted for display in public buildings, such as banks or stores, like an art exhibit.

Creating many of these items would be good student projects. Adults don't—and shouldn't—have to do it all.

Informational Brochures of Interest to Parents

All parents, but especially those who are new to the school or community, will appreciate brochures created on topics of interest to them, such as "Who Can Help When Your Child Has a Problem at School" or "Tips on Getting the Most from a Conference with Your Child's Teacher(s)." Often different brochures for grades and/or subjects are useful.

Even though the information may be available in a student handbook, parents will appreciate user-friendly brochures designed especially for them. Other questions parents might like to have answered include the following:

- What is my child expected to learn this year? Do certain standards have to be met? How do these compare with those in other schools? Where might I get a copy of the standards?
- How will my child be evaluated and when? What is the grading or assessment system in this school? When are report cards issued? Is there a special time for parent conferences? What standardized national or state tests will my child take? When are these scheduled? What does my

child have to do to pass a course or move up to the next grade?

- What can I do at home to help my child do better in school? Is there a homework policy in place?

- How will I know if my child is not doing his or her work? Whom should I contact to find out how my child is doing—the classroom teacher or guidance counselor?

- What will you do to help my special child? Is there a tutoring program or summer school for students who need a little extra help? What special education options are available? Are there special programs for gifted or talented students? How do I go about getting my child enrolled in one of these special programs?

- What extracurricular activities are available in this school? How can my child get involved?

- What regular communications can I expect from the school (school or class newsletter, etc.)? What regular or special meetings might I be interested in attending (parent organization, college information night)?

Other Ways to Communicate in Writing

Research has shown that parents who receive frequent and positive messages from teachers tend to become more involved in their children's education than those who don't. At the high school level, communication becomes more difficult because, unlike elementary teachers who have only one group of students all day, high school teachers may have five or even six different classes. Some strategies that help keep parents informed have been developed.

One high school had postcards printed in the school colors reading: "A Message from South Point High School." Both administrators and teachers sent these to parents and students when they had something positive to write, but they didn't wait until students had done something "great." The message might let the parent know that their child had been especially helpful to a new student, had presented a project that showed a lot of time and effort, or hadn't been tardy to class for the whole grading period. Both parents and students felt good when they got such nice mail from someone in the school. Grover's Corners High School parents also were pleased to receive postcards; many said it was the first time they had received such communications from their child's high school teachers.

Letters to parents not only provide information but also involve them in the instructional process when the letters explain classroom/homework procedures and units of study or give assignments that require students to interview parents. Grover's Corners social studies teachers kept parents informed about the new curriculum by writing many letters home to explain what students would be doing, what would be expected of them, and how the teachers would help them meet higher new standards.

Teachers also should consider writing letters to parents at three other times. Teachers might write to introduce a new unit of study, so that parents will know what their children are expected to do. The letter can serve as the cover sheet of the unit handout packet, with space at the bottom for a parent signature and comments or questions. Teachers also can write to let parents know how children have done. Here the note might be written on the test paper or project and sent home with the students for parent signatures. Third, teachers can write to tell parents something positive about the child's progress or participation. A small note can have a big impact—especially since many parents have come to expect to hear from teachers only when something is wrong.

Many parents will appreciate regularly published newsletters (free of jargon) with interesting and informative articles about what different teachers are doing. To ensure that they get to the homes, it is better for the school to get a bulk-mail permit than to send them home with students. Different teachers or classes (with samples of student work) can be featured, or some teachers may want to send their own class newsletters. Although high school teachers probably will not want to do one issue per week, as a fourth-grade teacher we know has done for years, they may find monthly issues are possible—and students can do most of the work. What better way for students to review and reinforce what they learn than to summarize it in an article for their parents to read?

Some schools and/or parent organizations have created e-mail lists or list-serves connecting parents and students to teachers and administrators. Newsletters and other school information can be sent as e-mail rather than "snail mail" to those who have computer access. Perhaps like one airline's frequent-flier program, the school can ask parents if they'd like to sign up to receive school information electronically. Teachers can communicate directly with parents who have e-mail addresses when they have general information to share or something personal about one student. Also, as mentioned earlier, in some communities anyone who wants to can sign up and participate in electronic discussions about school issues.

Sharing Student Work
with Board Members and Others

A strategy used by a high school English department chair to convince school board members not to increase the teaching load of English teachers can be adapted to "educate" parents and community members. The department chair brought in copies of students' writing and asked board members to read and respond to them as if they were teachers. After they saw how long it took to do one paper, they realized how much more time it would take English teachers to deal with the papers of a whole class and did not vote to add an additional class to teachers' workload. By providing diverse samples of student work to parents and others, teachers can show what students are learning. If they also give parents samples of questions from standardized tests, parents will see why test scores don't tell the whole story about student achievement.

Student work also can be exhibited in various places in the community, such as bank lobbies, libraries, and municipal offices. Including student writing in school newsletters can make them more interesting to read. These efforts have a double benefit: They inform adults at the same time they build students' self-esteem.

Engaging Stakeholders in
Discussions about Public Education

Public education has become a topic of national concern. Frightening articles about the problems of schools appear daily in newspapers and popular magazines. How are educators to know what citizens in their own communities think? Public discussions about the purposes of education, the role of the schools, what students should know and be able to do upon graduation from high school are—or should be—all topics of interest to everyone. Stakeholders will learn at the same time they share their perspectives—and they may even be able to suggest creative ways to address the needs of young people educators didn't think of. Many communities already have held such public forums.

PTA/Phi Delta Kappa Sponsor Community Forums

The PTA and Phi Delta Kappa (a professional educational organization) organized thirty forums (the first ones in 1995-96) to build support for improving education in a number of cities. John Jennings, the director of the Center on Education Policy, said the purpose of the forums was to have a frank and open discussion about schools. Forums combined small-group discussions with short general sessions to give basic information about the topics and to summarize what was discussed in small groups. Each forum was divided into three parts: (1) What is the purpose of the public schools? Why were they created? Are those reasons still valid today? (2) What are the public schools doing well? What are they not doing so well? (3) What can we do to improve the public schools?

People who attended the forums welcomed the opportunity to discuss their concerns and ideas with others. Jennings points out that when both supporters and critics of public schools were present, the forums were most successful. He suggests that it is important that most participants be non-educators. People who have no links to the schools or are critical of them will be reluctant to attend meetings dominated by educators and strong school supporters. Yet, he says, "It is precisely these people . . . who need to be part of the . . . discussion because their support (or opposition) to the schools will ultimately determine the fate of the public schools."[17]

Creating a Compact for Learning, Anytown, USA

President Bill Clinton challenged Americans in a 1997 speech to develop written compacts that would help every child learn to high standards. A compact, according to U. S. Secretary of Education Richard W. Riley, is "(1) a commitment to sharing responsibility for student learning and (2) an action plan for a family-school-community partnership designed to help children in school get a high-quality education."[18] To help people establish such compacts, the Department of Education has published a handbook with information, strategies, checklists, and, most helpful, examples of compacts developed at Jackson Preparatory Magnet School in St. Paul, Minnesota, and at Roosevelt High School in Dallas, Texas (the school profiled in Chapter 8). These compacts, which are signed by the student, staff member, and parent, clarify the commitment and responsibilities each pledges to uphold.[19]

Suggestions for Initiating Discussion

Instead of just talking "at" parents when they attend a meeting at school, educators can engage them in conversations that will help them see the need for some aspects of school reform or, put another way, that everything was not golden in the "good old days." (This strategy also may help teachers who question the need for change to rethink their perspectives.)

Parents in small groups should take a few minutes to remember their own school days and choose two incidents or experiences to share: one very positive, the other very negative. Then, as they share stories, a facilitator lists characteristics of these experiences on a two-column chart. For example, "made to feel like a dummy" might come from a negative experience while "felt proud to do the project because it was my own idea" might come from a positive one. The details on these lists (which can be combined to make a large-group list) then can serve as the basis for a discussion about which school practices are likely to foster student engagement and achievement and which ones are probably working against that desired end.

Questions suggested in the Education Commission of the States booklet, "Let's Talk about Education Improvement" as a focus for a group discussion about the best and worst school experiences include the following:

- What, if anything, do the best and worst experiences shared have in common?
- What do these memories suggest about the influence of particular experiences on people's perceptions of school and themselves as learners?
- What does this activity suggest about the way or ways school should be organized to maximize learning for all students?[20]

"Why Change?" is another activity suggested by the commission to help participants think about the ways the world has changed and what these changes might suggest schools need to do. (Once again, these responses can be discussed first in small groups and then shared with the large group.)

First, participants should be asked, "How are specific areas of your lives (such as your workplace, the kitchen, leisure time, etc.) different today than they were ten, twenty, or thirty years ago?" Then the group should discuss what these changes in people's lives tell about the need for changes in schools, how schools have changed in response to the current situation, and how they might change in response to changes in the future.[21]

Another question for discussion is "What should every tenth grader know?" This activity suggests the limitations of the curriculum as a set of facts and formulas students should learn in a particular subject. Because there is an ever-increasing base of knowledge, education today needs to emphasize the understanding and application of concepts and the development of essential skills rather than specific facts to be memorized.

In groups of four, participants determine the ten most important facts every tenth-grade student should know upon completing biology (or any other grade/subject). The groups should have ten minutes to complete the task and then be asked: "How did your group go about generating its list? What, if any, problems did the assignment present? How did you deal with these difficulties? Would you have been able to complete the task to your satisfaction if you have been given more time?" If any group has a hard time compiling a list of "facts" for a given curriculum, they should discuss this question: What does this activity illustrate about the shortcomings of a curriculum based on facts vs. one that focuses on essential ideas, skills, and the ability to gather and use information?[22]

The Importance of
Identifying and Involving "Opinion Leaders"

Authors Marjorie Ledell and Arleen Arnsparger believe that successful school change efforts require many groups to support the changes. These groups develop opinions based on information from newspapers, radio, and television as well as through listening to what a community's "opinion leaders" say. These leaders may or may not have children in the schools. Thus it is important to identify these leaders and make special efforts to keep them informed and to listen to their views on issues; since they usually have more information than others do, people often let them frame the topics for discussion and action.

The "opinion leaders," might be presidents of civic organizations or less-visible board members or political campaign workers. Some characteristics Ledell and Arnsparger suggest for identifying them include the following: (1) They are interested in important issues, including education. (2) They are well informed about the issues. (3) They are avid consumers of information in almost any form— newspapers, magazines, books, television, radio. (4) They are quick to try out new ideas and, if the benefit is apparent, to accept and recommend the ideas to others. (5) They are good organizers who can get other people to take action. (6) They read publications concerning their special areas.[23] The forums discussed earlier and other activities suggested in this chapter would be good ways to involve opinion leaders.

Creating and Fostering
Opportunities for Everyone to Learn

Throughout this book we have emphasized the importance of thinking of parents as learners. There are many ways to involve parents and community members in learning.

Involving Parents in Learning about New Practices

Parents favor classroom practices and teaching methods that they think will help their children develop the skills and knowledge needed to succeed in school and prepare them for the future. They oppose those that seem to them to hinder learning. So if educators can help parents see how an unfamiliar practice will help students learn, they will be more likely to support it.

Just as students must be active participants if they are to learn, parents must also be actively involved and engaged. They are unlikely to learn new ways of thinking about teaching and learning if their knowledge is limited to what they read in newsletters and other written communications from the school. And if these written communications are riddled with jargon, they are likely to be frustrated or further confused rather than informed. Parents can be given opportunities to learn about new practices in several ways.

First, educators may be able to transform traditional meetings with parents into opportunities for learning. At a PTA or booster club meeting, for example, organizers might use practices similar to those being used with students in the classroom, such as small-group discussions or informal writing, to conduct the business at hand. After parents have experienced one of these practices, the leaders can explain how that practice is used in the classroom to help students learn English, history, or biology. Parents also might gain new knowledge from routine conferences with teachers if the traditional format were modified to include some general discussion about the process of learning in relation to individual children. These conferences should be two-way conversations, however. Too often, parents receive information from teachers; they are not equal and active participants in an interactive exchange of views and concerns. The profile about the UCLA Parent Education Program in Chapter 8 is one example of how parents can learn about new practices. The following snapshots describe others.

Involving Parents in Learning with Teachers

As Chapter 8 showed, parents can learn along with teachers. As high schools have begun restructuring efforts, they have recognized the need to provide teachers with professional development to learn about recent research and how to change their teaching to reflect these findings. Of course, most parents would not be free to attend teacher workshops held on inservice days, but if one or two parents participated, they could spread the word to others.

The profile about the Gwinnett County Standards-Setting Project in Chapter 8 is one example of one such program. In a similar vein, Jean Konzal, one of the authors of this book—with a parent in the district who was also a published writer—once conducted a summer writing institute for parents and teachers. In the morning participants concentrated on their own writing, which they shared with each other. In the afternoon participants discussed the implications of what they were learning about the writing process for teachers' classroom practice. These parents—many of whom would later act as volunteers—and teachers easily developed a trusting relationship as together they planned changes in the way writing would be taught in the coming school year.

Involving Parents in Learning with Their Children

High schools can easily adapt the idea of "Family Math" programs found in many elementary and middle schools. Family Math brings parents and children together for after-school activities focused on math learning. The program goal is to encourage children who don't usually consider math-related careers—girls and members of minority groups—to do so. Parents who learn with their children can encourage them to consider math in a more positive light and also find out how math is taught today.

In a few instances high schools have opened the doors and invited parents in. For example, in Mendecino (California) High School, teacher Ed Murrell offered evening algebra meetings for parents and students as a response to parents coming to him with questions. The plan for the first evening meetings was to address questions about the math program; later sessions evolved to include algebra activities that students and their parents did together. While this program is no longer offered at this school, another high school offers a different version of "Family Math." Martin Luther King High School in Detroit sponsors a yearly one-night program for high school students and their parents. Over 600 family members—parents, grandparents, younger siblings, and high school students—turn out to participate in math activities together. It is not unusual to find classrooms with age ranges of three to seventy. The existence of programs like these challenges two myths: (1) that high school parents aren't interested in participating in their children's education and (2) that high school students don't want their parents around.[24]

More Meaningful Parent Conferences

Another common elementary school approach to make parent conferences more meaningful has been tried in a few high schools. In one school students regularly collect samples of their work in portfolios. Then, after five weeks of school, students review their work and write a reflection on what they have learned since the beginning of school. During the week of parent conferences, they do the same thing in letters to their parents. When parents come in, they already have an idea of what to look for in their children's portfolios and questions to ask the teacher. Students, too, assume more responsibility by being present to explain their work. This three-way conference with its focus on actual student work fosters better communication and cooperation among all participants than is true in the routine one-way conference where the parent hears only the teacher's opinion about a student's progress (or lack thereof).

Even if schools continue with the typical teacher-led conferences, it is important for them to listen to parents. When there is a disagreement between teacher and parent, teachers might ask themselves, "Do I want to be right, or do I want to resolve this problem?" Teachers are responsible for keeping parent conferences from degenerating into power struggles that do nothing to help students improve.

Parents Respond to Their Children's Writing

Deborah Jumpp, an English teacher in a Philadelphia high school, wanted to break down the commonly held assumption that inner-city parents "just don't care." She knew they did and wanted to find a way to give them an opportunity to demonstrate it. As part of a larger study about the use of portfolio assessment, she invited the parents of students in one of her English classes to be partners with her in researching the question "How can parents use portfolios?" Twenty-six of the parents—representing more than half of the students in the class—volunteered to participate. Students chose papers they had written to share with their parents. Parents read and discussed these papers with their children and then either wrote (or dictated while their children recorded) their responses. Jumpp found that some responses focused on grammatical concerns ("Daryl needs help with his grammar. He writes like he's talking to his friend on the corner.") Others were encouraging ("I liked the content of the essay. If someone knew nothing about Malcolm X, her essay would give them an informative, condensed version of his life."), and some were personal messages ("You have to be part of the solution not the problem. Be more open and think positive.").

Both parents and students enjoyed the experience. Students said: "My mom surprised me by her getting into my schoolwork. I should probably try to get her into more of my schoolwork" and "We both should do this more often even if she has to write and I respond to what she say." Parents said, "I had to meet the teacher that did this. I kind of like this" and "Thank you for allowing me to participate in Warren's education."[25]

This approach may be good for other teachers to adapt because it enables parents to be involved without having to go to school. Even working parents or those without transportation can participate.

Parents and Students Doing Homework Together

An innovative project called TIPS (Teachers Involve Parents in Schoolwork) Interactive Homework process, originally designed for the elementary grades, was extended to middle schools—and may be something high schools could try. Researchers at Johns Hopkins University and teachers in Maryland, Virginia, and Washington, D.C., developed homework assignments that require students to talk to someone at home about something they are learning in school. For example, students might interview a family member or ask for his or her reactions. Family members are not expected to "teach" the children. All TIPS activities include a section for the family member's response to the activity and comments or questions for the teacher. The TIPS process "is designed to keep all families aware of what their children are learning in school, including parents who work outside the home, have little formal education, speak languages other than English, [or] have many children at home."[26]

Results of one study of the project (focusing on writing) show that almost all parents thought that TIPS helped them understand what their children were learning and about 90 percent wanted the program to continue. More than half of the students reported that they liked the TIPS activities better than their usual homework assignments. Six of the eight teachers said they would continue the project even without any assistance or support from researchers. The researchers also report that students' achievement and attitudes improved when they did TIPS activities at home. Yet they also note that it will take more than homework to help students meet their goals for learning and success.[27]

This type of project could also work at the high school level, especially at the eleventh- and twelfth-grade levels when students are beginning to think about their futures in the workplace and college. Both parents and teens may be grateful to have something noncontentious to discuss with each other.

Involving Parents through Their Children

Schools and even classroom teachers alone can do a great deal to help parents understand and support innovative practices by making sure that students understand what teachers are doing. Most parents get their information about school from their own children, but as noted earlier children can be unreliable informants. Teachers can increase the chances that parents will get "good" information by making sure students understand the purpose of what they are learning and the methods teachers are using. If, for example, teachers explain why they have chosen to ask students to discuss a book in small groups or why it is not important for them to worry about spelling errors on the rough draft of a writing assignment, then students will be better able to explain these practices to their parents.

The following snapshot describes how one high school involved students—and through them, their parents—in their decision to change their schedule to a block schedule—ninety-minute classes instead of typical forty minute classes.

Under the direction of principal Joe Buzanowski, Iroquois High School in northwestern Pennsylvania undertook a year-long study of scheduling and possible changes. High schools nationwide were switching to block schedules—some without much support from teachers, parents, or students. In fact, a neighboring high school introduced block scheduling only to quickly rescind it because of a parental uprising. Before making any changes, Iroquois High School decided to go slowly and to involve every teacher, as well as students and parents, in the process.

Teams of teachers and students visited a number of schools where block scheduling was in place. They met with staff and students at these schools to gain an understanding of what worked well and what didn't. They used this information to craft a plan that they thought would work well for them. The students who were involved were able to explain the new schedule and what went into planning it to other students and, most important, to their parents. In addition, parents were invited to learn about the new schedule at morning coffee klatches as well as evening meetings. The principal and the teachers knew that it was important that parents get the students' views, so at these meetings students presented their perspectives about the proposed schedule. The result was that the new block schedule was introduced to the high school with support from everyone.[28]

Parents as Resources and Teachers

Parents are important resources for schools. They know their communities and their children well. When new teachers arrive at the school, parents may be the best ones to orient them to the community—its history, places of interest, and values. This is especially important when the new teachers represent a culture different from the cultures of the students.

In her book *Kwanzaa and Me,* Vivian Gussin Paley describes how she asked parents of African American children in her primarily white kindergarten classes to help her understand what they thought about racism and schools. She also invited parents from different backgrounds to come into her class to tell stories about their childhood.[29] While this is an example from a kindergarten class, parent stories most likely could fit into many high school social studies and English class studies.

Many parents have knowledge, skills, and abilities from which teachers and students can benefit. Some could be invited to offer professional development for teachers, as did the parent mentioned earlier, who used his experience as a published writer to cofacilitate the workshop on writing.

Mentor parents, trained at the Stockton, California, school district's parent resource center, spent 5,000 hours helping school staff improve family-school communication and parent involvement in their children's learning. Among other activities, mentor parents conducted four workshops on obstacles to parent involvement with schools and on teacher bias, which may result from cultural or language differences among teachers and parents.[30]

Parents are more likely to listen to other parents than to educators—even in school communities that are working to tear down the boundaries between parents and teachers. An important question to ask then is, "How can parents who are involved in the school help other parents to understand what goes on in the school and suggest ways they might be involved?"

The Right Question Project, based on the idea that "you can't get what you want unless you know what to ask for," empowers parents by teaching them the "right" questions to ask to find out how well the school is meeting their children's needs. If the school is not meeting those needs, they learn what they can do about it.

Other questions include the following: What is my child learning? What does my child need to learn? Is the teacher teaching what my child needs to learn? Is my child learning what he or she needs to learn? If not, what can I do? If so, what else can I do?[31]

In addition to finding out how to make things better for their own children, these parents are also shown how they can conduct workshops for other mothers and fathers. Educator Deborah Cohen describes a two-and-a-day session in Paterson, New Jersey:

> [P]roject trainers helped about twenty parents in this primarily low-income minority community come up with questions ranging from who sets school standards to what an A means on a report card. The trainers then put parents through the paces of stimulating mock sessions for their peers, who offered feedback and constructive criticism.
>
> "Yesterday, you wouldn't have caught me up here. My hands were cold and clammy—I was so nervous," says Joanne Vaccaro, one of the participants. "But now I think I would be able to do it with a smaller group."[32]

The Right Question Project, which reaches parents through other organizations and is funded in different ways, can be found in other communities. Consultant Donna Muncey, who evaluated the project, believes that the "approach is sound, works well with disparate groups, and properly keeps the focus of the discussion on guiding parents to their own solutions." While she worries that parents who get excited about conducting workshops may not get many participants, she notes that "one study in rural Massachusetts found that thirteen parents held workshops for 256 parents within eight months of being trained."[33]

Reading Controversial Books Together

This snapshot is an example of action research in an elementary school that could be adapted by high schools. Here parents and teachers work together to resolve—or, in some cases, to prevent—a problem in schools.

Controversy is no stranger to high schools. Researcher William Boyd suggests that schools operate within a "zone of tolerance" when it comes to making decisions about controversial matters. Because these zones are bounded by the perceived norms and values of the community, schools are free to make changes as long as they do not step beyond these boundaries. Because going beyond the "zone of tolerance" is likely to generate opposition and conflict, teachers and administrators are cautious about moving beyond these lines, especially if they've been burned before by parental resistance to school decisions.[34]

The idea of teacher and parents together reading controversial books in a small inner-city elementary school began as a result of teachers' concerns about possible parental resistance. Teachers were reluctant to assign sixth-grade students the controversial award-winning book *The Giver* by Lois Lowry because it dealt with issues of sexuality and genocide. In response to this concern, university researchers Dennis J. Sumara and Brent Davis suggested that teachers come together with parents to read and discuss the book. And so, most of the school's teachers and eleven parents did just that. The results were surprising. Parents did not find the book objectionable. As one parent said: "That stuff was pretty tame . . . and besides, these are things that the kids are thinking about anyway. There's no sense pretending that they can be protected from this information."[35]

Thanks to their shared reading and discussion, these parents and educators came to respect each other's views and perspectives. Rather than assuming they knew the parents' "zones of tolerance," the teachers in this group found out about them firsthand—and may have prevented parent opposition by inviting them to participate in choosing children's reading books. This is another example from lower grades that high schools might consider adopting. Thanks to television talk-show host Oprah Winfrey, more adults are reading and joining reading groups. Parents of high school students might welcome an opportunity to read and discuss some interesting books at the same time they share in deciding what their children might read in school.

Many parents are too busy with their work and family commitments to fully participate in action research. There are other less time-consuming ways to involve them, such as simply inviting them to give their opinions about the issue. As one parent said: "If they were to come to me and ask me my opinion, as you did, I would be very willing to do that. I would be very willing to give it. But because of time constraints and my activities surrounding my son outside of school, I'm not sure how much more I could do."

Educators might consider adopting the focus group model that business and industry depend on for consumer feedback. When changes, such as the introduction of an interdisciplinary course, are contemplated, educators could bring together a representative group of parents to explore the concept. Through their discussions, parents might begin to understand the potential benefits of practices that are unfamiliar to them, and educators could learn what concerns parents have about the practice.

One of the most important implications of our studies is that educators need to talk to parents to find out what they actually think and what they misunderstand or need to know. Results from survey data may be misleading or incomplete. Just knowing that parents oppose a particular practice or program, for instance, isn't very helpful because there are many reasons a parent might be critical. By listening carefully, it may be possible to find, almost hidden within critical comments, the key to resolving the conflict. If surveys are used to collect data, educators also should consider gathering some more in-depth personal responses by interviewing some participants in their homes. High school students could gain some valuable hands-on experience and relevant learning by helping educators in this regard. Phone interviews will provide more information than printed forms, but parents are likely to be most comfortable and

Assess Your School's PPPQ*
(Parent Perspectives and Participation Quotient)[36]

Directions: Circle at least one response for each item. If, in some cases, more than one response describes your school, circle as many as apply.

1. Most of our written communications, such as informational letters or school newsletters, could best be described as
   a. jargon-free.
   b. "jargon-lite."
   c. jargon-infested.
2. When we begin discussing the possibility of starting a new program or changing a practice, we usually
   a. make sure parents and community members are included in the planning discussions from the start.
   b. make sure we inform everyone before the change actually takes place.
   c. hold informational meetings and/or issue news releases when the change is around the corner or underway.
3. We get information on parents' perspectives about effective classroom practice primarily from
   a. parents who respond to surveys that we may follow up with some in-depth interviews and/or focus groups with parents who represent the full range of political perspectives and socioeconomic and ethnic/cultural categories in our community.
   b. those parents who speak at open meetings.
   c. parents who have conferences with teachers or contact the school when they have a question or concern.
4. At meetings to acquaint parents with new practices, we most often
   a. provide opportunities for parents to understand and perhaps actually experience new practices for themselves (involving parents as learners).
   b. describe planned changes and encourage discussion in small groups (listening to parents).
   c. explain changes and answer questions (talking at parents).
5. Most of our parents
   a. have visited classes when they are in session and/or served as volunteers, guest speakers, or substitute teachers.
   b. come to school for conferences, open house, or athletic and other school activities but rarely when classes are in session.
   c. never or rarely come to the school at all (except perhaps when there is a problem).
6. Most of our parents probably get most of their information about classroom activities and assignments
   a. from participating in some assignments and regularly seeing samples of their children's work.
   b. from letters and newsletters sent home by individual teachers.
   c. from informal conversations with their children.

---

* The questionnaire that follows, developed by co-author Anne Wescott Dodd and based on data collected from parent interviews, is intended only as an informal, unscientific way for educators to assess what the local school currently is doing to get information about parents' perspectives and to involve them in making decisions about school practices. In responding, readers may discover other ways they can and probably should involve parents in the life of the school.

7. Teachers in our school would probably say that
   a. parents and students both need to understand the reasons teachers have chosen particular curriculum and teaching methods used so they will know why and how these will help students learn.
   b. students can probably benefit from knowing the importance of their curriculum and why teachers have asked them to do assignments in a certain way, but this knowledge, although nice, isn't necessary.
   c. parents and student should trust teachers to make these decisions and probably don't really care about knowing the reasons for the curriculum and methods chosen as long as the students seem to be doing okay.

8. When a parent is critical of a program or practice, our usual approach is
   a. to explore this parent's criticism in depth so that we can be sure we understand the nature of his/her concerns, look for ways to solve the immediate problem, and use this information to consider what we may need to do for parents more generally.
   b. to explore the nature of this parent's concern so that we can find a way to resolve the immediate problem.
   c. to minimize the conflict as quickly as possible by finding some way to appease the critical parent.

9. A fair estimate of the number of our parents who have had a *personal* and *positive* contact with a teacher or principal during this school year would be
   a. more than half of all parents, including some from every political, socioeconomic, and ethnic/cultural group in our community.
   b. about half of all parents, but most of these could best be described as mainstream middle-class.
   c. fewer than one-half of all parents, and few or none from some segments of our community.

10. Our school regularly provides the following opportunities for parents *to share their ideas and/or concerns* with the school:

[List activities, such as open discussion at parent meetings, conferences, surveys, etc., but don't include any one-way communications, such as a school newsletter, on your list.]

Scoring

For each A response, score 3 points; B = 2 points: C = 1 point. For question number 10 score one point for each item listed. Then add the points together to get your total.

30 +   You are probably building parents' support for change.
16-29   The embers of dissent may be smoldering and could flame up at any time, especially if you have not been involving all segments of the community.
below 15 Keeping parents so distanced from school is likely to become very problematic—if you aren't facing an outright conflict right now.

open about sharing their views if they can do so on their own turf, as was the case with Roosevelt High School. This point may be especially important with regard to those parents whose past involvement with the school usually has been the result of their children's school problems.

Involving More People in Making Decisions

Seymour Sarason argues that parents should be involved in school decision making because they—and their children—are directly affected by the decisions being made. However, he warns against creating legislative bodies where special-interest groups are pitted against each other. Many schools have recently begun to use a site-based management approach, which shifts decision making from a district's central office to school councils comprised of teachers, parents, administrators—and, in some instances, students. A few districts, most notably schools in Chicago, created councils where parents have the majority of votes and the power to hire and fire the principal. Some attempts at site-based management have not proven to be successful because they have just added one more layer to a cumbersome bureaucracy or because principals have maintained control over the councils. In the places where this approach has worked, perhaps it is because researcher Mary Henry's advice was followed: School councils operated within the context of a school climate of caring and responsive relationships.

Kentucky Education Reform Act

Under the Kentucky Education Reform Act, most schools must now have a school council made up of the principal, three teachers, and two parents. The council is charged with making decisions to improve student learning, such as determining the curriculum, assigning students to classes, and deciding how time and space will be used. Schools also may have other committees that work on specific topics, such as the school budget, and report to the council.

Lynn Townsend, a mother who went to the open house at Laurel High School in London, Kentucky, to see how she could get her daughter into a Latin class she needed, ended up joining the school's committee on restructuring. She now thinks all parents should have the opportunity she has had: "This type of involvement makes you understand what ownership really means." Principal Roger Marcum agrees and works to get parents more involved than baking cookies or raising money. He gives an example of the value of parents' perspective: "When parents participate in interviews for school personnel, they ask, 'Is this the type of person I want my child to spend time with every day? Would my child enjoy having this person as a teacher?'" Marcum believes that "the quality of parent involvement at Laurel High School is high because parents' viewpoints are valued and their contributions are meaningful."[37]

Parent Participation in Illinois

In the large Carpentersville, Illinois, school district northwest of Chicago, parents have served on teams that selected textbooks, created new courses and report cards, considered dress codes, changed the form of parent conferences, redesigned student orientation programs, and developed technology plans. According to parent June Cavarretta, "More than 400 parent volunteers in my district have been trained to participate in . . . children's education through shared decision making." The district's school improvement model involves stakeholders with a variety of roles working together to create shared visions at each school. Using this model, the schools already have accomplished major reforms, such as the adoption of block scheduling at the high school.

This shift from educators working alone to sharing the work with others didn't happen all at once. Cavarretta recalls an early planning meeting activity for sharing school successes in which "[t]eachers enthusiastically participated while most parents sat in silence. . . . Finally, in the midst of all the praise, one brave parent said, 'My child comes home from school and cries.'" First there was silence and then others shared similar accounts. Cavarretta now sees that "as a breakthrough moment when highly disparate individuals moved an inch towards listening to one another."[38] The work has been hard, but she says, "I cannot think of another volunteer experience . . . that has been as meaningful as my participation in school improvement. My work counts. My voice is heard. I've made a difference."[39]

Giving Parents a Voice in Assessing Teachers (and Schools)

Rochester, New York, is among the districts that are trying to figure out how to give parents a voice in evaluating their children's teachers. Although everyone agrees that parents can offer useful insights, there is some disagreement about the ability of noneducators to assess teaching abilities. Some parents, however, argue that they know who are the good teachers—and the bad ones—in their schools and should have a voice in evaluating them. When researcher and author Gloria Ladson-Billings began her study of successful teachers of African American children, she recognized the value of parents' knowledge and asked parents in the community as well as educators to nominate outstanding teachers. She chose to study those teachers about whom teachers and parents agreed.[40]

One way to avoid an impasse on such sensitive issues with teachers' unions is for districts to focus survey questions on communications with the home and on school climate, not on individual teachers. And even if survey results are not used in the formal teacher-evaluation process, the information gathered will be helpful in developing closer ties with parents and creating a more welcoming atmosphere in the school for both parents and students.

Whole-School Reform

The best kind of reform is, of course, not a collection of random innovations but a thoughtful plan to change a whole school—and to do so not merely by changing programs and structures but also by redefining roles and relationships. Over the past fifteen years, many whole-school reform programs have been developed. These approaches are built on the assumption that tinkering with one part of the school's program or another will never achieve the desired changes in achievement for all children. Rather, advocates argue, the entire school—its structure, curriculum, teaching methods, governance, parental involvement—needs to be changed.

One well-known example of this approach is James Comer's School Development Program, which makes parental involvement central in schools from kindergarten through grade 12. Comer established the School Development Program in 1968 in two elementary schools in New Haven. These schools served poor African American children poorly. Comer found that much of what was going on in these schools kept teachers and parents from working together to improve children's achievement. He found that a major factor contributing to the problem was the troubled relationships between and among parents, teachers, administrators, and students. To change this, he called for parents to be an integral part of the school improvement process and for relationship building to be a major part of what schools do. The changes educators made in the program schools have led to higher student achievement and better relationships all around. Even though much of the work has been done in elementary schools, we believe, once again, that any high school can learn from it.[41]

The Responsive Schools Project, begun in 1994, is another example of a project that involves parents, community members, teachers, and administrators in whole-school reform efforts. Working in grades kindergarten through 12, schools in Chicago, Illinois; Flambeau and Milwaukee, Wisconsin; Harts, West Virginia; Las Cruces, New Mexico; Boston, Massachusetts; and Cleveland, Ohio, consultants from the Institute for Responsive Education led these schools through a process of community engagement and school improvement. They assisted in creating partnership teams, conducted communitywide focus groups, identified student competencies, set priorities for improvement, planned for improvement, and implemented and assessed the improvement plan.[42]

The Alliance Schools Initiative, a partnership between the Texas Interfaith Education Fund and the Texas Education Agency, works to engage parents and the community in reforming schools. The profile of Roosevelt High School in Dallas in Chapter 8, is one example of how Alliance schools operate. Alliance schools help parents learn about new practices in a variety of ways. They include parents in the same workshops as teachers. Ernesto Cortes, Jr., the Southwest regional director of the Industrial Areas Foundation, a network of grass-roots organizations working to restructure local schools, said: "[W]hen parents become full partners with teachers, they become as interested in innovative educational theories as the educational experts themselves. In his several visits to Alliance Schools, Harvard University professor Howard Gardner discovered that Spanish-speaking parents from low-income communities were asking the same questions about learning and assessment methods as were his education researchers."[43]

Finally, author and high school reform advocate Ted Sizer's Coalition of Essential Schools began as a focused approach for changing high schools. It includes parents as a component—but in a less prominent way than does Comer's approach—in a restructuring plan for high schools. A national network of public and private schools has been formed, and many high schools have used Coalition principles as the basis for making changes.[44]

Because there are so many different whole-school projects and networks, it is easy for reform-minded educators, parents, and community members to find out what others have done to change the old model of school. And reading about others' work may inspire something wonderful yet to be tried. The resource list in Appendix A and the notes for this chapter provide information for contacting these groups and others.

What Can Local Schools Do?

We hope that among the many ideas we have highlighted in this chapter, some have given readers—whether educators or parents—an incentive to do more in local high schools. We do not believe that parent involvement at the high school level is an "impossible dream." Given the right leadership, commitment, and creativity, high schools can be just as successful as elementary schools and middle schools in involving parents—although the participation may come in different forms. We encourage readers to share their ideas with people in other schools and communities. There is much we can all learn from one another.

From Parent Involvement to Community Building: A Call to Action

> Meaningful public engagement is a long-term process requiring a patient investment of sustained effort. Rather than being just one part of a strategy to improve public education, public engagement should be at the center of the effort. It is not a question of bridging the gap between "leaders" and the public: It is a matter of making the public the leaders in education reform.
>
> —Ernesto Cortes, Jr.

> There is no better place to create a community of caring than in our schools—the heart of our future.
>
> —Patricia Gándara

Both educators and teachers want children to succeed. Both want society tomorrow to be better than it is today. Because the future certainly will be characterized by constant change, a Model T education will not serve children. High schools must improve because the schools Americans remember will not adequately prepare children to live and work in an uncertain future. As educational researcher Carl Glickman once said, "Things that don't change are dead things."[1] Who wants to pay for "dead" schools? Or public schools that educate only *some* children?

To reduce the widening gap between the haves and the have-nots in the United States, some argue that only public schools are in a position to offer equal opportunities for everyone. In fact, educational scholar Linda Darling-Hammond warns, "If we cannot build such schools at this moment in history, I believe that a deeply stratified society—one divided by access to knowledge and the opportunity to learn—could undo our chances for democratic life and government."[2]

No one has *the* answer for improving high schools. What works in one community may not be what is needed in another. In each town or city neighborhood, people will have to come together to create a common vision of how high school should be and then to figure out how to translate that ideal into school programs and classroom practices. This process must include everyone—from all social classes, ethnic backgrounds, and philosophical perspectives.

Schools themselves should become democratic communities because, as researchers Michael Apple and James Beane point out, "The most powerful meaning of democracy is formed not in the glossy political rhetoric, but in the details of our everyday lives."[3] Perhaps the model for such schools should not be a factory but a village. In such schools children can, as John Dewey suggested, practice democratic living as they learn.

If the public high school is to be a truly democratic institution, all stakeholders—not just parents—must participate in the discussion about "good" schools. If there are people who don't respond to an invitation to participate for the purpose of maintaining a democratic ideal, perhaps an appeal to baser motives might motivate them to do so. Even though the schools cannot be blamed for social problems because they only mirror those in the larger society, they can help to solve them. The consequences when Americans fail to nurture and educate all children adequately—high unemployment rates, increased demand for welfare and drug treatment programs, the need to hire more police and build more prisons—affect the lives of all citizens. Educators have no way—and some feel strongly that they have no right—to change children's home environments, but the public can make changes in its schools.

An increasing number of people believe that the current public education system cannot and will not make needed changes. As we pointed out earlier, many people have turned to alternatives in the public high school: An ever-growing number of parents has chosen home schooling, private independent schools, or parochial schools for their children. Furthermore, according to David Mathews, president of the Charles F. Kettering Research Foundation, the current relationship between schools and communities is greatly in need of repair: "[T]here may be so few people supportive of the idea of public schools—so small a community for these inherently community institutions—that school reform may need to be recast as community building. The success of reform efforts, and even the survival of the public system, may rest on an all-out effort to build a new compact between the public and its schools."[4]

What do educators need to do to create more effective and more democratic school communities? How can they invite parents and community members to participate? These questions have no easy answers.

Challenges to Building a Democratic School Community

As explained in Chapter 2, *community* as an idea is both complex and problematic. Creating a true school community will be difficult, and there are few maps to guide the process. Changing the school from a place where only white middle-class students and parents feel truly at home to one that values and fully includes students and parents from diverse ethnic, racial, social, and economic backgrounds will be challenging. In addition to the fact that public high schools tradition-ally have not been such inclusive and caring places, there are other complicating factors.

One obstacle to overcome in this process is likely to be what author Robert Bellah calls "communities of memory." The feeling of longing for the idealized small town people often have, Bellah says, is really "a longing for meaning and coherence."[5] People often talk as if they could turn back the clock and make life as perfect as it was in the past. But these places that people recall may never really have existed. So instead of trying to re-create a past people think they remember, they should focus on the characteristics of the increasingly multicultural and geographically mobile society in which Americans live and turn their attention to creating a more inclusive community for today.

Another obstacle is that people belong to many communities simultaneously, and in today's society individual communities often want to maintain their separate identities. These communities may represent differing, even contradictory values—values that many people will not be willing to give up. The idea of the United States as a melting pot no longer applies; instead the country now is more like a salad bowl. Somehow Americans must figure out a way for these many communities to exist at the same time people join together to create a new shared idea of community in the public schools. As noted earlier, researchers Carol Merz and Gail Furman acknowledge the fact that all people belong to many communities—such as neighborhood, workplace, nation, and world—and suggest that we need to learn to live "with the ambiguity associated with divided affiliations."[6] With no models for guidance, stakeholders of any given school will have to come together to develop their own.

If educators are forced to emphasize efficiency and cost effectiveness and operate with the belief that people can be managed and controlled, efforts to transform high schools in truly positive ways will fail. As Chapters 2 and 3 explained, this perspective on institutions, which has its roots in Frederich Taylor's ideas of scientific management, has led to bureaucratic schools that function too much like factories. Merz and Furman describe this obstacle as a paradox: Schools need to be both more organized and more personal.[7] These conflicting goals will cause schools to operate at cross-purposes unless the idea of school is reconceptualized in new ways. Educational philosopher Jane Roland Martin, for example, argues that because many children need caring and nurturing as much as they do academic knowledge and skills, Americans should think not of school *houses* but school *homes*. Using early childhood education pioneer Maria Montessori's model of the school, (which was used to educate impoverished street children in Rome), Martin explains in *The Schoolhome: Rethinking Schools for Changing Families* how schools can foster the personal and academic development of children by adding the three Cs—caring, concern, and connection— to the teaching of the three Rs.[8]

No matter what model a community adapts or creates to improve its high school, we believe, as did John Dewey, that every school community should serve as a model for students' future lives in society. Because actions always speak louder than words, people need to remember that they are teaching their children as they discuss and debate these tensions, paradoxes, and community members' differing values and perspectives. Children will remember what they learn from this "hidden curriculum" better than history or math. The ultimate paradox is that the process any community uses to decide how to educate its children may itself be the most important part of their education.

Caveats: Other Important Ideas to Keep in Mind

To improve high schools for students, parental involvement is essential. However, just as educators cannot do the job alone, neither can only parents and teachers working together. Public high schools are the public's schools, and to serve any community well, every school should work to involve all stakeholders. Full participation by everyone in the community in school discussions and activities—even by representatives of all the various constituent groups—is unlikely, but voters from all of these groups have the power to decide how much public support and funding any school will get. If people know more about schools and they like what they hear, they will be more likely to vote yes on budgets and bond issues. We believe these points are important to keep in mind.

First, no one should underestimate the power of an invitation and a friendly environment. People like to be included on the guest list even if they can't attend. And, like children who don't get asked to a party, they may become very resentful, even vindictive, when they feel left out or ignored. Lois White, president of the national PTA, noted that for years there has been a "wall between parents and educators. That wall is breaking down, and we've [the parents] been the ones with the hammer."[9]

One study concluded that one of the greatest barriers for parents is the school's attitude toward them. Researchers found that "rude secretaries, unfriendly atmospheres created by principals and teachers, and poorly timed activities discouraged many parents from participating . . . in their children's schools."[10] Researcher Jean M. Norman says, "I don't think schools are malicious . . . but they are negligent." She once walked into a school where duct tape marked the floor in front of the office counter with the message: "Do not cross."[11] It doesn't take a genius to see that parents—indeed, perhaps even the students—would not feel welcomed there! In another school, a table was parked right at the top of the entrance stairs. Although there was no indication of its purpose, parents said, "The principal put that table there to keep us out." On the other hand, a few schools have set aside a room for parents and volunteers (or one for alumni, who often have children in the same school they attended). Here people can gather informally, have a cup of coffee, and chat.

Second, educators should remember that although one-on-one, day-to-day interactions may seem small and insignificant, as chaos theorists remind us, small events can lead to big effects. The secretary answering the phone, the teacher who calls to tell a parent her son's project was superb, the hallway walls hung with student work—these may be what one principal calls "small practices." They have power because they shape the mental models people develop of our schools. Everyone in the school—from the custodian and cafeteria worker to the department head and guidance counselor—should be aware that, as the song goes, "Little things mean a lot."

Third, public relations—something that often has a negative connotation and that most schools do very little with—is an essential first step to the more important process of public engagement. The whole community needs to know the positive things a high school and its students are doing. Although the local media will quickly publicize any problems, spreading the word about "good works" is left to teachers and parents. Educators need to recognize that every contact with a parent or member of the public may be multiplied many times over. If, for example, parents leave a private or public meeting at the school with concerns or complaints, they probably will share them with neighbors, friends, and even the store clerk or barber. Teachers should think of their students as messengers because what most parents know about school comes from their own children. If the students are confused or discouraged, parents get negative messages.

By making public relations a part of their routine, principals and teachers can increase the good news people get about school. Tony Wagner, an expert on school/family relationships suggests, however, that such public relation strategies may just be a beginning. More important and effective for one Vermont school district was inviting the community to join in a conversation about schooling.[12] One of the important lessons learned here was that "[p]ublic engagement begins with listening." Wagner notes that in many communities "there is a pent-up need to share concerns; educators' willingness to hear these issues is the most important first step in improving the image of schools."[13]

There is a difference between *public relations* and *public engagement*, as Deborah Wadsworth, executive director of Public Agenda (public policy research organization), explains, commenting that "public relations is an honorable endeavor," but it differs from public engagement in several ways. The ultimate point of public relations, which most think of as keeping people informed, is "to bring people around to a particular point of view." In contrast, public engagement is a much more complex and collaborative process. It presupposes that individuals and groups will together think through issues and struggle to arrive at solutions.[14]

In an ideal world the public would always be engaged. They would, for example, participate in making decisions, not just hear about them after they have been made. In the real world, however, public engagement seems to evolve. Daniel Yankovich, Public Agenda cofounder, developed a seven-stage model to show how this happens: (1) People develop an awareness of a problem, usually through some action, such as the publication of international comparisons of students' achievement showing that U.S. students did not fare well. (2) An urgent belief that something must be done develops. (3) A search for answers begins. (4) Various obstacles appear that can lead to some serious public resistance. (5) If this stage comes (which it doesn't in all cases), leaders suggest alternatives and help the public to understand them. (6) People appear to accept a change intellectually but are not yet ready to put it in place. Wadsworth cites the need for higher standards as an example, and, as we said earlier, even though some parents said they liked the idea of higher standards, they were resistant when these standards were applied to their own children.) (7) The process ends with behavior change or full acceptance.[15]

Deborah Wadsworth sends a clear message to educators who hope eventually to get to stage 7: "I have attended countless meetings . . . in communities struggling with education reform, and I continue to be amazed by educators' inability to listen to the public's concerns while insisting that only they themselves have the true solution."[16]

Finally, echoing Wadsworth, we believe that no one should ever assume what anyone thinks. Two-way communication is always essential. For example, teachers often think parents don't care, but Linda Moore of the Institute for Educational Leadership says, "Clearly, parents are interested and care about their children's education. . . . Just as clearly, the lack of time in their own lives is a big stumbling block to that involvement." Even so, a majority of parents in one study said they checked almost every day on their children's homework.[17] It is also important to recognize that parent involvement can take many forms. As Jean Norman points out, "Teachers still do not realize that you don't have to see parents for parents to have a meaningful involvement in their children's education."[18]

The tendency to assume that parents don't care may be greater in schools with poor and minority students. In a study that compared two urban schools—one affluent and one working class—researchers found that cultural and social differences, not a lack of parent interest, accounted for less parental involvement in the working-class school. The researchers cautioned that an "emphasis on parental involvement 'may transform cultural *diversity* into cultural *deficiency*'" (italics in the original).[19] It is important to remember that people may have different definitions of *parent involvement*.

Some may assume that black and white parents have different priorities for themselves and their children, but a recent Public Agenda study reports that both groups care more about "high standards than achieving integration." In fact, they have "'strikingly similar visions of what it takes to educate kids.' Parental involvement was a key ingredient in many answers to researchers' questions . . . 91 percent of blacks and 95 percent of whites [consider] mastering . . . [the] basics [reading, writing, and arithmetic] to be absolutely essential." Like the parents we interviewed, 86 percent of the black parents, despite the national debate over Ebonics, also consider it essential that all children learn to speak and write standard English "with proper punctuation and grammar." Surprising to many will be the finding that only 28 percent of black parents "considered standard tests to be culturally biased against blacks" and "[n]early eight black parents in ten wanted results of such tests made public as a way to spur school reforms."[20] Also, as the profile in Chapter 8 showed, a diverse group of parents in Los Angeles (white, African American, Asian, and Latino) had many of the same concerns as those of white parents in a rural New England town.

People's opinions are complex and idiosyncratic; the same words can have different meanings. So, in order to understand what either a school critic or fan is really saying, we educators usually need to hear more. Genuine dialogue may be the best means for dissipating dissension.

Essential Principles

As schools attempt to involve all parents—not just a few of the most powerful and controlling ones—and community members in ongoing and continuous conversations, there will be many challenges. We believe that four principles, which draw on other points made earlier, are essential to keep in mind if the goal of improving the high school is ever to be achieved. Because no map exists to point the way, these principles are also challenges for each individual school community. As members build relationships and make decisions, they will forge their own paths.

Find Ways to Build a Bridge between Educators' Professional Perspective and Parents' More Personal Perspective

Teachers think mostly about what is good and fair for *all* children while parents focus on what is good and fair for their children. Surprisingly, some changes reformers advocate for improving the high school may provide one key for closing this gap. Because some innovative practices make learning more personal for individual students, they actually address parents' concerns that education be "good and fair for my child." But if educators don't include parents as full participants in the community of learners, parents may not know that this is the case. Without an understanding of the new and unfamiliar practice, they will continue to believe that the way they learned is the best way for school to be.

By engaging parents in conversations, by listening to their concerns, and by giving them experience with unfamiliar practices, educators can learn how parents understand and interpret new teaching methods. Parents may begin to realize that practices unlike those that they remember from their own school days might be better for their children. When learning is viewed as a personal and individual process, what is good and fair for all children is also good and fair for their children.

Recognize that Parents and Teachers Are Knowledgeable in Different Ways

Both parents and teachers bring important knowledge to the discussion about "good" schools. A growing number of teachers have an increased and in-depth understanding about the evolving body of knowledge about teaching and learning. Parents, on the other hand, who know their own children, their community, and their culture, realize that some innovations just won't work in their schools. As we explained in Chapter 3, two calls for reform, *teacher-as-professional* and *parent-as-active-participant*, may be viewed as competing and contradictory and thus block any meaningful reform. Carl Glickman from the University of Georgia argues that "professionalism must complete—not compete with—democracy."[21] Just how this can be done isn't clear, but Deborah Wadsworth sees the need to involve "ordinary citizens" in the process:

> A well-established phenomenon in contemporary American life is the growing dependence on experts and professionals to solve our social problems. A striking consequence of this development has been the loss of real dialogue among most citizens about issues that are significant to the vitality of the nation. . . . No challenge can be

greater than reengaging the nation's citizens in the effort to improve the education of all children.[22]

We believe no challenge is more important.

Without a climate that supports ongoing conversations among parents, community members, and educators—a climate that allows people to learn with and from each other—teachers will attempt innovations that, as did many reforms in the past, are doomed to disappear.

Provide Ways for Teachers and Parents to Share Perspectives

People should shift the focus from talking about ways to share *power* to providing opportunities for teachers and parents to share *perspectives.* Most people think of power as a limited commodity—power given to someone means power must be taken away from someone else. But talking about redistributing power makes school change a win-lose situation. Instead, Americans should adopt the idea of perspective sharing, because the sharing of multiple perspectives will foster the development of a community where relationships between parents and educators can be equalized—a community where both parents and educators respect and value each other's views.

Sharing perspectives is an important first step because as researcher Lisa Delpit says, "we all interpret behaviors, information, and situations through our own cultural lenses; these lenses operate involuntarily, below the level of conscious awareness, making it seem that our view is simply 'the way it is.'"[23]

Even hard-held beliefs can change when people really try to understand the perspectives of those with whom they disagree. Lynn Langer Meeks, who resigned her job as an English-language arts coordinator at the Idaho State Department of Education as a result of "conservative Christians . . . [derail]ing many of the . . . reforms" she instituted, wrote an article about this experience. What happened as a result of the writing surprised her.

> It started out to be an angry diatribe against conservative Christians
> and what I considered their narrow-minded, anti-intellectual, anti-

scholarly views. But something happened. As I wrote, I began to understand—in a way that I have never understood before—the basis for the deeply held fears and concerns of conservative Christians. What I began as an "exposé" has turned into an explanation and a plea for tolerance.[24]

Even when there is no easy resolution of conflicting or contradictory points of view, people can learn, as Meeks did, from understanding points of view with which they disagree.

Remember that in the Best High Schools Everyone Learns and Everyone Cares

No one has a magic bullet for making high schools better, and no high school will ever be a perfect place. People need to see high schools as always being in the process of improving; Americans—parents and educators—need to see themselves as always being in the process of learning how to do that.

This collaborative effort and the schools themselves will be more effective if the climate for learning is characterized by genuine caring. Just as the quality of the relationship between students and their teacher can make the difference in whether students learn or not, so too will the relationships adults build with each other impact high schools in positive ways. Failure to do so will perpetuate the status quo. Perhaps in their roles as learners, all members of school communities have as much to learn about relationships as they do about high school reform. In the end, learning is central both as the goal of reform and as a component of the process to reach that goal.

In particular, we believe that it is essential for schools to think of parents as co-learners. Parents often object to changes because the new practices are unfamiliar. They do not see how these innovations will help their children learn what they need to know. Thus we believe that learning—and caring—for everyone is at the heart of every good high school. Parents and educators must agree to disagree about important issues because the high school will always be an arena where societal tensions are played out. We believe that people can find new ways to resolve these tensions through discussion—and sometimes debate—if they use a little humor and share human stories with others they have come to know. By listening to and learning from the views of others, even from those with whom people think they have great differences of opinion, they may be able to find small but important points on which they do agree. From these small common ideas and through continued conversation, they can begin to bridge their differences and to find common patterns within their multiple perspectives.

Because more democratic and effective schools offer the best hope for creating stronger communities and a better world tomorrow, perhaps everyone will come to see that all Americans must cooperate to make schools work for every child. Ultimately what is good and fair for any high school student will depend on doing what is good and fair for all high school students. As John Dewey said, "What the best and wisest parent wants for his own child, that must the community want for all of its children. Any other ideal for our schools is narrow and unlovely; acted upon, it destroys our democracy."[25] Americans should accept no less for any child than they would demand for their own.

What Principals Can Do

Be accessible to parents when they want to talk to you.

Make sure your school is parent friendly.

Ask parents what you can do to make your school more welcoming for them.

Invent many different ways that parents can participate in your school—one way doesn't fit all parents.

Invite a cross-section of parents to be on committees planning new programs.

Conduct focus groups regularly to find out what parents think about the school's programs.

Hold informal coffee klatches with parents.

Meet with parents on their turf—in their homes, at community events, in public buildings other than schools.

Support your teachers when they reach out to parents.

Encourage all teachers to keep parents informed and to welcome their interest and involvement.

What Teachers Can Do

Talk with your students about why you teach the way you do.

If you live in the community, talk with your friends and neighbors about what you do in the classroom.

Think of every interaction you have with parents as an opportunity to listen to and to learn from them.

Invite parents to visit your classroom.

Ask parents to share what they know about their children's learning styles and interests.

Send letters home to parents explaining your curriculum and teaching methods.

Let parents know when a child has done something well.

Keep parents regularly updated on their children's progress in your class.

Let parents know how and when they can contact you.

Invite parents to help you with a class project.

Invite parents to student recitations and presentations.

Plan ways for parents to actively learn about new teaching practices you use (or plan to use) in your classroom.

Ask parents for their opinions about new teaching practices.

Ask parents to help you assess the impact of new teaching practices on their children.

Invite parents to join a parent-teacher study group.

Invite parents to conduct action research projects with you.

What Parents Can Do

Talk to your child about their work and activities at school.

Find out as much as you can about the school and the teachers.

Ask questions when you are confused or uncertain.

Don't hesitate to call someone at the school when you have a concern.

Contact the teacher at the first sign of a potential problem.

Meet your child's teachers in person.

Tell teachers what you appreciate about them.

Write a letter to the principal applauding teachers' efforts.

Visit the school when it is in session, if you can.

Be an active participant in parent-teacher conferences: Ask questions, share your views, and find out what you can do to help at home.

Attend school activities—athletic competitions, art shows, drama productions.

Volunteer, even occasionally and in small ways, maybe as a chaperone for a school event, a guest speaker on career day, or booster club member.

If you are qualified, consider serving as a substitute teacher.

Become active in the parent-teacher organization and encourage others to join.

Serve on school or district committees and maybe even run for election to the school board.

Let elected (school board members, legislators) and appointed officials (the superintendent) know what *you* think.

Increase your knowledge about teaching, learning, and schools by reading books and articles and Web browsing.

Join a study group to learn and share ideas with other parents and teachers.

Appendices

APPENDIX A: RESOURCES

Internet Resources

The following Internet sites provide links to everything anyone ever wanted to know about education and parent involvement—and more.

www.ed.gov
> For e-mail information from the Department of Education, subscribe to EDInfo by sending an e-mail message to: listproc@inet.ed.gov Then write either SUBSCRIBE EDINFO YOURFIRSTNAME YOUR-LASTNAME in the message, or write UNSUBSCRIBE EDINFO. (Please turn off any signature blocks.) Then send it!

www.ed.gov/BASISDB/EROD/direct/SF
> The Education Resource Organization Directory. The directory is intended to help people identify and contact organizations that provide information and assistance on a broad range of education-related topics.

www.ed.gov/free
> This collaboration of more than thirty-five federal agencies makes hundreds of Internet-based education resources easier to access for student and teachers. The U.S. Secretary of Education said it "offers one-stop shopping for a treasure trove of historical documents, scientific experiments, mathematical challenges, famous paintings."

www.accesseric.org:81
> Educational Resources Information Clearinghouse (ERIC) is a federally funded national information system that provides, through its sixteen clearinghouses, a variety of services and products on a broad range of education-related issues. One service is the Ask ERIC e-mail: askeric.org. E-mail questions and ERIC will reply.

www.npin.org

    The National Parent Information Network (NPIN), a project sponsored by two ERIC clearinghouses, provides information to parents and those who work with parents. Includes the Resources for Parents section, the Parents AskERIC question-answering service, and the PARENTING-L electronic discussion list.

www.familyeducation.com

    Family Education Network. This site's mission is to "help parents help their kids learn." In addition to other things, this site offers information about curriculum trends and educational policy.

members.aol.com/pledgenow/appleseed/index.html

    Project Appleseed. The National Campaign for Public School Improvement. This site provides parents and educators information on parental involvement. Resources include the Parental Involvement Checklist, community partnership development, parental involvement provisions of Title I of the Improving America's Schools Act of 1994, extensive parental involvement research, a decentralization primer, parents' frequently asked questions, and more.

Organizations with an
Interest in Parent Involvement

Many of these organizations sponsor parent involvement programs; publish newsletters, magazines, or journals; and offer books for purchase. Some provide support to schools reaching out to parents; others provide support to parents reaching in. Others do both. If you have access, try the Internet sites first (http://).

Academic Development Institute
Center for the School Community/
Family Education Center
121 North Kickapoo Street
Lincoln, IL 62656
217-732-6462
adi@adi.edu
www.adi.org

American Association of School
Administrators
1801 North Moore Street
Arlington, VA 22209-9988
703-528-0700
1-888-782-2272 (to order publications)
www.aasa.org

Annenberg Institute (Office of
Public Engagement)
Brown University
Box 1985
Providence, RI 02912
401-863-7990
www.aisr.brown.edu

Association for Supervision and
Curriculum Development (ASCD)
1703 North Beauregard Street
Alexandria, VA 22311-1714
703-578-9600 or 1-800-933-ASCD
www.ascd.org

Center on School, Family, and Community Partnerships
Johns Hopkins University
3003 North Charles Street, Suite 200
Baltimore, MD 21218
410-516-8800
www.csos.jhu.edu

Education Commission of the States
(ECS)
707 17th Street, Suite 2700
Denver, CO 80202-3427
303-299-3692
www.ecs.org

The Home and School Institute
1500 Massachusetts Avenue, NW
Washington, DC 20005
202-466-3633
www.megaskillshsi.org

Institute for Responsive Education
50 Nightingale Hall
Northeastern University
Boston, MA 02115
617-373-2595
www.resp-ed.org

Interfaith Education Fund
(The Alliance Schools Project)
1106 Clayton Lane
Suite 120 West
Austin, TX 78723
512-459-6551

Mexican American Legal Defense
and Education Fund
Community Education and Public
Policy
634 South Spring Street
Los Angeles, CA 90014
213-629-2512
www.maldef.org

National Association of Secondary
School Principals (NASSP)
1904 Association Drive
Reston, VA 22091
703-860-0200
www.nassp.org

National Black Child Development
Institute
1023 15th Street, NW, Suite 600
Washington, DC 20005
202-387-1281
www.nbcdi.org

The National Coalition for Parent
Involvement in Education
Institute for Educational Leadership
1001 Connecticut Avenue, NW,
Suite 310
Washington, DC 20036
202-822-8405 x 53
www.ncpie.org

National Community Education Association
3929 Old Lee Highway, Suite 91A
Fairfax, VA 22030-2401
703-359-8973
www.ncel.com

National Council of La Raza
1111 19th Street NW, Suite 1000
Washington, DC 20036
202-785-1670
www.nclr.org

National Network of Partnership Schools
3003 North Charles Street, Suite 200
Baltimore, MD 21218
410 516-8800
www.csos.jhu.edu/p2000

The National PTA
330 North Wabash Avenue, Suite 2100
Chicago, IL 60611-3690
312-670-6782
www.pta.org (e-mail: info@pta.org)

National School Boards Association
1680 Duke Street
Alexandria, VA 22314-9900
703-838-6722
www.nsba.org

National Urban League
120 Wall Street, 8th Floor
New York, NY 10005
212-558-5300
www.nul.org

Parents as Teachers National Center
10176 Corporate Square Drive, Suite 230
St. Louis, MO 63132
314-432-4330
www.patnc.org

Phi Delta Kappa
408 N. Union
P.O. Box 789
Bloomington, IN 47402
1-800-766-1156
www.pdkintl.org

Project Appleseed, Inc.
National Campaign Headquarters
7209 Dorset at Midland Boulevard
St. Louis, MO 63130-3017
pledgenow@aol.com
appleseed@k12mail.com
members.aol.com/pledgenow/apple-seed/index.html

Public Agenda Foundation
6 East 39th Street
New York, NY 10016
212-686-6610
www.publicagenda.org

A Sampling of Print Resources on Parent Involvement

Many of the programs mentioned in the text and the organizations listed below publish how-to guides and materials for schools and parents. These are just a sampling of those available.

Arnsparger, Arleen, et al. *Building Community Support for Schools: A Practical Guide to Strategic Communication*. Denver: Education Commission of the States, 1997. Guide for establishing a strategic school or school district communication plan with a team comprised of representatives from key constituent groups. Includes specific suggestions for selecting team members, conducting meetings, and deciding what is important in an effective plan.

Center for the School Community. *Alliance for Achievement Planning Guide* and videotapes. Kickapoo, IL: Center for the School Community. The planning guide includes nineteen meeting agendas for a "school community council" consisting of the principal and representative teachers and parents. The guide and videotapes also feature dozens of community-building activities.

Center for the School Community. *The School Community Journal*. Kickapoo, IL: Author. This journal publishes material from and for educators, scholars, teachers, school board members, parents, and others interested in the school as a community.

Council for Basic Education. *How Does Your School Measure Up?* Washington, DC: Author, 1996. Information on standards.

de Kanter, Adriana, et al. *A Compact for Learning: An Action Handbook for Family-School-Community Partnerships*. Washington, DC: U.S. Department of Education, 1997. Accompanies a kit with samples and reproducible pages— everything a community needs to know to develop its own compact.

Education Commission of the States (ECS). *Let's Talk about Education Improvement*. Denver: Author, 1996. Guide for educators, policymakers, and community members for using conversations to build community partnerships. Includes resource list.

Education Commission of the States/CPB Math and Science Project. *What Communities Should Know and Be Able to Do about Education*. Denver: Author, 1993. Suggestions for building community support, worksheets, and examples of programs already in place in several communities.

Epstein, Joyce L., et al. *School, Family, and Community Partnerships: Your Handbook for Action.* Thousand Oaks, CA: Corwin Press, 1997. Comprehensive framework for building school, family, and community partnerships. Includes how to form an action team, how to plan and conduct workshops, as well as sample agendas and planning and evaluation forms.

Institute for Responsive Education. *Building a Learning Community.* Boston: Author, 1996. A set of four guidebooks that includes suggestions for changing schools; rethinking teaching, curriculum, assessment, and school structures; creating family driven school-linked services; and reaching out to families.

Ledell, Marjorie, and Arnparger, Arleen. *How to Deal with Community Criticism of School Change.* Alexandria, VA: Association for Supervision and Curriculum Development and the Education Commission of the States, 1993. Good suggestions for preventing, minimizing, and responding to criticism. Includes a very useful list of "Educational Terms That Can Be Misinterpreted."

Moles, Oliver, ed. *Reaching All Families: Creating Family-Friendly Schools.* Washington, DC: U.S. Department of Education, 1996. Specific suggestions for policies and programs, including some that deal with working with special groups, such as parents with limited English skills and fathers. Lists many resources available from the U.S. Department of Education.

Partnership for Family Involvement in Education. *Employers, Families, and Education.* Washington, DC: U.S. Department of Education, 1997. Suggestions for and examples of business working to encourage parent involvement with schools. Includes a good resource list.

Pritchard, Ivor. *Judging Standards in Standard-Based Reform.* Washington, DC: Council for Basic Education, 1996. More on standards.

The Regional Laboratory. *Creating New Visions for Schools: Activities for Educators, Parents, and Community Members.* Andover, MA: The Regional Laboratory for Educational Improvement of the Northeast and the Islands, 1994.

Shartrand, Angela M., et al. *New Skills for New Schools: Preparing Teachers in Family Involvement.* Cambridge, MA: Harvard Family Project, 1997. Suggestions for developing and descriptions of existing and promising programs for training teachers to work with parents and families.

St. Paul Foundation. *Lessons Learned: Supporting Diversity in Schools through Family and Community Involvement.* St. Paul, MN: Author, 1996. A very useful booklet printed in three languages (English, Spanish, and Hmong) describing an effective program for working with culturally and linguistically diverse parents and families.

U.S. Department of Education. *Strong Families, Strong Schools: Building Community Partnerships for Learning.* Washington, DC: Author, 1994. Citing research studies, this booklet offers examples of programs in place as well as other suggestions for parents, educators, businesspeople, and policymakers. Includes an extensive bibliography on parent and community involvement.

U. S. Department of Education. *America Goes Back to School: Partners' Activity Kit.* Washington, DC: Author, 1998. This resource gives suggestions for involving community members and parents in "America Goes Back to School" events. These events are held to raise awareness about education issues in local communities, to find ways for dealing with these issues, and to take action.

Information on Academic Standards

Setting standards nationally, statewide, and locally is gaining public attention. The following organizations have been particularly active in the standards-setting movement. Business organizations and those representing government officials are interested in the relationship of high standards to the strength of the nation's economy and thus have been major supporters of the standards-setting efforts. Other groups, such as the National Center for Fair and Open Testing, want to make sure that in the effort to set standards, some groups are not unfairly impacted. People interested in parental involvement in standards-setting should start with these groups. Find the Internet sites at http://.

Achieve
444 North Capitol Street, NW,
Suite 422
Washington, DC 20001
202-624-1460
www.achieve.org

American Federation of Teachers
555 New Jersey Avenue, NW
Washington, DC 20001
202-393-5676
www.aft.org

Business Coalition for Education
Reform
c/o National Alliance of Business
1201 New York Avenue, NW, Suite
700
Washington, DC 20005
1-800-787-2848
www.bcer.org

The Business Roundtable
1615 L Street, NW, Suite 1100
Washington, DC 20036
202-872-1260
www.brtable.org

Council for Basic Education
1319 F Street, NW, Suite 900
Washington, DC 20004
202-347-4171
www.c-b-e.org

Council of State School Officers
1 Massachusetts Avenue, NW,
Suite 700
Washington, DC 20001
202-408-5505
www.ccsso.org

National Center for Fair and Open
Testing (FairTest)
342 Broadway
Cambridge, MA 02139
617-864-4810
www.fairtest.org

National Education Association
1201 16th Street, NW
Washington, DC 20036
202-833-4000
www.nea.org

National Education Goals Panel
1255 22nd Street, NW, Suite 502
Washington, DC 20037
www.negp.gov

National Governors' Association
444 North Capitol Street, NW
Washington, DC 20001
202-624-5300
www.nga.org

U.S. Department of Education
400 Maryland Avenue, SW
Washington, DC 20202
1-800-USA-LEARN
www.ed.gov

The following Internet sites contain information on and examples of standards:

Eisenhower National Clearinghouse's "Standards and Frameworks":
http://www.enc.org

Mid-Continent Regional Educational Laboratory (McREL):
http://www.mcrel.org

Putnam Valley Schools:
http://www.putwest.boces.org/standards.html

Professional Organizations:
The Content Areas and Special Education

These organizations, while not focusing on parent and community involvement, recognize its importance. Most have developed standards in their disciplines. People particularly interested in parental involvement and one of the specific disciplines or special education might want to contact these organizations. Find the Internet sites at http://.

American Council on the Teaching
of Foreign Languages
Six Executive Plaza
Yonkers, NY 10701
914-963-8830
www.actfl.org

Council for Exceptional Children
(Special Education)
1920 Association Drive
Reston, VA 20191-1589
1-888-CEC-SPED/TTY 703-264-
9446
www.cec.sped.org

Music Teachers National Association
The Carew Tower
441 Vine Street, Suite 505
Cincinnati, OH 45202-2814
513-421-1420
www.mtna.org

National Art Education Association
1916 Association Drive
Reston, VA 22091-1590
703-860-8000
www.naea-reston.org

National Council for the
Social Studies
3501 Newark Street, NW
Washington, DC 20016
202-966-7840
www.ncss.org

National Council of Teachers of
English
1111 West Kenyon Road
Urbana, IL 61801
217-328-3870 or 1-800-369-6283
www.ncte.org

National Council of Teachers of
Mathematics
1906 Association Drive
Reston, VA 22091-1593
703-620-9840
www.nctm.org

National Science Teachers
Association
1840 Wilson Boulevard
Arlington, VA 22201-3000
703-243-7100
www.nsta.org

APPENDIX B: DESCRIPTION OF STUDIES

Study Design and Methodology
(Anne Wescott Dodd)

To investigate parents' beliefs about the nature of teaching and learning, Anne Wescott Dodd interviewed twenty-five parents of students in grade 11 who studied English in a heterogeneously grouped American Studies course in a small high school in Southern Maine. When the interviews were conducted in the spring of 1993, educators in this school had been involved in efforts to restructure the classroom for several years, but they had not yet included parents in the process. Twenty-five participants were selected randomly from a categorized list of all students enrolled in grade 11. The sample represented the full range of parents in the population (parents of grade 11 students) with regard to educational background and social-economic status. One interview lasting an average of one hour and ten minutes was conducted with each parent. Follow-up phone calls were made in some instances.

Beliefs, as defined for this study, are comprised of the classroom practices parents preferred because they would best help their children learn, the explanations they gave to support their preference for or opposition to specific practices, and the assumptions about the nature of teaching and learning that appeared to underlie their preferred practices.

The data were analyzed in three phases. The first phase was primarily descriptive and provided a basis for later examining the data at a more abstract level. Anne first summarized the practices parents preferred and the explanations they gave. She further analyzed the explanations to determine the criteria parents used to evaluate the practices they preferred and the origins of these criteria. Then, to determine the assumptions underlying preferred practices, she used six dilemmas about teaching and learning (from a list developed by Berlak and Berlak[1] and developed a framework for rating parents' responses. These results were used to construct a portrait of the beliefs of parents as a group. Placeholder profiles marking four positions on a continuum showed how parents' beliefs differed when they were positioned relative to one another. Following a principle of grounded theory research, she used the data as the basis for creating and naming her own beliefs categories.

Of the three major limitations of this study, the fact that the data were collected entirely from interviews probably had the greatest effect on the results. Only one interview was conducted with each parent, and the interviews varied. Some parents talked more than others. Some of the interviews were interrupted by phone calls, a baby needing attention, or a barking dog. Anne's lack of experience conducting interviews may have influenced parents' responses, especially in the first few interviews. Moreover, as Rokeach[2] and others note, people cannot express all that they believe, because some beliefs are buried below the level of their awareness. On the other hand, most parents seemed quite comfortable after a few minutes and did not hesitate to say what they thought. Several were clearly enthusiastic about, and thanked her for giving them, the opportunity to think and talk about their children's learning.

As in any qualitative study, the researcher's social position and personal beliefs also influenced both the data collection and analysis. Because some people may have viewed her as a representative of the school, they may have felt the interview was a test of their knowledge about schools and been reluctant to talk. Others may have hesitated to express opposition to current school practices, as seemed to be the case with a former educator. He waffled when first asked about grouping, but further probing finally led him to acknowledge that, in contrast to the prevailing view in professional circles, he would choose only honors classes for his son if he had it to do over. To encourage parents to talk candidly, Anne made every effort to make them feel comfortable by conducting interviews in their homes or, in two cases, at other sites they chose. She was also careful to avoid using educational jargon, and she dressed informally. Several procedures, including the use of peer reviewers, were followed to minimize the effects of researcher bias and to make the study as valid and reliable as possible.

Finally, this study was limited by the small number of parents included, although the parents of 38.7 percent of the students in grade 11 were interviewed. The participants, ranging from a parent who dropped out of school in grade 4 to one with two advanced degrees, quite fairly represented the full range of parents of grade 11 students in this school. Despite best efforts to select a cross section of parents, however, methods to do so were inexact. It is likely that the sample was not representative of parents in this community as a whole. Parents with college degrees were under-represented in this sample: while 32.2 percent of persons over twenty-five in Eastland are college graduates, only 20 percent of the sample had completed college. It is not clear what effect this factor may have had on the results of the study.[3]

Study Design and Methodology (Jean Konzal)

This is an interpretive case study that tells the story of how parents and educators in one small-town New England high school—Grover's Corners—understand new teaching and learning practices. Based on Elliot Eisner's[4] work, and using the metaphor of *researcher-as-artist* rather than *researcher-as-scientist* to inform her work, Jean Konzal conceptualized this study as an educational criticism. Educational criticism, according to Eisner, is a two-part process. First one appreciates[5] the phenomena under study, and then one makes this appreciation public by re-presenting it. Appreciating a phenomena is a private experience. Re-presenting what is learned makes it public.[6]

Appreciating

In order to gain an appreciation of parent-teacher understandings of new teaching and learning practices in Grover's Corners High School, Jean spent six weeks on-site. While there she conducted a telephone survey of a randomly selected set of parents of seniors (specifically, students who had fully experienced both the new math curriculum and the new social studies curriculum), conducted thirty-eight personal interviews with parents of seniors and juniors in their homes or in local restaurants; interviewed twenty high school and district teachers and administrators; reviewed documents about the new math and social studies curriculum, as well as documents related to the on-going restructuring efforts; attended parent-teacher meetings related to the school and district change efforts; and sat in on math and social studies classes. In the final analysis, while the knowledge she gained through the other methods of collection supported what she learned through the interviews, it was the thirty-eight personal interviews with parents and the twenty interviews with teachers and administrators that most extensively informed her study. Jean's interviewing approach was characterized by open-ended conversations guided, within the broad topic of inquiry, by the interests of the person with whom she was talking. By allowing them to take the lead, their voices were more clearly heard than had Jean insisted that they answer a predetermined set of questions. Jean assumed a stance of co-constructor of knowledge with the person with whom she was speaking, rather than one of objective interviewer.[7]

Re-Presenting

As Jean listened to the tapes of her conversations with the parents, she became convinced that the passion and the emotion heard in their voices called for a portrayal different from a typical narrative report. Therefore, she re-presented her findings in the form of two readers' theater scripts. Readers' theater is minimalist, a form of representational theater that presents ideas without the aid of costuming, sets, or props. The idea is to engage the audience in the words—not the actions—of the players, in order to encourage them to discuss, debate, and take action on important social issues. Educational researchers use readers' theater as a way of making research more accessible to practitioners, scholars, and the general public. The analysis presented in this book is drawn from those scripts as well as from additional analysis of the interview transcripts.

The process of script construction resembles that of more traditional qualitative research processes. Interviews are read and coded as a way of discovering themes that run through the interviews.[8] Once themes are identified, they are organized in a way that best tells the story. Jean approached the script construction process differently for the two scripts. For the first script she wanted to demonstrate how individual past experiences influenced personal mental models about what goes on in good schools. Therefore, she needed to present specific individuals rather than composites. To do so she decided to identify parents who were representative of all those she interviewed. After reading and coding each parent interview, and identifying themes in each one, she chose the voices of sixteen parents to represent the themes found in all thirty-eight interviews. She created a grid to compare these sixteen parents with the original thirty-eight to make sure that there was a broad representation of parents within this group. She then compared the parents to see if any major themes from the group of thirty-eight were omitted from the perspectives of the sixteen; there were no significant omissions. She was satisfied that she could use these sixteen voices without losing any of the major themes represented in the total group.

The second script was easier to deal with. Since it addressed the differences between parent and educator perspectives and the barriers that separated them, Jean could deal with themes and choose representative quotations—rather than specific individuals—to represent the themes: for the parents, the differences among parents and their past experiences attempting to communicate with educators; for the educators, the differences that existed among educators and the questions they had about how parents should be involved in schools. Her intent was to decenter the prominent voices of the professional and to provide more room for parent voices. Her intent, however, was not to privilege parental voices over professional ones, but rather, by allowing them more space, to recognize the importance of both parental and educator voices.

Interpretive qualitative studies cannot be evaluated by the same criteria as quantitative studies. Noreen Garman[9] suggests that questions such as: "Does the work ring true?," "Is the work structurally sound?," "Is there sufficient depth of intellect?, " "Does it make a contribution to the field?," "Is it important, meaningful, nontrivial?," and "Is it enriching, pleasing to anticipate and experience?" are more relevant for works that acknowledge the interpretive nature of research. It is by these criteria that this study should be judged.[10]

Notes

Preface

1. These scripts can be found in *The School Community Journal* (Fall/Winter 1996), pp. 93-130.

Introduction

1. Pseudonym.

Chapter One

1. Robert C. Johnston, "Just Saying No," *Education Week*, April 9, 1997, p. 1, 26. In an attempt to garner more support for the eleventh grade test, Michigan officials later changed the rating scale and labels; for example, "proficient" (highest level) became "1, endorsed, exceeded Michigan standards." See "Mich. Adopts New Terms for Proficiency Testing," *Education Week*, May 20, 1998, p. 23, for more details about the changes.
2. Ann Bradley, "Requiem for a Reform," *Education Week*, June 1, 1994, p. 21.
3. Dana Mack, *The Assault on Parenthood: How Our Culture Undermines the Family* (New York: Simon and Schuster, 1997); and E. D. Hirsch, *The Schools We Need and Why We Don't Have Them* (New York: Doubleday, 1996).
4. Philip Schlechty, *Inventing Better Schools: An Action Plan for Educational Reform* (San Francisco: Jossey-Bass, 1997), p. xi.
5. Ibid.; Roland Barth, *Improving Schools from Within* (San Francisco: Jossey-Bass, 1990); and Ann Leiberman, address to the Southern Maine Partnership, University of Southern Maine, May 30, 1991.
6. James S. Coleman and Thomas Hoffer, *Public and Private High Schools* (New York: Basic Books, 1987), reported by Lynn Olson, "Parents as Partners," *Education Week*, April 4, 1990, p. 22.
7. See Herbert M. Kliebard, *The Struggle for the American Curriculum*, 2nd ed. (New York: Routledge, 1986); and Lawrence Cremin, *The Transformation of the School* (New York: Vintage, 1961).
8. Jonathan Kozol, *Savage Inequalities* (New York: Crown, 1991).

Chapter Two

1. Kieran Egan, *The Educated Mind* (Chicago: University of Chicago Press, 1997), p. 10.
2. Lawrence A. Cremin, *American Education: The Metropolitan Experience 1876-1980* (New York: Harper & Row, 1988), p. 176.

3. Ibid., pp. 176-177.
4. Ibid., p. 187.
5. Ibid., p. 192.
6. Ibid., pp. 236-237.
7. Allan C. Ornstein and Daniel U. Levine, *An Introduction to the Foundations of Education*, 3rd ed. (Boston: Houghton Mifflin, 1985), pp. 150, 152.
8. Myra Pollack Sadker and David Miller Sadker, *Teachers, Schools, and Society* (New York: Random House, 1988), p. 186.
9. Cremin, *American Education*, pp. 499-500.
10. Sadker and Sadker, *Teachers, Schools, and Society*, p. 186.
11. Ornstein and Levine, *Introduction*, p. 152.
12. Ibid., p. 159.
13. Ibid., p. 161.
14. Ibid., p. 13.
15. David B. Tyack and Elisabeth Hansot, *Managers of Virtue: Public Leadership in America, 1820-1980* (New York: Basic Books, 1982), p. 21.
16. Ibid.
17. Ibid.
18. Ibid., pp. 21-22.
19. David B. Tyack, *One Best System: A History of Urban Education* (Cambridge, MA: Harvard University Press, 1974), p. 16.
20. Alan Peshkin, *Growing Up American: Schooling and the Survival of Community* (Chicago: University of Chicago Press, 1978), p. 208.
21. Tyack, *One Best System*, p. 17.
22. Ibid.
23. Ibid.
24. Ibid., pp. 17-18.
25. Herbert M. Kliebard, *The Struggle for the American Curriculum*, 2nd ed. (New York: Routledge, 1995), p. 1.
26. Lawrence A. Cremin, *The Transformation of the School* (New York: Vintage, 1964), p. 20.
27. Ibid., p. 21.
28. Tyack and Hansot, *Managers of Virtues*, p. 17.
29. Ornstein and Levine, *Introduction*, p. 166.
30. Gerald L. Gutek, *Education and Schooling in America*, 2nd ed. (Englewood Cliffs, NJ: Prentice-Hall, 1988), p. 29.
31. Tyack, *One Best System*, p. 230.
32. Ibid., pp. 24-25.
33. Ibid., p. 32.
34. Ibid., p. 229.
35. Arthur G. Powell, Eleanor Farrar, and David K. Cohen, *The Shopping Mall High School: Winners and Losers in the Educational Marketplace* (Boston: Houghton Mifflin, 1985).
36. Gutek, *Education*, p. 2.
37. Ibid., p. 3.
38. John Dewey, *Democracy and Education* (New York: Free Press, 1916), p. 9.
39. Robert D. Putnam, "Bowling Alone: America's Declining Social Capital," *Journal of Democracy* 6, no. 1 (1995): 65-78.
40. Peshkin, *Growing up American*.

41. Carol Merz and Gail Furman, *Community and Schools: Promise and Paradox* (New York: Teachers College Press, 1997), p. 10.
42. Ibid., p. 9.
43. Ibid., p. 5.
44. Robert Bellah, *Habits of the Heart* (Berkeley: University of California Press, 1985).
45. Merz and Furman, *Community and Schools*, p. 25.
46. Ibid., p. 89.
47. Ibid., p. 91.
48. Ibid., p. 97.
49. Ibid., p. 8
50. Dewey, *Democracy*, p. 360.
51. Seymour Sarason, *Parental Involvement and the Political Principle* (San Francisco: Jossey-Bass, 1995).
52. Kenneth A. Strike, "Professionalism, Democracy, and Discursive Communities: Normative Reflection on Restructuring," *American Education Research Journal* 30, no. 2 (1995): 273.

Chapter Three

1. David Tyack and Elisabeth Hansot, *Managers of Virtue* (New York: Basic Books, 1982).
2. National Commission on Excellence in Education, *A Nation at Risk: The Imperative for Educational Reform* (Washington, DC: U.S. Government Printing Office, 1983).
3. See, for example, Linda Darling-Hammond, "Policy and Professionalism," in Ann Lieberman, ed., *Building a Professional Culture in Schools* (New York: Teachers College Press, 1988), pp. 55-77.
4. *Webster's Encyclopedic Unabridged Dictionary of the English Language* (New York: Gramercy Books, 1989).
5. Linda Darling-Hammond as cited in Linda Darling-Hammond and A. Lin Goodwin, "Progress Toward Professionalism in Teaching," in Gordon Cawelti, ed., *Challenges and Achievements of American Education: 1993 Yearbook of the Association for Supervision and Curriculum Development* (Alexandria, VA: Association for Supervision and Curriculum Development, 1993), p. 20.
6. Darling and Goodwin, "Progress," p. 22.
7. Ibid.
8. D. E. Mitchell and C. T. Kerchner, 1983 and K. K. Zumwalt, 1988, as cited by Darling and Goodwin, "Progress," p. 25.
9. See, for instance, Kenneth Strike, "Is Teaching a Profession: How Would We Know?" *Journal of Personnel Evaluation in Education* 4 (1990): 91-117.
10. Seymour Sarason, *Parental Involvement and the Political Principle* (San Francisco: Jossey-Bass, 1995), p. 23.
11. Kenneth Strike, "Professionalism, Democracy, and Discursive Communities: Normative Reflections on Restructuring," *American Educational Research Journal* 30, no. 2 (1993): 255-275.
12. Sarason, *Parental Involvement*.
13. Strike, "Professionalism," p. 261.

14. Robert L. Crowson, *School-Community Relations, Under Reform* (Berkeley, CA: McCutchan Publishing Corporation, 1992), pp. 9-10.

15. Jean Konzal, *A Study of a School District in Transition: Including Parents in the Schooling Discourse,* Unpublished manuscript. University of Pittsburgh, 1994.

16. Steve Farkas, *Divided Within, Besieged Without,* 1993; Jean Johnson and John Immerwahr, *First Things First: What Americans Expect from the Public Schools,* 1994; and Jean Johnson et al., *Assignment Incomplete: The Unfinished Business of Education Reform,* 1995. All three reports are published by and may be ordered from the Public Agenda, 6 East 39th Street, New York City, NY 10016.

17. Johnson and Immerwahr, *First Things First,* p. 17.

18. Ibid.

19. Ellen Condliffe Lagemann, "Parents—A New Keyword in Education," *Teachers College Record* 94, no. 4 (1993): 677-681.

20. Myra Pollack Sadker and David Miller Sadker, *Teachers, School, and Society* (New York: Random House, 1988), pp. 321-322.

21. Ibid., p. 322.

22. Ernest Boyer, *High School: A Report on Secondary Education in America* (New York: Harper & Row, 1983).

23. John Chubb and Terry Moe, *Politics, Markets, and America's Schools* (Washington, DC: The Brookings Institution, 1990).

24. D. Lindsay, "Wisconsin, Ohio Back Vouchers for Religious Schools," *Education Week,* July 12, 1995, pp. 1, 14.

25. Paul Berman, et al, *A National Study of Charter Schools: Second-Year Report* (Washington, DC: Office of Educational Research and Improvement, 1998).

26. Lindsay, "Wisconsin," p. 14.

27. Annette Lareau, *Home Advantage: Social Class and Parental Intervention in Elementary Education* (London: The Falmer Press, 1989).

28. Strike, "Professionalism."

29. Michelle Fine, "Parent Involvement: Reflections on Parents, Power, And Urban Public Schools," *Teachers College Record* 94, no. 4 (1993): 682-709.

30. Sarason, *Parental Involvement,* p. 67.

31. Ibid.

32. Fine, "Parental Involvement," p. 684.

33. Joyce Epstein, "Perspectives and Previews on Research and Policy for School, Family, and Community Partnerships," in Alan Booth, Judith F. Dunn, Judy Dunn, eds. *Family-School Links: How Do They Affect Educational Outcomes* (Mahwah, NJ: Lawrence Erlbaum, 1995).

34. See, for example, Sarason, *Parental Involvement.*

35. See Robert L. Crowson, *School-Community Relationships* and Mary Henry, *Parent-School Collaboration: Feminist Organizational Structures and School Leadership* (Albany, NY: State University of New York Press, 1996).

Chapter Four

1. Jean Johnson, *Assignment Incomplete: The Unfinished Business of Education Reform* (New York: Public Agenda, 1995), p. 20.

2. Jean and John Immerwahr, *First Things First: What Americans Expect from the Public Schools* (New York: Public Agenda, 1994), p. 17.

3. See Peter Senge, *The Fifth Discipline* (New York: Doubleday, 1990) for more information about mental models.

Chapter Five

1. Ann Berlak and Harold Berlak, *Dilemmas of Schooling* (New York: Methuen, 1981).
2. Michael Fullan (with Suzanne Stiegelbauer), *The New Meaning of Educational Change* (New York: Teachers College Press, 1991).

Chapter Six

1. Robert Hilliard quoted in *Engfo* 5, no. 1 (1989). Colorado Department of Education.
2. Kiplinger Washington Editors, *Prepare Now for the 21st Century: Kiplinger's Guide to 2000 and Beyond* (Washington, DC: Kiplinger, 1997), p. 13.
3. Michael Young and Patrick McGeeney, *Learning Begins at Home* (London: Routledge & Kegan Paul, 1968).
4. Richard Whitmire, "Critics Say the Latest Methods Do Not Compute." *USA Today*, November 24, 1997, p. 5D.
5. Grover's Corners High School, *Grover's Corners Social Studies Curriculum Guide* (1994).

Chapter Seven

1. *ASCD (Association of Supervision and Curriculum Development) Update* 36, no. 3 (March 1994): 4.
2. John Immerwahr and Jean Johnson, *American's Views on Standards: An Assessment by Public Agenda* (New York: Public Agenda, 1996), p. 10.
3. Ibid., p. 9.
4. Education Commission of the States (ECS), *Listen, Discuss and Act: Parents' and Teachers' Views on Education Reform* (Denver: Author, 1996), p. 12.
5. Ibid., p. 16.
6. Ibid., p. 32.
7. Ibid., p. 5.

Part III

1. Mary Henry, *Parent School Collaboration: Feminist Organizational Structures and School Leadership* (Albany: State University of New York Press, 1996), pp. 5-6.
2. Betty Shockley et al., *Engaging Families* (Portsmouth, NH: Heinemann, 1995), p. 91.

Chapter Eight

1. The Bay Area Writing Project was part of a national series of programs developed to give teachers an opportunity to learn more effective ways of teaching writing by engaging in the writing process in the same way they would later have their students do.

2. Information for this profile comes from an interview with Lois N. André Bechely and from Lois N. André Bechely and Stuart Bernstein, "Building Parent Leadership in Curriculum Reform Through School/University Collaboration," Paper presented at the annual meeting of the American Educational Research Association, San Diego, CA, April 1998. We thank Lois for reading the draft and making necessary changes and additions.

3. Information for this profile comes from an interview with Kate Kirby-Linton and from Kate Kirby-Linton, Nancy Lyle, and Susan White, "When Parents and Teachers Create Writing Standards," *Educational Leadership* (December 1996/January 1997): 30-32. We thank Kate for reading the draft and making necessary changes and additions.

4. The Partnerships for Achievement in Learning Project was supported in part by Cooperative Agreement H023L1008 from the U.S. Department of Education, Office of Special Education and Rehabilitative Services/Office of Special Education Programs. Points of view or opinions stated do not necessarily represent official agency positions.

5. Information for this profile came from an interview with Pam Kay; from Jeanne Backhaus and Patricia Woodward, *Partnerships for Achievement in Learning* (Burlington, VT: University of Vermont, 1995); and from Pamela J. Kay and Martha Fitzgerald, "Parents + Teachers + Action Research = Real Involvement," *Teaching Exceptional Children* (September/October, 1997). We thank Pam for reading the draft and making necessary changes and additions.

6. These quotes are found in Kay and Fitzgerald, "Parents + Teachers + Action Research = Real Involvement," p. 11.

7. Information for this profile came from telephone interviews with Melvin Traylor, Brenda Shell, and Mary Beth Larkin; and from Ernesto Cortes, Jr., "Making the Public the Leaders in Education Reform," *Teacher Magazine on the Web* (November 22, 1995). To find this on the Internet, go to *Education Week* at http://www.edweek.org and run a search through the archives. Information also came from "Roosevelt High School (The Alliance Schools Initiative): An Inner-City High School Joins a Statewide Effort, Dallas, Texas," *Family Involvement in Children's Education* (October, 1997), found on the Internet at http://www.oeri.ed.gov/pubs/FamInvolve/rhs.html. We thank Melvin, Brenda, and Mary Beth for reading the draft and making necessary changes and additions.

8. Cortes, "Making the Public the Leaders in Education Reform," p.2.

9. From telephone interview with Mary Beth Larkin, September, 1998.

Chapter Nine

1. Robert Samuelson, "My Turn," *Newsweek* (December 4, 1995): 61.

2. The following findings are quoted from MetLife, *The Metropolitan Life Survey of the American Teacher 1998: Building Family-School Partnerships: Views of Teachers and Students* (New York: MetLife, 1998), pp. 3-5. Available free (while supplies last) or found on the Internet at http://www.metlife.com.

3. Ibid., p. 45.

4. Michael G. Fullan (with Suzanne Stiegelbauer), *The New Meaning of Educational Change* (New York: Teachers College Press, 1991).

5. Sarah Lawrence Lightfoot, *Worlds Apart: Relationships Between Families and Schools* (New York: Basic Books, 1978), p. 189.

6. Patricia Sullivan, "The PTA's National Standards," *Educational Leadership* 55, no. 8 (May 1998): 43.

7. For another article on the PTA standards, see Lois Jean White, "National PTA Standards for Parent/Family Involvement Programs," *The High School Magazine* 5, no. 3 (January/February 1998): 8-12. This issue contains several other articles about parent and community involvement, including "Meeting Across the Divide: Effective Parent-Professional Collaboration" by Jacqueline Thousand et al. The introductory note to this article reads: "Often meetings between parents and the professionals serving them end in confusion, boredom, or even hostility. What can be done to make these accounts more productive?"

8. For more information, contact the Center on School, Family, and Community Partnerships, 3505 North Charles Street, Suite 200, Baltimore, MD 21218; telephone: 410-516-8818; or look on the Internet at http://scov.csos.jhu.edu/p2000/p2000.html.

9. Andrew Trotter, "Parents, Educators Make New Connection with the Internet," *Education Week*, April 23, 1997, p. 10.

10. Ibid.

11. Ibid.

12. U.S. Department of Education, Partnership for Family Involvement in Education, "America Goes Back to School" (Washington, DC: Partnership for Family Involvement in Education, 1997), brochure.

13. Debra Viadero, "School Hot Line Found to Boost Parent Involvement," *Education Week*, June 4, 1997, p. 8.

14. Ibid.

15. Ibid.

16. Eric Bloom, "Teachers Say Personal Phones Allow Instant Feedback for Parents," *Portland* (ME) *Press Herald*, February 24, 1998, pp. 1, 4A.

17. "About the Forums," *Our Children: The National PTA Magazine* (May/June 1997): 16-17. For a more detailed description of a forum and suggestions from participants in Chicago, see E. Arthur Stunard, "The Chicago Forum," *Phi Delta Kappan* 78, no. 10 (June 1997): 774-776. This issue also contains several other informative articles about public engagement.

18. Adriana de Kanter et al., *A Compact for Learning* (Washington, DC: Partnership for Family Involvement in Education, U.S. Dept. of Education, 1997). (See Appendix A for address and phone number.)

19. Ibid.

20. Education Commission of the States, "Let's Talk about Education Improvement" (Denver: Author, 1996), p. 6. The booklet's appendix contains more specific information for facilitating discussions.

21. Ibid., pp. 8-9. A "Why Change?" list on p. 9 in the booklet can be made into an overhead and used to focus discussion for this activity.

22. Ibid., p. 8.

23. Marjorie Ledell and Arleen Arnsparger, *How to Deal with Community Criticism of School Change* (Alexandria, VA: Association of Supervision and Curriculum Development and Education Commission of the States, 1993), pp. 8-9.

24. For more information about Family Math programs, contact Virginia Thompson at the University of California, Berkeley: (510) 642-6859 or e-mail: equals@uclink.berkeley.edu.

25. Deborah Jumpp, "Extending the Literate Community: Literacy over a Life Span," in Members of the National Writing Project Urban Sites Network, *Cityscapes: Eight Views From the Urban Classroom* (Berkeley, CA: National Writing Project, 1996), pp. 133-143.

26. Joyce L. Epstein et al., "Involving Parents in Homework in the Middle Grades," *Phi Delta Kappa Research Bulletin* 18 (September 1997): 1.

27. Ibid., pp. 3-4.

28. Information from an interview conducted with Joe Buzanowski by Jean Konzal, August 1997.

29. Vivian Gussin Paley, *Kwanzaa and Me* (Cambridge, MA: Harvard University Press, 1995).

30. U.S. Department of Education, Partnership for Family Involvement in Education, "America Goes Back to School," cited above.

31. Deborah L. Cohen, "Beyond Question," *Education Week*, November 22, 1995, p. 27.

32. Ibid., pp. 27-28.

33. Ibid., p. 28.

34. William Boyd, "Local Influences on Education" in Harold Mitzel et al., eds., *Encyclopedia of Educational Research* (New York: Macmillan, 1982), pp. 1118-1129.

35. Dennis J. Sumara and Brent Davis, "Enlarging the Space of the Possible: Complexity, Complicity, and Action-Research Practices," in Terrance R. Carson and Dennis J. Sumara, eds., *Action Research as a Living Practice* (New York: Peter Lang, 1997), pp. 299-312.

36. This questionnaire was originally published in *Educational Leadership* 53, no. 7 (April 1996).

37. Karen Rasmussen, "Making Parent Involvement Meaningful," *Education Update* 40, no. 1 (January 1998): 1, 6, 7.

38. June Cavarretta. "Parents Are a School's Best Friend," *Educational Leadership* 55, no. 8 (May 1998): 14.

39. Ibid., p. 15.

40. Gloria Ladson-Billings, *The Dreamkeepers: Successful Teachers of African-American Children* (San Francisco: Jossey-Bass, 1997).

41. For further information, contact Charlene Vick, School Development Program, 55 College Street, New Haven, CT 06510. Telephone: (203) 737-4016. E-mail: charleneivk@yale.edu. On the Internet at http://info.med.yale.edu/comer.

42. For more information, contact the Institute for Responsive Education, 50 Nightingale Hall, Northwestern University, Boston, MA 02115. Telephone: 617-373-2595. On the Internet at http://www.resp-ed.org.

43. See *Teacher Magazine*, November 22, 1995. On the Internet at www.edweek.org/tm/tm.htm and "Roosevelt High School (The Alliance Schools Initiative)." On the Internet at http://oeri.ed.gov/pubs/faminvolve/rhs.html.

44. For further information, contact Coalition of Essential Schools, Amy Gerstein, Executive Director, 1814 Franklin Street, Suite 700, Oakland, CA 94612. Telephone: (510) 433-1451. E-mail: agerstein@ess.scl.org. On the Internet at http://www.essentialschools.org.

Chapter Ten

1. Carl Glickman in an address at the annual conference of the Association of Supervision and Curriculum Development, New Orleans, March 17, 1996.
2. Linda Darling-Hammond, "The Right to Learn and the Advancement of Teaching: Research, Policy, and Practice for Democratic Education," *Educational Researcher* 25, no. 6 (1996): 7.
3. Michael Apple and James Beane, *Democratic Schools* (Alexandria, VA: Association for Supervision and Curriculum Development, 1995), p. 103.
4. Cited in Education Commission of the States, *Transforming the Education System: The 1997 Education Agenda* (Denver: Author, 1997), p. 12.
5. Robert Bellah, *Habits of the Heart* (Berkeley: University of California Press, 1985).
6. Carol Merz and Gail Furman, *Community and Schools: Promise and Paradox* (New York: Teachers College Press, 1997), p. 97.
7. Ibid., p. 89.
8. Jane Roland Martin, *The Schoolhome: Rethinking Schools for Changing Families* (Cambridge, MA: Harvard University Press, 1992).
9. Kevin Bushweller, "Parenthood in the 90's," *Educational Vital Signs 1995*. Published by *The American School Board Journal* and *The Executive Educator* (December 1995): A9.
10. Ibid.
11. Ibid.
12. Tony Wagner, "The New Village Common—Improving Schools Together," *Educational Leadership* 54, no. 5 (February 1997): 25.
13. Ibid., p. 28.
14. Deborah Wadsworth, "Building a Strategy for Successful Public Engagement," *Phi Delta Kappan* 78, no. 10 (June 1997): 750. This issue contains several other articles related to this topic.
15. Ibid., p. 751.
16. Ibid., p. 752.
17. Bushweller, "Parenthood," p. A7.
18. Ibid., p. A9.
19. Ursula Casanova, "Parent Involvement: A Call for Prudence," *Educational Researcher* 25, no. 8 (November 1996): 31.
20. Associated Press, "Survey Finds Integration Takes Back Seat to Standards, Discipline," *Portland* (Maine) *Press Herald*, July 29, 1998, p. 3A.
21. Glickman, March 17, 1996, speech. op. cit.
22. Wadsworth, "Building a Strategy," pp. 749, 752.
23. Lisa Delpit, *Other People's Children: Cultural Conflicts in the Classroom* (New York: The New Press, 1995), p. 151.
24. Lynn Langer Meeks, "When Worldviews Collide: The Curriculum Explodes," *English Leadership Quarterly* 18, no. 4 (December 1996): 7.
25. John Dewey, *The School and Society* (Chicago: University of Chicago Press, 1900/1990), p. 7.

Appendix B

1. Ann Berlak and Harold Berlak, *Dilemmas of Schooling* (New York: Metheun, 1981).

2. Milton Rokeach, *The Open and Closed Mind* (New York: Basic Books, 1960); and *Beliefs, Attitudes, and Values* (San Francisco: Jossey-Bass, 1968).

3. The full study is reported in Anne Wescott Dodd, "Parents as Partners in Learning: Their Beliefs about Effective Practices for Teaching and Learning High School English." Unpublished doctoral dissertation, University of Maine, 1994.

4. Elliot W. Eisner, *The Enlightened Eye: Qualitative Inquiry and the Enhancement of Educational Practice* (New York: Macmillan Publishing Company, 1991); "Forms of Understanding and the Future of Educational Research" *Educational Researcher* 22, no. 7 (1993): 5-11; "Is Arts-Based Research an Oxymoron?" (Paper presented at the Annual Meeting of the American Educational Research Association, San Francisco, CA, 1995), 1-8.

5. "Appreciation" in this context means "gaining intimate knowledge of" rather than "approving of."

6. Elliot W. Eisner, *The Enlightened Eye,* 1991.

7. Michael F. Connelly & Jean D. Clandenin, "Stories of Experience and Narrative Inquiry," *Educational Researcher* 19, no. 5 (1990): 2-14; Patti Lather, "Critical Frames in Educational Research: Feminist and Poststructural Perspectives," *Theory into Practice* XXXI, no 2 (1992): 87-99; Elliot G. Mishler, *Research Interviewing: Context and Narrative* (Cambridge: Harvard University Press, 1986).

8. Robert Donmoyer and June Yennie-Donmoyer, "Data as Drama: Reflections on the Use of Readers Theater as a Mode of Qualitative Data Display," *Qualitative Inquiry* 1, no. 4 (December, 1995): 402-428.

9. Noreen Garman,. "Qualitative Inquiry: Meaning and Menace For Educational Researchers," in *Proceedings of the Conference on Qualitative Research,* The Flinders University of South Australia, Adelaide, August 5. 1994.

10. The full study is reported in Jean L. Konzal, "Our Changing Town, Our Changing School: Is Common Ground Possible?" Unpublished doctoral dissertation, University of Pittsburgh, 1995.

Index